AN INTRODUCTION TO PROBLEMS IN THE PHILOSOPHY OF SOCIAL SCIENCES

KEITH WEBB

PINTER

PINTER
A Cassell imprint
Wellington House, 125 Strand, London, WC2R 0BB, England

First published in 1995

British Library Cataloguing in Publication Data

A CIP catalogue record for this book is available from The British Library

ISBN 0 85567 290 1 (hardback)
 1 85567 291 X (paperback)

Typeset by Mayhew Typesetting, Rhayader, Powys
Printed and bound in Great Britain

CONTENTS

ACKNOWLEDGEMENTS

I would like to thank Professor Michael Nicholson for his stimulating writing and conversation about methodology over the years. Also I would like to express gratitude to my colleagues and former students at the University of Kent. In addition, gratitude is owed my wife who has helped me a great deal. Finally, thanks to my friends and fellow philosophers at the Share and Coulter, Herne Bay, without whose company this book would have been finished much sooner.

INTRODUCTION

Posing the questions

This book is an introduction to the problem of certainty and uncertainty in social science. It asks the question 'How do we know what we know in social science?' Several responses are given. First, that while there can never be absolute certainty in our understanding of other people and society, there are good reasons to treat some of what we believe as knowledge rather than as ephemeral opinion. The key phrase here is, of course, 'good reasons'; what is to count as a good reason for belief? Ultimately this comes down to the acceptance of 'criteria of validity', or those methodological beliefs that give us cause to believe in something. For example, if an item of knowledge is congruent with and supportive of what we already believe we know, there is some reason to accept it. Or if a proposition, such as 'revolutions never succeed where the military supports the established government in an undivided manner' remains unfalsified by empirical observation (that is, there are no counter-examples), then we may have reason to accept it at least tentatively.

But there are two qualifications here. While we make recourse to criteria of validity to demonstrate a case, not all of our criteria will point in the same direction. Hence uncertainty can arise not only about whether to accept something as 'knowledge' but also as to the correct means for evaluating it. More of this later. Further, it is an error to equate 'knowledge' with 'certainty'. The belief in absolute certainty is only attainable in the realms of logic or mathematics — or possibly religion — but is not possible in the empirical world. Many things that I may believe I 'know' may in fact be wrong, even though I am willing, for good reasons, to accept them as being true for the time being. This means, therefore, that the realm of knowledge is constantly revised and developed. Human beings, lacking omniscience, are in the business of investigation, discovery, reinterpretation, re-evaluation, and thus constant contestation. This does not mean, however, that there are not good reasons at particular points of time to prefer one proposition to another. The lack of certainty and the probability of change does not conflict with there being good reasons to believe.

Second, it is suggested here that there is no one acceptable overall 'position' in social science. The disciplines of social science are composed of 'schools', 'paradigms', 'research programmes', 'approaches', or theories, none of which has a monopoly on knowledge however much they may claim it. A knowledge of social science involves acceptance of eclecticism and a multitude of ways of knowing. Social scientists in both the past and present have argued for particular ways of viewing the world or segments of the world. They have attempted to build coherent and comprehensive theories of their area with a view to explaining developments and events in that area. Hence, to simplify, there are monetarists, Keynesians, and Marxists in economics; realists, pluralists, and Marxists in international relations; and behaviourists, Freudians, and Gestalt theorists in psychology. These are sometimes seen as mutually exclusive 'paradigms', where to accept one is necessarily to reject the other approaches. The same kinds of divisions are found in all the social science disciplines.

However, it is the nature of theory to present a simplified abstraction of processes in the 'real' world, and in the process of simplification violence is necessarily done to the complexity and multi-faceted nature of the social world. The consequence of this is that no single theory can hope to 'explain' fully all the events within its domain, since those factors which it singles out to be of major importance are only some of the factors that exercise influence. A corollary of this is, then, that the social scientist must draw on different theoretical ideas to explain and understand events and processes happening in the world. Hence, while a rational actor model may be a good starting point for explaining why nations go to war, the gaps and imprecisions resulting may need supplementing with theories of perception or ideology.

An obvious response to this difficulty is to ask: 'Why don't social scientists build big theories which incorporate all the factors that affect events?' The problem here is that if such a theory were devised that incorporated all the different stresses (approaches etc.) within one discipline, and also the interference effects of other disciplines, the resultant theory would be so complex that it would be little use in analysis. A theory of everything is a theory of nothing. We are left, then, with little alternative to intelligent eclecticism if we wish to avoid the aridity of theoretical dogmatism.

The aim of the book, therefore, is to argue for a balanced and eclectic scepticism, rather than either dogmatic acceptance and advocacy or the philosophical rejection of the possibility of knowledge. The fact that certainty cannot be guaranteed is not reason for the adoption of dogmatic postures, nor is it a good ground for cynicism about social science, or despair and rejection of social science. All of these responses are based ultimately on a naïve false belief that the social scientific activity is only justifiable where there is certainty with respect to its outcomes and discoveries. But to say there is no certainty, in any absolute sense, is not the same as saying that what we believe we know is of no value. Social science may be of value as an intellectual activity in its own right — such as archaeology or the study of ancient languages; here it would be seen as part of the growth and development of civilization. Or it may be of value in terms of changing interpretations of society at a time of rapid and continual change; here the function would be akin to that of some forms of literature. Or it may have value as a socially applicable area of study, something that can aid in the achievement of desired outcomes. Or, and this is the opinion of the author, it may have value in all of these ways.

There is a further consequence of looking at social science in the eclectic manner advocated here which reflects on the traditional debate about the scientific or non-scientific nature of the study of society. And it is that the study of society shares certain features with natural science but also necessarily has within it elements of humanistic interpretation. It is, therefore, neither 'scientific' nor 'non-scientific' but will opportunistically draw on different traditions of scholarship, investigation, and understanding as the particular problem demands. It is, for example, interesting that 80 per cent of wars are won by those instigating the war; that the capacity to fight effectively declines with distance; that war is more likely in the five years succeeding an alliance formation; that great power intervention in Third World conflicts tends to reinforce existing schisms and cleavages; or that the willingness to accept third-party mediation will tend to increase when a 'hurting stalemate' occurs. These are the kind of findings that are typically established by 'scientific' and quantitative analysis, by the analysis of large numbers of cases. However, such propositions are thin and bald, merely describing the surface features of events. To understand them more fully we need to go to a different kind of analysis, one that is very much more dependent on the interpretation and understanding of how actors perceive, assess, and evaluate the world within which they are acting. We move much closer to historical and narrative forms of analysis, to an understanding of the rules and norms that govern social behaviour. For example, what do we mean by a 'hurting stalemate'? A situation where both sides in a conflict can make no progress on the battlefield but are incurring large costs. From an observer's point of view, a hurting stalemate may be perceived, but actors will vary enormously in their willingness to accept costs, this dependent on resources, group cohesion and beliefs etc. In order to understand particular cases, it is usually necessary to supplement generality with the specificity that is derived from the subjective evaluations of participants in their situations. It is thus not the case that there is any opposition between different ways of doing social science; in reality all forms of knowledge are complementary.

A final aspect of this view of social science is that debate, argument, discussion and difference are themselves seen to be of value. As Edmund Burke noted: 'He that wrestles with us strengthens our nerves and sharpens our skill. Our antagonist is our helper.' It is through debate and argument that new knowledge, perspectives and approaches are discovered, and old approaches are refined and changed. To 'know' in social science will never equate with fixed, rigid and doctrinaire dogma, but rather is being aware of a range of alternative ways of viewing the social universe. It is more a case of understanding the human possibilities of the world rather than a comprehension of some fixed, static and unchanging world. In this sense, the more approaches there are, even though they may be incompatible, gives us access to more insights. A theory will usually draw attention to empirical features of phenomena that seem significant from a point of view. The more theories we have, therefore, the greater the empirical content of our knowledge about segments of the world, and the greater the number of points of view they encompass.

An overview of this book

With these precepts in mind, that there are good reasons for belief, that sceptical eclecticism is to be prefered, that social science is a blend of investigative traditions and recognition of the value of diversity, the method of the book is to examine some of the 'problems' of social science. The book is not 'progressive' in the sense that there is a development through the book. Rather, there is discussion of a number of areas of traditional social scientific philosophical dispute that are intended to elucidate and demonstrate these points.

Chapter 1 examines the argument that ultimately the human condition can be explained in terms of biology. If this were true, there would be an objective base from which to view human societies. Social science would therefore be a branch of biological science. It is noted that there are, in fact, a number of biological arguments rather than just one biological argument such as traditional Darwinism, ethology, psychological approaches, including statements of 'human nature', and sociobiology. Not all of these approaches are saying the same thing, even though they all argue that the ultimate determinants of human fate are to be found at the level of biology. While some influence of biology can never be entirely discounted — this perhaps reflected in the continual resurgence of biological theories in different guises over the years — a number of arguments are advanced that question the usefulness of the approach. For example, do biological explanations tell us anything about human behaviour that we did not know from the observation and understanding of human behaviour? That is, do they provide any *novel* insights? It is suggested that they do not but have the further effect of intellectual closure. Further, it is argued that there are richer and more fruitful explanations of human behaviour cast at the level of human reason and understanding. The conclusion is that we cannot locate certainty about human behaviour in biological approaches.

Chapter 2 is a discussion of the problem of relativity and the foundationalist and anti-foundationalist dichotomy. The argument here has been that all social perception is related to the social background of the perceiver, background usually seen in class, ethnic, cultural or linguistic terms. It is an argument that has been with social science since its inception, and the consequence of the argument is that, if true, there can be no general or independent position from which to view society. This would mean that social science cannot in any sense be a generalizing activity, that is, able to make statements that transcend particular social situations, a view that would restrict many contemporary views of social science. The argument this chapter suggests is that this dichotomy between relativity and 'objectivity' may be too stark, and that it is a contingent rather than necessary feature of social perception. Arguments for relativity are presented, and then logical and substantive arguments against relativity are examined. The chapter concludes with a discussion of the learning faculty of human beings and how this reflects on the question of relativity.

Chapter 3 looks at the problem of language in social science, and by extension, classification. The traditional concern with definition and classification is outlined — the thesis that social research begins with definition and social reality can be 'captured' by the appropriate use of language and classification. A number of problems in this view of language are then discussed, such as the idea of social science being cumulative, and the necessity for a trade-off between linguistic innovation and the comparability of research. Further, the idea of 'essential contestability' is examined, the notion that there are some terms that cannot be defined in an uncontested manner. It is suggested both that there are limitations to contestability and that contestability is a rich source of creativity.

Chapter 4 is concerned with the critique of social science that sees it as a form of ideology, or even indistinguishable from ideology. In evaluating this argument a usage of 'ideology' is developed that allows comparison with social science. It is argued that there are similarities between ideology and social science, particularly with regard to the incorporation of values and the nature of embedded prescriptions. However, it is noted that they are functionally very different, and they differ markedly in other ways. In particular, rather than social science being in any sense more value-free than ideology, it gains its special and distinct character by having additional values not found in ideology.

In Chapter 5 the idea of social science as a science is discussed. It is suggested that social scientists in general have been rather naïve in their ideas of science, in particular, in their belief that there *is* such a thing as *a* scientific method. Rather, there are a number of competing typifications of science, each of which draws attention to different criteria of validity. The chapter then examines five 'models' of science and elicits the criteria of validity. The central theme of this chapter is that it is irrelevant whether one considers social science to be a science or not; that debate is seen as arid and sterile. What is important are the criteria of validity by which one evaluates the products of social science. There are such criteria, but there is also the additional problem that at times they conflict, giving rise to further uncertainty.

Chapter 6 is somewhat more historical than other chapters. It discusses the rise of positivism and its practical application, behaviouralism. Both are related to historical social and intellectual developments. Positivism is the belief that the study of society can be 'scientific', that there is a unity of method between natural and social science. Positivism is distinguished from other forms of empiricism by emphasis on four principles, all of which are seen to be problematic. A number of critiques of behaviouralism are noted. While the 'movement' failed, it none the less made an important contribution to the development of social science, particularly with respect to the emphasis on methodology.

In Chapter 7 the question is asked: 'What does it mean to explain in social science?' Explanation is defined as 'the reduction of the unfamiliar to the familiar'. This involves a discussion of what is known as the 'covering-law model' — the idea being that something is explained if it can be related to and seen as a case of a class of similar phenomena. A distinction is made between the strong and weak versions of the theory. In a weak sense this is seen as an adequate view for the explanation of social phenomena. A distinction is made between two models of explanation, the 'cause and effect' and the 'reason and action' model. It is suggested that both are appropriate to social science in different ways and that the weaker version of the covering law view is applicable to both.

Chapter 8 looks at the problem of prediction in social science. According to some views the status of a discipline as a science is dependent on its capacity to predict; indeed, prediction is sometimes seen as closely related to explanation. It is argued that in social science (and in everyday life) it is impossible not to predict but that often our predictions will be wrong. That our predictions are often wrong is frequently unsurprising. The reasons why predictions are often wrong are investigated: such as the Oedipus effect, the zebra principle, chaos and catastrophe theory, the scope and range of prediction, and the role of contingency, among other factors. Two further arguments are introduced.

First, that while we may not always be able to predict events, we can often predict the responses to events. Second, that there are various ways in which we attempt to ensure the future by controlling it. Attention is drawn here to the role of power, interest, and trust. It is suggested that the frequent failure of prediction does not reflect on the status of social science.

The penultimate chapter asks the question: 'What use is social science?' This question is based on the assumption that if thousands of people world-wide study and practice social science, there must be some belief in its usefulness beyond merely being a way to earn a living. The chapter looks at what the study of social science has to offer the social practitioner or the policy-maker. The answer given is much more tentative than that often given, and the idea that the social scientist can be some kind of 'applied social engineer' is completely dismissed. Rather, the social scientist can offer a menu of possibilities, act as a critical audience, evaluate potential consequences, and sensitize to change. What the social scientist cannot do is either take over the policy-making process with a legitimacy derived from being a social scientist, or act as an *eminence grise* behind the policy-making throne while pretending to remain a social scientist.

The final chapter considers the emergence of postmodernism in social science. Emphasis is placed on sceptical postmodernism, which most forthrightly denies that there is any basis for objective knowledge in social science. Various aspects of postmodernism are noted such as the methodology, the idea of logocentricism, and intertextuality in both its linguistic and theoretical senses. The conclusion is that postmodernism is unjustified in its rejection of the more traditional forms of social science.

1
SOCIAL SCIENCE AND BIOLOGICAL EXPLANATION

....

Science and social science

The biological explanations of human behaviour are an attempt to treat human behaviour as phenomena that are amenable to scientific analysis and explanation. The purpose of this chapter is to examine these claims with respect to the biological explanation of aggression and violence. What is true of biological explanation in the context of conflict, however, will also be true when applied in other cases.

The introduction of a scientific mode of analysis into the study of society was an attempt to cope with the uncertainty surrounding the study of social life. Science, at least to the non-scientist, appeared to deal in certainties, while social science was full of debate, dispute, and contradictory interpretations. A scientific study of society has been a dream of scholars for many years — Comte, Marx, Durkheim, and Weber being early dreamers — and the high point in this quest came in the 1950s and 1960s in the guise of what became known as the 'behavioural revolution' (see Chapter 6). Accompanied by changes in the technology of research, the advocacy of the scientific mode of analysis became predominant.

Thus, while social science could not easily find validation through experiment, application, and prediction as could natural science, none the less adoption of the scientific *method* would guarantee results in a way that could not otherwise be achieved. Methodology *per se* thus became an independent and significant area of inquiry, since the validation of results was seen to be a consequence of the manner of establishing those results.

However, while the debate about the use of scientific methods in the study of society was intense, it centred on the use of quantitative techniques such as surveys, statistics, and modelling, and rarely included the transfer of scientific models from other disciplines to social science. The former stressed the transfer of *methods*, while the latter emphasized the actual transfer of substantive explanatory theories. The critique of 'scientism' in social science has, for some obscure reason, tended to omit or overlook biological 'scientific' theories. In general, particular disciplines can in some cases be enriched by the use of analogical models from other contexts — examples might be the dramaturgical analogy, or the application of systems theory — if only to the extent that the debate ensuing clarifies or extends understanding even if this is to lead to the eventual rejection of particular analogies. The application of biological theory to social science is not just a simple transfer of method, nor just the adoption of an heuristic analogy: it is ultimately an attempt to subsume social science under the umbrella of biology. This, however, is not a new project; Destutt de Tracy in the Enlightenment coined the word 'ideology' to describe the attempt to derive ideas from biological origins,[1] while in the nineteenth century 'social Darwinism' as an explanation of relations between nations and relations between classes had many adherents.

The new incursion of biology

The aim of this chapter is to suggest that biological approaches of all kinds are of little relevance to the study of conflict and that any further consideration of such approaches should be abandoned forthwith. To many this will seem so obvious as to render this chapter redundant, while to deny the relevance of biology is for others absurd. Thus in recent contributions to the study of society Gurr feels constrained to include a contribution from Davies on biology and conflict, while in an even more recent work concerned with 'understanding social science' Trigg includes a chapter on sociobiology.[2] Even more recently, Shaw and Wong and Reynolds *et al.* write books that attempt to explain international behaviour in terms of biological factors.[3] Whether these authors and others agree or disagree wholly or partially with the thesis that there is a biological influence on human conflict behaviour is irrelevant; the significant point is that there is still discussion of the subject that is taken seriously as a contribution to the discipline.

It was perhaps understandable in the nineteenth century, under the impact of early Darwinism, that this impressive and intellectually exciting theory should have been extrapolated to human society either as a biological explanation of class or as a biological explanation of race and nation. Indeed, Western thought in the nineteenth century was imbued with the ideas of development, progress, and evolution, whether one looks at the writing of Comte, Marx, Mill, or Hegel. It is significant that Marx felt there to be sufficient analogical similarity between his work and Darwin's to seek a foreword to *Das Kapital* from the latter. It is also understandable that some of these ideas should have maintained themselves in the political ideologies of the right in the twentieth century or in the socialized prejudices of the politically unsophisticated, and even intruded unconsciously into the thinking of comparatively recent liberal developmental theorists. What is incomprehensible is that biological approaches still have sufficient credence to warrant serious discussion in contemporary social science. The quixotic aim of this chapter is to assemble a number of arguments and approaches that have influenced the writer in his absolute abandonment of any notion that biological approaches have any use whatsoever in explaining human conflict.

Inherency and contingency in conflict

At the beginning of this chapter it was noted briefly that one of the aims of science was to establish certainty. The application of this desire in the field of conflict is further noted here. Much time and effort has been spent in determining the bases or origins of conflict. In this section a debate will be reviewed which importantly affects the way we view conflict. As will be shown, this is far from a mere academic debate, but one which significantly affects the mode by which society operates. Broadly, we can subsume various approaches, with only a little conceptual violence, into two broad classes, the inherent perspective and the contingent perspective.[4]

Something is contingent if its occurrence depends on the presence of unusual (we might say aberrant) conditions that occur accidentally, conditions that involve a large component of chance.

Something is inherent either if it will always happen (e.g., entropy) or if the potentiality for it always exists and actuality can only be obstructed.

According to Eckstein, the resolution of the inherency–contingency problem in conflict is an example of what he refers to as 'problemation' or 'the discovery of the most fundamental problem requiring solution if a progressive development of theory about a subject is to occur'. By implication, then, unless the inherency–contingency debate is resolved, there will be little or no progress towards an understanding of a subject area and hence a limitation upon our ability to resolve or control the more undesirable aspects of human behaviour. In the study of conflict the problem posed by the inherency–contingency dichotomy can elicit a response on several levels. Here we tackle the problem at the level of biology, but it can also be answered in terms of psychology, sociology, political science, and international relations. Further, there are circumstances where to decide between an inherency or a contingency approach may be far from easy. For example, if the biological thesis is advanced that aggression is not innate in man as such, but that the potential for aggression has a very low threshold or that aggression can be elicited by large numbers of environmental cues, a contingency view is being advanced the effects of which are almost indistinguishable from an inherency argument. In general, however, we might suggest that over-arching biological views of conflict have little use if they do not establish an inherency that is general in nature. And we would, in fact, expect them to do this since they are rooted in the universal biological inheritance of man. There are occasions, however, where we might be prepared at the level of the individual to cede a role for biological factors, where, for example, there are personal biochemical imbalances, but here the behaviour is explained by the aberrant and unusual factor and is hence clearly contingent in nature.

However, while Eckstein is concerned to resolve a difficulty in the contemporary study of conflict, and uses notions drawn from the philosophy of science such as the Popperian 'crucial experiment' (see Chapter 5), it is clear that the dimensions of inherency and contingency can be usefully discussed as organizing categories for most of the significant classical political theoretical contributions to the understanding of conflict.[5] The political theory of Hobbes, for example, would clearly be seen as an inherent perspective, while the approaches of Marx or Rousseau are examples of contingency. Hence Eckstein, while writing in a modern social science idiom, is articulating a very old and important debate.

The debate is of crucial importance for the discussion of conflict in general because the perspective adopted will vitally affect the manner in which the conflict is managed or resolved. To the extent that an inherent perspective is adopted, management, control, and the reduction of opportunity are all that can be hoped for (though in more or less humanitarian modes); while if a contingent approach is adopted, the satisfaction of needs and wants becomes possible and conflicts can be resolved, settled, or managed. If, like Hobbes, it is believed that there is an inherent striving after scarce resources, whether these be material or honorific, then needs, desires, or wants can never be satisfied in their entirety but the struggle for them only controlled. This perspective underlies the central thesis of Hobbes. Such control may be exercised through legitimized ideology or social doctrine, backed by coercion. An emphasis, however, is always placed on coercion and control, and a relaxation of these will lead to an outburst of conflict and protest. Hence, from this point of view the social fabric is delicate and liable to be destroyed through an excess of demand; demand must therefore be controlled and law and order emphasized.

If, however, conflict is perceived as being a contingent phenomenon, the response is very different. Rather than control, the satisfaction of demands is the way to social quiessence. To damp down demands through coercion is to reduce the legitimacy of the regime and merely store up trouble for the future. Conflict is not inherent in human nature but rather in the condition of man. We can envisage two kinds of hydraulic model here symbolizing the two approaches, the 'gusher' model and the 'kettle' model. The gusher model is constant pressure, like a capped oil well or a rumbling volcano, where the pressure can merely be contained and held in check; the kettle model also has pressure, but this can be released and dissipated harmlessly through appropriate manipulation of the environment. Thus Marx saw conflict as rooted in the class structure or in the relations between man, and if the conditions of man were changed, so also would be the relations of conflict; conflict is not inevitable but is a consequence of particular structures of society. Hence the social policies adopted by a contingency theorist will be very different from those adopted by an inherency theorist and would be aimed at response and satisfaction. While politicians are rarely sufficiently sophisticated theoretically to state their beliefs in this manner, yet the policies and ideologies of political parties, in so far as these are articulations of beliefs about human nature, reflect this divide.

The argument that there is a biological basis to human conflict behaviour is not just one argument but comes from a number of sources. The most simple and perhaps most widely believed view derives from simple Darwinian theory. In the distant past when man was involved in a desperate competitive struggle for survival, the chances of survival were better in so far as a man was stronger and more aggressive. The more aggressive he was, the better the chances of his mating, feeding, and defending his offspring. Thus in evolutionary terms, the selection of the fittest meant the selection of the more aggressive. Hence, over the millennia of human existence, and before the development of settled agrarian communities, aggression had been genetically bred into man.

With respect to within-group pressures, aggression was related to the ability to mate and to gain access to scarce resources. Between groups, however, population pressure and access to hunting grounds was also a selective pressure. Those groups of a more pacific nature would lose out to the more aggressive social units with the result, again, that a selective pressure existed for the breeding of aggression. There would be a biological aspect to this, but also it is possible to think of 'cultural evolution' in that a selective pressure existed for the survival of the most aggressive cultures within which the most pressure towards the selective breeding for aggression had taken place. As a natural result of success in the struggle for survival between species, there was an increase in the size of the human population, with a consequent increase in levels of conflict. Pressure of numbers on the resources available led again to competition and the elimination of some groups. As Malthus argued, later to be reiterated in more complex fashion by contemporary neo-Malthusians, population increases always lead to pressure upon resources with the result of 'famine, vice, and misery' at least part of which is caused by the occurrence of war in the struggle for resources.[6]

Another strand of the argument comes from ethology, a field of study that specializes in the extrapolation from the animal kingdom to the world of mankind. Here man, like other animals, has instincts and imperatives derived from his nature as an animal, and insights can be gained into those imperatives through the study of simpler creatures. Thus it has been argued that there is a 'territorial imperative': man will fight to gain and to defend territory just as seals on a beach do or birds seeking to mate.[7] Similarly, according to Konrad Lorenz, not only is aggression an innate drive that needs a periodic release of pressure, but the animal world can be divided up into two kinds of animal, those with intra-specific inhibitions to killing and those without.[8] In general, animals with powerful killing weapons also have submission gestures the use of which prevents the stronger animal from killing the weaker. Animals without such weapons typically rely on flight to escape a stronger opponent. Humans, being physically weak, have no such inhibitions to killing their own species, and yet through the power of their brains have developed weapons of frightening efficiency. The consequences of an imbalance between nature and efficacy in a nuclear age are held to be potentially catastrophic. But, while the Lorenzian theory has been rejected on empirical grounds — intra-specific aggression and killing are common to many animals other than man — its resonance lingers on supported by the prestige of the Nobel Prize-winning biologist.

A more recent addition to the basket of ideas supporting a biological basis to conflict comes from genetics in the form of the 'selfish gene', an idea that has become married to sociobiology and represents a contemporary expression of Darwinian thinking. Sociobiology is defined as 'the systematic study of the biological bases of all forms of social behaviour . . . in all kinds of organisms including human'.[9] A problem existed in traditional Darwinian theory in that according to that theory each animal was supposed to act to maximize its survival. Since any one animal had 100 per cent of its own genes, it was rational for each animal to act to ensure its own survival. In fact, however, animals will often sacrifice themselves and behave 'altruistically'. Mothers will often die defending their offspring even though each of the offspring has only 50 per cent of her genes. A shift in conceptualization was then made from the genes of the individual to the 'gene pool': survival of the fittest no longer referred to the individual but to the group of individuals who were the carriers of the genes shared with the individual.

By this means altruism could be explained in genetically self-interested and rational terms. It could make sense for a man to go to fight with a good chance of dying if by so doing he guarantees the survival of his genes in the shape of his offspring, his brothers and sisters, and his cousins. The number of his genes that they carry as a genetic group is larger than those that he alone possesses. But there is a further problem here: the number of people to whom we are genetically related is in fact far smaller than the social units to which we give allegiance and for which we are willing to fight and die. If the basic biological framework is accepted, the selfish gene can readily explain the basis of many conflicts, particularly if the social organization is the extended family, small tribe, or clan, since in many cases the gene pool will be co-extensive with the social organization. Protection of the social organization is also protection of the gene pool. But when we start to move to complex society, the gene pool is no longer co-extensive with the social unit. A brief consideration of the roles of conquest and assimilation and immigration and emigration makes this very clear. How can the idea of the 'selfish gene' aid in the explanation of altruistic heroism on behalf of those with whom there is no genetic relationship? Here two notions are introduced, the idea of 'reciprocal altruism' and the idea of evolved predisposition to loyalty. Altruism is reciprocated to the extent that the survival of one's own genes is dependent upon the goodwill of other groups. It is thus genetically rational to fight to defend not only one's own gene pool but also those other gene pools with whom reciprocal relations have been established and which increase the potentiality for the survival of one's own gene pool.

There is a further argument to support the defence of the wider gene pool, and this derives from the assumed nature of evolution. Mankind (including of course womankind) through much of his earlier history was part of an extended kinship group which was coterminous with the tribe. Loyalty and allegiance to the group was thus the same as loyalty and allegiance to the genetic pool. Shaw and Wong comment:[10]

If so, decision rules of thumb may have evolved as cultural enabling mechanisms to assist the operation of epigenetic rules in maximizing an individual's inclusive fitness and group solidarity. In the case of kin, this process may have been enhanced by mental channels attuned to heed physical and symbolic markers. Thus, biological relatedness may have given way to cultural ethnicity today, but in the human mind, the latter typically invokes images of blood relatives and a common homeland, language, and customs.

The extreme *readiness* of human beings to give without reserve allegiance to a social group, even though it is not a genetic group, is merely an evolved capacity. Thus, nationalism and patriotism are explained within the theory but at the cost of divorcing the explanation from any direct linkage with the altruistic gene. In Chapter 5 we will describe this procedure as a 'conventionalist strategy'.

Another addition to this collection of ideas comes from psychology, both psychoanalytical and clinical. The clinical suggestion — that man shares certain brain structures with animals and thus in some conditions will share behaviours — I will consider later. The psychoanalytic perspective, however, argues from the observation of man as patient that aggression is innate. Freud is clearly the most famous exponent of this view, and in his renowned correspondence with Einstein in 1932 wrote: '. . . the tendency to aggression is an innate, independent, instinctual disposition in man . . . constituting the most powerful obstacle to culture . . . there is no likelihood of our being able to suppress humanity's aggressive tendencies.'

In this judgement, of course, Freud was echoing Edmund Burke, and came to much the same conclusion with the concurrence and approval of Lorenz: the defence against the anarchic and aggressive tendencies of man was the protection and defence of culture and civilization. In this belief they were all probably wrong, if the analyses by Quincy Wright and Pitirim Sorokin are to be accepted.[11] Here the argument is that the lethality of aggressive behaviour both inter- and intra-group is positively related to advancing 'civilization', and that societies at the height of their cultural development tend to be more aggressive than at other times.

Yet a further approach, which we may call the 'clinical psychological', argues that the structure of the human brain is an evolved feature. MacLean argues, with Davies, that the human brain is layered by evolutionary stages with rationality marked only in the later development of the brain and overlaying the far more primitive part with the implication,[12] '. . . that, to the extent that the primitive and limbic systems 'dominate' overt behaviour, people may not be totally aware and in control of their reasons for behaving as they do, notably in times of stress that attend conflict'.

MacLean concludes:[13]

I will close with one more thought. It is traditional to belittle the role of instincts in human behaviour. But how should we categorise those actions that seem to stem from a predisposition to ritualistic, compulsive, or imitative behaviour, or to a proclivity to prejudice and deception, or to a propensity to seek and bow to precedent? Although not discussed, the display studies that were described bear directly on the question of the neural substrate of imitative behaviour and indicate a basic involvement of the striatal complex. With worldwide television, the matter of imitation looms more importantly than ever in human affairs, not only as it applies to fads, fashions, and drug cultures, but also, and of more dire consequence, to mass political action.

Thus there are a number of approaches that argue that there is a biological and innate predisposition to aggression. These tend to overlap and support each other; the ethological approach is not entirely separate from Darwinian or, neo-Darwinian perspectives, or, indeed, from clinical and psychoanalytic views. All of them would suggest, though, that the basis of conflict is inherent in that it will always happen and that its actuality can only be obstructed.

The frequency of conflict as a basis for biological belief

Part of Eckstein's definition of inherency refers to frequency of occurrence — something is inherent 'if it will always happen'. As far back into human history as we care to look we can observe conflict of all kinds, and a brief glance cross-nationally and intra-nationally will demonstrate a great deal of contemporary conflict. Conflict, therefore, is a frequent occurrence. To what extent, though, are we justified in going from the statement that conflict is a very frequent phenomenon to a belief that because of this it has a biological origin, except in the trivial sense that our biological inheritance does not preclude engagement in conflict.

We are, of course, in this exercise, making reference to an inductivist model of science.[14] Such a model has severe epistemological limitations. None the less, the frequency of past occurrence does have an impact particularly with respect to future expectations. Indeed, much of our behaviour is experientially conditioned. Thus, if it is established through an inductive methodology that violent conflict and war are part of the human condition and have always been so, then expectations and behaviour will be altered with respect to the future. Further, and more dangerously, in so far as our behaviour is based on such perceptions, even though they may not be true, we may well set into effect a malign spiral of self-fulfilling expectations.

A distinction needs to be made before going further. Conflict *per se* is probably an ineradicable feature of human life. The mere existence of desire and the non-uniformity of desires would seem to indicate the permanence of conflict in a situation where resources and potential outcomes are in limited supply. But it should also be noted that conflict is in some circumstances fun and is actively sought. Further, progress is often brought about by conflict; the green issue in contemporary politics, for example, is highly conflictual given the vested economic interests in the maintenance of pollution but is undoubtedly progressive with respect to the common good. What we are interested in, therefore, is not the eradication of conflict, but the eradication or limitation of those forms of conflict that utilize violence. It is this expression of conflict that kills and maims and has such terrible costs in developmental terms for other human goals. For the purpose of this chapter, therefore, violence is taken to mean the behavioural use of force or coercion.

First, however, in order to examine the inductivist case, we need to make some kind of estimate of the amount of violent conflict there actually is, even if this estimate is necessarily drawn with rather broad brush strokes. For example, all of us engage in conflict some of the time, but none of us engage in conflict all of the time. The potentiality for conflict resides in all of us (like watching television) but we do not utilize this potentiality all of the time. If, for example, we were to conduct a Weberian 'mental experiment' and divide our daily time into five-minute packets and monitored our behaviour and thoughts, we would discover that the amount of time we actually spend in conflict, even if we included conflictual thoughts and feelings with no behavioural manifestation, was in fact very small. And of this set, violence would normally be a small and often empty sub-set. The fact that we spend so little time in conflict, however, is no guarantee of a lack of biological origin; a stag, after all, spends only a small portion of his annual time actually fighting for mates.

If we continued our personal monitoring over days and weeks, we would discover further that our conflict manifestations were not even or constant; there would be pockets of high conflict engagement and periods of no conflict engagement. What is true of us as individuals is also true of collectivities. Sorokin, for example, looks at a number of nations and states, and while making allowances for changes in boundaries over time, concludes that taken over several hundred years there is considerable variation in the number of 'war years' of different states. Wright also notes 'oscillations' in magnitude of war and the increased likelihood of war at different stages in the development of a civilization.[15] Similarly, if we consider the contemporary era, there is variation in the participation in war and conflict of particular states at different times: Sweden, for example, from being deeply engaged in violent international conflict from the fifteenth to the seventeenth centuries has gone for nearly two hundred years without voluntary involvement in war. Even countries with a relatively high number of war years over a thousand years of history, such as France, show variation in their participation. It should also be noted as an important methodological point that high levels of war years historically must not be equated with the nature of modern war; in terms of days actually spent in violent conflict the First World War was probably longer than the Hundred Years War, with the consequence that Sorokin's data probably overstates considerably the amount of inter-collectivity violence.

To further the analysis on the relationship between frequency and inherency, we can turn to some of the quantitative studies of conflict and war. Melvin Small and J. David Singer writing out of the Correlates of War project note:[16]

If we calculate the number of nations that have existed since the end of the Napoleonic Wars in 1815 to 1985, and the number of years each has been a sovereign state, we find that the world *could* have experienced about 16,000 nation years in which war was underway. Yet there have been, in those 170 years, only 120 major international wars, averaging about one year in duration and four participants, for a total of 'merely' 600 nation-years, or less than 4 percent of the *possible* total.

What is then of interest is not the outbreak of war but the proportion of cases which did *not* result in war. If, for example, one is studying the occurrence of avalanches, and ideal conditions are isolated for an avalanche to happen, and it does not happen, then the non-occurrence becomes more interesting than the occurrence. There were in this period many more conflicts and crises than there were wars. It is clear, therefore, that necessity appears to be absent and that human choice, decision, and experience are significant factors and that any biological (or any other) deterministic model is inadequate.

It would appear, therefore, that if we reject genetic variation between parts of the human species (ie, France and Sweden), that rather than conflict emerging from some internal pressure, such as suggested by the Gusher Model, it is a response to events in our environment that we desire to control in some way. We then have the problem, whatever our views on the frequency of occurrence, of explaining how a factor which is posited as a universal is able to explain variations in the level of conflict; how can a constant explain a variable? Clearly as an explanatory mode biology would need additional support drawn from non-biological frameworks in order to make it work. Van den Berghe quoted in Trigg comments:[17]

What many social scientists have long tried to do is to explain the movements of the dog by rubbing out the man and the leash. What the sociobiological paradigm is suggesting is that we regard man, leash, and dog as an integrated system in which the motions of the dog are always to be explained by interrelated motions of the man and the dog mediated by the leash. What we can legitimately argue about is whether we are dealing with a Great Dane held by a toddler, a Chihuahua held by a Sumo wrestler, or some more likely pairing in between.

If it were the case that the influence of biology on society was similar to that of the Sumo wrestler with a Chihuahua, then presumably variation would be slight and the influence of exogeneous variables relatively slight. If, however, biology was the toddler and society the Great Dane, then autonomous factors exogenous to biology would be the dominant influences in conflict. Since, in order to explain the degree of variation we observe in conflict, we need to make massive use of non-biological factors, we may conclude that if there is any biological influence, it is so slight as to be negligible and that, quite properly, we may exclude it from consideration. If this argument is to be rejected, it is up to the proponents of the biological thesis to provide us with means to evaluate in some reasonably precise manner the effects of biology on behaviour.

Examining our personal experience, and observing the historical record, would then lead us to conclude that the notion of violent conflict being 'natural' and 'inherent' in mankind has little evidence to support it if our criteria of inherency is mere frequency. It occurs quite often, but also, far more often, does not occur. But, through a strange quirk of perception, the non-event of its absence is not taken into account. What seems to happen often is a violation of a basic methodological rule, the principle of non-vacuous comparison.[18] This rule states that a statement of condition only has meaning in relation to and compared with some other actual or potential relevant condition. In so far as the existence and occurrence of violent conflict is rarely compared and contrasted in a disciplined manner with non-violent conflict, our perception will be distorted with respect to its frequency and importance.

In one sense we might expect our perception of the ubiquity of conflict to increase both as our awareness of it grows and due to changes in the nature of the contemporary world. The former factor refers to a kind of tunnel vision that can occur to scholars specializing in particular areas; they tend to see what they are interested in everywhere and to attribute more importance to that facet than other scholars would. The latter factor refers to the enormous increase in interdependence that has occurred over the last few hundred years, accompanied by an explosion in communications. The consequence is a vast increase in the nature and kind of interactions that both individuals and collectivities engage in and also of our awareness and knowledge of these interactions. The number of conflictual relations will tend to increase with the number of interactions, at least until and if some form of integration occurs. This does not mean that more interactions are conflictual as a proportion of total interactions but merely that as the number of interactions on a regular basis increases we may expect the sub-set of conflictual relationships also to be larger. And, because both as human beings and scholars we give great emphasis to conflict, the impression is left that everywhere there is conflict.

The really interesting question then becomes this: why, given that violent conflict relations are a limited proportion of total relations, do we attribute such importance to them? In contemporary life people probably spend more time and energy watching television than engaging in conflict, yet no one as yet has argued that watching television is 'inherent' or 'natural' or an ineradicable part of 'human nature'. What happens, then, is that from the total range of human actions and behaviours a small segment of human experience is selected out and given disproportionate emphasis. The fundamental reasons for the excessive emphasis on conflict resides, first, in the effect of violent conflict itself on the participating actors; second, on the seriousness that often attends the outcomes of violent conflict.

There is very little by way of generalization that we can make about human nature, other than to note its enormous complexity, adaptability, and variability. But one point we can make with considerable empirical justification is that in general (but by no means universally) people prefer life to death and pleasure to pain. Conflict, as a form of human experience, enjoys special attention due to the threat it holds to this basic generalization regarding death and pain avoidance. In addition, it should be noted that conflict relations are sometimes sought rather than avoided, the goal being the excitation that comes through conflict, the communication that is sometimes achieved through conflict, the prestige that comes through a successful public participation in conflict, or the feelings of solidarity that sometimes accompany participation in group conflict. Particular social conditions may encourage or discourage participation in conflict at either the individual or the group level. For example, the type of recruitment to ritualized conflict — sport — varies in relation to the material and symbolic rewards and alternative channels of mobility provided by society. Similarly, Chagnon notes the care with which Yanomamo Indian boys are socialized into aggressive behaviour, a necessity given the structural conditions of Yanomamo life.[19]

The second reason conflict is emphasized is due to the effects of conflict in both personal, domestic, and world terms. Personally we have all engaged in conflict and this may at various stages of our lives have had dramatic consequences ranging from parent–child conflict, or workplace conflict, to divorce. And, if we look around us, we can see many people engaged in personal conflict with other people all the time. The recognition of this is that both within and between societies we have conflict-regulating mechanisms in the form of systems of morality and law, both usually backed up by some form of sanction. Similarly, if we look at either the historical record or the current scene, we see conflicts in the form of the prosecution of interests or the pursual of causes everywhere and at all times; and again many of these conflicts had and have the effects of dramatically altering the manner of people's lives. However, it is also the case that not everyone is in conflict with everyone else all the time and most of the time is not in conflict with anyone; it is also the case that while there is always protest, social movement formation, and interest pursual in society, these are always a small minority of the number of potential conflicts given the range of interactions. Thus while as a sub-set of human action, conflict interactions are indeed relatively few, their effects can be great. In similar vein, in an international context, as Michael Howard points out, war was responsible for the shape of Europe as we know it today,[20] just as it was for the division of Africa into nation-states and the structure of the international system. An awareness of the consequences that have attended violent conflict accentuates our awareness of the importance of this form of interaction. Thus, as we progress from the seventeenth century to the present, while the number of wars have decreased, their destructiveness has increased until annihilation is a real possibility. An interest in and emphasis on the use of human violence is thus not misplaced, but the interpretation of this stress in terms of ubiquity is, what would be called in other areas, a simple sampling error.

The fact that violent conflict is not as frequent as is sometimes assumed and that it is not a constant and ever present factor in all human relationships, while not of itself being a denial of the biological thesis, is at least suggestive of error. The error here would appear to be of the class of errors known as 'ecological fallacies', where inference is made from one level of analysis incorrectly to another level of analysis. Because, viewed at the macro-level, conflict appears to exist at all times and places, and is thus perceived as inherent and unavoidable, the inference is that it must be related to the nature of man. While there is always violent conflict on a world scale — there has not been one day since the end of the Second World War when there has not been a war going on somewhere (and hence the world is always 'at war') — this does not mean that individual states, communities, or societies are always at war. In fact, both individuals and leaders of collectivities always have choices about the courses of action they undertake, and the decision to engage in conflict (of which violent conflict is a small sub-set) is taken on the grounds that given the available strategic options in relation to goals and resources, the conflict/violent conflict option is the perceived best means.

To summarize this section. I have argued that conflict is not the ubiquitous phenomenon it is sometimes thought to be but that because of the type of thing it is and its consequences, it has received attention far in excess of its relative frequency as a class of human action. In conclusion, therefore, there is no good reason to go from a statement of the frequency of violent conflict to a statement of inherency, with or without the baggage of biological arguments brought in to sustain the inherency perspective.

Biological argument as intellectual closure

There are many works in social science that we know to be at fault and yet which still qualify as 'great works'. Three such works are Marx's *Capital*, Mosca's *Ruling Class*, or Michels' *Political Parties*. Each of these works can be criticized on a number of grounds and a considerable literature has grown up around each. Why, then, are these books still consulted and referred to even while flawed? One reason is that they are admirable merely as intellectual edifices, regardless of the significance or contemporary relevance of their content. A further reason is that they have within social science an historical relevance in the sense that they are landmarks within the development of particular fields. A full comprehension of some of Weber's work would not be possible without a recognition of the intellectual climate previously created by Marx, while the development of democratic elitism as a school through Schumpeter and Dahl was in the context set by writers like Mosca and Michels. But most social scientists are neither literary critics nor historians of social science but are scholars seeking answers to difficult and important questions. The real or major reason that we still look at these writings is that they attempted to answer important questions, and even their errors were instructive and provoking with respect to further research. In other words, the responses they gave to important questions were *fruitful* in terms of the development of the discipline.

Ultimately there is no way that we can choose among competing explanations of the world. Karl Popper would have us use falsification as a criterion for deciding between theories, but theory change, *ad hoc* modification, and the actual practices of scientists, as well as the problem that in social science we would have remarkably few theories left render this approach very suspect at any level above the simple hypothesis (see Chapter 5). Thomas Kuhn would urge us towards the development of conformity. And, while Lakatos frankly admits that there is no decisive way that choices can be made between 'progressive' and 'degenerative' theory, a preference is expressed for 'progressive' theory.[21]

Let us say that such a series of theories is theoretically progressive (or constitutes a theoretically progressive problemshift) if each new theory has some excess empirical content over its predecessor, that is, if it predicts some novel, hitherto unexpected fact ... Finally, let us call a problemshift progressive if it is both theoretically and empirically progressive and degenerating if it is not.

Put crudely, a theory or an approach is progressive if it leads somewhere and stimulates something, and degenerative if it does not. The 'great works' noted above were progressive in the sense of leading to new and further significant work and, even where wrong, were wrong in big ways that excited additional comment and research.

The discussion above relates directly to the topic of biology and conflict, for it is undoubtedly the case that a biological explanation of conflict is degenerative in the sense specified by Lakatos, while non-biological approaches are far more progressive in the sense of stimulating new and interesting work. The number of important questions that can be asked within a biological framework are very limited and almost always relate merely to an increased or more detailed formulation of what is already asserted rather than to any investigation of new social data. Hence, the social and non-biological approaches are superior in that not only do they have greater empirical content, but they also stimulate further and interesting work. A similar point can be made with respect to the fundamentalist interpretation of the historical geological biological record in contrast to a Darwinian evolutionist view; much of the same data can be 'explained' by the fundamentalist view, but having done so there is nowhere else to go and nothing else to do. Development, growth, and progress is at an end, a perspective that historically looks very dubious unless we arrogantly consider ourselves to be in some way far superior and more astute than the generations of scholars who will succeed us.

The problem with the biological approach to violent conflict is that it simplifies and creates a false clarity, a certainty about the world that is pernicious in that being rooted in man's biology nothing can be done about it. Embedded in the biological explanation of human affairs is a fatalism about the future possibilities of existence. The remedies for a potentially deteriorating social order are always modes of control that reinforce the prevailing social order; because of the nature of the theory, creativity and social invention are excluded.

The explanatory efficacy of biology in comparison to alternatives

The thrust of this argument follows from previous points relating to the ubiquity of conflict as a source of belief in its biological origin and the theoretically degenerative nature of biological perspectives. There we suggested that the reasons for conflict are at least, if not more, widely distributed than the cases of conflict. The general point following from this is that if biology is to be utilized as a mode of explaining conflict, it has to be compared with other modes of explanation and shown to be better. The term 'better' can be interpreted in two ways. First, the usage has to be more explanatorily efficacious in regard to particular cases, and second, it has to be more fruitful with respect to increased empirical content and theoretical and research development. Here, by way of example, I will take two cases and merely ask whether they are any better than a biological explanation.

Given that there are large variations in participation in conflict, does it not make much more sense to look for explanations that account for variation in reasonable terms rather than in terms of an articulation of drives the linkage of which to action is assumed rather than demonstrated. 'Reasonable' is used here in the sense of referring to human motives, desires, reasons, perceptions, and construals of the world. The clue to a fruitful non-biological mode of explanation comes from a variety of sources: it is that the probability of conflict increases with increases in the degree of interaction that takes place outside of a legitimized management process. For example, Chagnon, commenting on the war propensity of the Yanomamo Indians notes:[22]

However, there are many variations in the intensity of warfare as one moves from the tribal periphery to the tribal centre. Simply stated, warfare is more intense and frequent at the centre resulting in a different kind of cultural adaptation there . . . Briefly, villages at the centre, because of the relative proximity of neighbours, are not free to migrate into new areas at will. Instead they must confront each other politically and militarily.

The argument is not confined to isolated tribes of Indians but is suggested as an important explanatory factor in modern international relations. Kenneth Waltz, for example, keen to rebut the globalist thesis, notes that: 'Interdependent states whose relations remain unregulated must experience conflict and will occasionally fall into violence. If regulation is hard to come by, as it is in the relations of states, then it would seem to follow that a lessening of interdependence is desirable.'[23]

Additionally, were we to attempt an explanation of the prevalence of war in the relations of France and Britain between 1815 and 1950 when compared with all other nations, exactly the same kind of explanation can be proffered. Similarly, we may note that something in the region of 80 per cent of violent international conflicts occur between neighbours and that the probability of such conflict decreases statistically with geographical distance. A great deal of empirical content seems to be encompassed. Further, there are numerous models available that give good explanations as to why there should be a strong relationship between interaction and conflict; the relationship not only exists but the reason for its existence can explained in reasonable human terms.

Let us take another case, that of territoriality. For example, Lorenz notes the ability to fight increases as an animal approaches the centre of its territory, and the fighting ability of the aggressor decreases the further it gets from its territory.[24] Here the phenomenon is explained by means of instincts. The territorial factor is important in many animal species in order to disperse the species with respect to food supply, both for the individual and for its offspring, and thus to encourage perpetuation of the species. The importance of territory is emphasized by citing evidence about rats killing other rats who intrude on their territory or the fact that wolves have territories marked out by urine deposits.[25] Similarly in this context, the experiment by C.R. Carpenter with Rhesus monkeys on Santiago Island, where they initially set up territorially based units before one group engaged in conquest and colonization, might be noted.[26] It is indisputable, given the evidence, that for many animal species territory is of extreme importance, and it is also indisputable that for human groups territory plays an important role. But is it the *same* thing in animals as it is in humans, or are there other and better explanations for territoriality in humans? Can the same facts be explained in other ways that make more sense? With respect to human war, it has been noted that the ability to fight and the probability of success declines with distance from the home territory. This *could* be explained in biological terms as an analogy to animal behaviour or it could be explained by reference to reasonable human factors.

First, we might note that a great weakness of an extrapolation from animals to humans is that human territorial behaviour is very much more variable and complex than is animal territorial behaviour. There are variations in territoriality within the same animal species, but these are specific and predictable variations based upon the instincts of the creatures observed and admit of little voluntaristic invention or variation. In contrast, conceptions and types of human territoriality have varied enormously in response to changed conditions which may either be cultural, structural, or a response to scarcity. In a recent work Sack points out with examples the operation of these factors and plausibly argues that with humans territory is not about instinct but is about power and that to redefine a territorial boundary is to make an assertion about a change in the nature of power and control.[27] 'Power' is a statement about the relations between humans and in at least some of its forms takes note of moral relations which immediately divorces the phenomenon from any connection with amoral life forms.[28]

Territoriality in humans is best thought of as not biologically motivated, but rather as socially and geographically rooted. Its use depends on who is influencing and controlling whom and on the geographical contexts of place, space, and time. Territoriality is intimately related to how people use land, how they organise themselves in space, and how they give meaning to place. Clearly these relationships change, and the best way of studying them is to reveal their changing character over time.

Just as Sack is able to account for human territoriality in general in terms that are comprehensible and meaningful in *human* terms, so Bueno de Mesquita is able similarly to explain the decreased fighting capacity of a nation at distance by reference to logistics, technology, the maintenance of morale when directly perceived national interests are not involved as well as the nature and unfamiliarity of the terrrain.[29]

It does not matter very much from the point of view of the argument if any of these reasonable explanations are correct or if all of them are partly correct. What does matter, however, is that there are fruitful alternative explanations to biological explanations that are far more powerful and which relate to human experience in a way that biological arguments cannot.

Linguistic quibbles and the nature of human conflict

One of the more famous of ethological works was the popular best seller by Desmond Morris entitled *The Naked Ape*.[30] The title is instructive in that it has within it some very common assumptions about the nature of human beings in relation to the animal kingdom that underlie a great deal of ethological work. These are frequently made assumptions all of which are extremely weak when looked at clearly. The first is the confusion inherent in the statement that 'man is part of nature', and being part of nature can usefully be viewed analogically in the context of the rest of nature. The second is that reductionism yields valuable insights, and the third is that 'instincts' have any significant role to play in the explanation of human action.

The simple observation of a relationship between biology and conflict is sometimes rhetorically bolstered by the statement that man is 'part of nature' and to believe that he is in some sense independent of his biology is to engage in monstrous and wholly unjustified anthropomorphic arrogance. As MacLean argues:[31]

There are those who argue that one has no right to apply behavioural obser-vations on animals to human affairs, but they may be reminded that man has inherited the basic structure and organization of three brains, two of which are quite similar to those of animals. They evolve somewhat like a house to which wings and superstructure are added.

The belief that man is 'part of nature' and thus must share characteristics that are useful in explaining his conduct with other living creatures rests in part upon confused conceptions of 'nature' and in part upon heavy but often disguised normative assumptions. First, what is 'natural' is believed to be good, whether one is talking about face cream, the countryside, or wheat germ; and what is natural is opposed to what is contrived or manufactured. In this sense, cholera and typhoid are natural and immunization unnatural, a logic that is indeed adopted by some fanatical religious groups. A related sense of 'natural' is connected to man's relationship with 'nature' broadly defined as the organic environment with which man interacts and shares the planet. It is in this sense that naturists who shed their clothes and opt for simplicity are behaving 'naturally', or those who seek to preserve the organic environment as a human resource think of man as a part of nature. A further sense in which 'natural' is used is dependent upon what we are used to; hence the family is seen as a normal and natural mode of procreation (in spite of the fact that there are other organized ways of human breeding, caring for, and socializing children). To act 'unnaturally' is to deny the norms and beliefs conventionally accepted; thus homosexuality, child abuse, and ungrateful children are unnatural in spite of the fact that they are frequently observed. Yet another sense of 'natural' relates to the idea of natural law in science but probably predated it by several millenia; something is 'natural' if it always or often happens. Those things that occur all the time everywhere are held to be 'natural' — why else would they occur? Conflict, therefore, is as natural as sex, and so must be built into the nature of the human creature.

However, it must also be noted that altruism, bad habits, and taking baths are just as widespread. Would we then want to argue that these are 'natural' in the same way as conflict and aggression? Why not? In this sense we could suggest that anything that happens with considerable frequency is 'natural'. How else could it occur if it were 'against nature'? Whereas the first sense of 'natural' rests upon an overtly romantic view of the world, the second upon a systemic and interactive perception, and the third upon particular cultural values, this sense of natural is profoundly conservative with respect to human nature and human potential. What has always happened will always happen, a state of affairs that the anti-behaviouralists referred to as 'the dominance of fact over possibility'. A human regularity is a regularity because of the way that human beings view the world, just as a social structure is a structure not because of some immanent stability but because of the nature of human beliefs about obligations, rights, and sanctions. There is no sensible reason whatever to go from the statement that 'man is part of nature' in an interactive, organic, or biological sense to the proposition that he must therefore be in essential characteristics the same as other parts of nature. We may as well study trees to discover what light they throw on human behaviour.

Indeed, *The Naked Ape*, taken here merely as a popular exemplar, makes the perceived linkage between mankind and other species very clear. But the form of argument upon which these approaches rest is scarcely very impressive when viewed logically, for an understanding of human behaviour is held to have increased to the extent that behaviours are shared. Hence MacLean, as noted above, argues for a layered brain on the basis that a part of the human brain performs the same functions as are performed by the reptilian brain. Thus, to the extent that humans and reptiles appear to do the same things, and that there is some brain state in both cases correlating to these functions, the latter is held to be useful in explaining the former. Similarly, the behaviour of fishes or rats, or even primates is supposed to give indications as to human behaviour.

On a simple point of logic the usefulness of the approach declines greatly. Supposing we had a wheelbarrow and a Concorde airplane; both are used to transport materials, but how much about the latter could we find out by examining the former?

Thus it is with delight that the ethologist learns that infant monkeys prefer a soft mother to a wire frame or that animals are capable of deception.[32] The delight is engendered by the thought that because some animals share some characteristics with humans, we can extrapolate to humans from animals. This leads to consequent absurdities such that a genetic theory that has considerable explanatory value for simple creatures, such as parental investment theory, has, when applied to human beings, a profoundly ideological flavour involving the subjugation of one half of the human race by the other.[33] Very little, in fact, can be learned, partly because what is claimed to have been 'learned' about humans is usually due to the imposition of an inappropriate framework by the observer to establish what we already know anyway through the observation of humans; has any mother ever really doubted that her baby preferred a soft cuddle to a wire frame? In the main, what we 'learn' from the study of animals about human beings we already know from the observation of people; in fact, because we have access to the meanings that people bring to their behaviour we know far more. Further, to note that two or more objects share the same characteristics is not to establish any kind of common identity between them unless the characteristics so specified are in some sense necessary to the recognition of all the objects. Hence it is an error to suggest that man is 'only' or 'merely' a more complex kind of animal: first, because there is a qualitative difference between even the most advanced primates and man and, secondly, because in the specification of characteristics, those that are shared would not adequately characterize man. This is not an argument from arrogance, but rather an argument from essentialism: those things that essentially characterize the human species — moral behaviour, inventiveness, symbolism, etc. — are so far divorced from anything observed in the animal world that any such comparison is foolish.

The basic absurdity of the linguistic reductionism embedded in 'merely' or 'only' arguments is matched by transference of the word 'instinct' to describe human behaviour. Instinct, as used to describe animal behaviour, is patterned and genetically prescribed behaviour. Thus, the weaver bird, which builds a nest of incredible architectural complexity, could do so even if hatched in isolation from all others of its kind. There are three reasons for rejecting any instinctivist thesis with respect to man.

First, the behaviour that is described by the word 'instinct' in animals is only inappropriately applied to the human race. We could perhaps accept that people are born with certain instincts or drives such as the breast-sucking imperative, the need for food and drink, or the desire for self-preservation, but what is genetically endowed soon becomes so heavily overlaid with culture that it can no longer be considered as genetically driven. Take sex and procreation, for example. The forms and the varieties of sexual arrangement through time and space cannot be explained by genes and evolution but only by culture and history. All we can say about sex from a genetic point of view is that 'there will be sex' but how much, when, who between, and its relationship to a plethora of other social norms, rules, and institutions are questions that can only be answered through cultural study. In this sense, therefore, there is very little relationship between the instinctual drives of the weaver bird and human behaviour. The word 'instinct' is misapplied.

Second, a human being's relationship to instinct differs from animals in a fundamental and significant way: humans can deny instinct. Do humans have an instinct of self-preservation? Most of us most of the time act to preserve ourselves in times of danger, and even such a hard-nosed thinker as Hobbes ceded this right to the individual against the sovereign. But Bobby Sands starved himself to death for a cause. Monks in southeast Asia have practised self-immolation to make political points. The same kind of evidence could be brought forward with respect to all the so-called instincts, drives, or needs; they can all be suppressed or denied or over-ridden by an act of human will.

Third, while the thrust of David Hume's comment, 'Reason is and ought to be the slave of the passions' (leaving aside the question of the relevance of the 'ought' if it 'is' and is unchangeable) can be explained by the context in which he was writing and the need to explain the origin of the energy for human action, there is little doubt that the passions of men and women vary and are dependent on the social context within which they live. The way people perceive the world and construe reality will affect the nature of the imperatives which drive them to act. Further, many of these imperatives are symbolic and moral in nature and dependent upon particular construals of the world and people's relation to it. Many men and women have died over questions of 'honour', a moral abstraction which prescribes ideas of right and wrong in the relations between people and which cannot be reduced to ideas of status and 'pecking orders'. Similarly, many have placed themselves in jeopardy on behalf of others for beliefs they hold which cannot be explained in terms of either 'instinct' or 'reciprocal altruism'. Could the behaviour of the small group of Germans and Poles who sought at great personal risk to rescue and hide Jews prior to and during the Second World War be explained in biological terms? In general, we can argue that there is no human action of any importance which does not become imbued with moral and normative significance and hence develops an abstract and symbolic dimension.

To summarize: there is a yawning chasm between the world of even the most sophisticated animals and human beings, and to engage in reductionism on the basis of very limited similarities is to extend analogies misleadingly, and to apply a similar term to describe the motives for action in humans and animals quite clearly distorts our perception of the data unacceptably. Further, to engage in such an exercise is liable to breed a fatalism which is quite at variance with the facts of human existence and the ability to make choices independently of genetic endowment.

Notes

1. Roucek, J.S. (1944) 'A History of the Concept of Ideology', *Journal of the History of Ideas*, 5, 479–88.
2. Davies, J.C. (1980) 'Biological Perspectives on Human Conflict' in Gurr, T.R. (ed.) *Handbook of Political Conflict*, New York: The Free Press, 19–68; Trigg, R. (1985) *Understanding Social Science*, Oxford: Basil Blackwell.
3. Shaw, R. Paul and Wong, Y. (1989) *Genetic Seeds of Warfare: Evolution, Nationalism, and Patriotism*, London: Unwin Hyman; and Reynolds, V., Falger, V.S.E. and Vine, I. (eds) (1987) *The Sociobiology of Ethnocentrism: Evolutionary Dimensions of Xenophobia, Discrimination, Racism, and Nationalism*, Beckenham: Croom-Helm.
4. Eckstein, H. (1980) 'Theoretical Approaches to Explaining Collective Violence' in Gurr, T.R. (ed.) *Handbook of Political Conflict*, New York: The Free Press, 135–67.
5. See Webb, K. (1986) 'Movimento Sociali: Fenomeni Contingenti o inerenti?' in Melucci, Alberto (ed.) *Movimenti Sociali e Sistema Politico*, Milan: Franco Angeli; and Webb, K. (1986) 'Conflict: Inherent and Contingent Theories', *World Encyclopedia of Peace*, Vol. 1, Oxford: Pergamon Press, 169–74.
6. Malthus, T. (1970) *An Essay on the Principle of Population*, Harmondsworth: Penguin; and Meadows, D.H. *et al.* (1972) *The Limits to Growth: a Report for the Club of Rome's Project on the Predicament of Mankind*, London: Pan Books.
7. Ardrey, R. (1961) *African Genesis*, New York: Dell Books.
8. Lorenz, K. (1966) *On Aggression*, New York: Harcourt Brace and World Inc.
9. Wilson, E.O. (1978) 'Introduction: What is Sociobiology?' in Gregory, H.S., Silvers, A. and Sutch, D. (eds) *Sociobiology and Human Nature*, London: Jossey Bass.
10. op. cit., p. 85.
11. Wright, Q. (1965: rev. ed.) *A Study of War*, Chicago: University of Chicago Press, 116–42; and Sorokin, P.A. (1962) *Social and Cultural Dynamics*, Vol. III, New York: Bedminster.
12. Davies, J.C. (1980) 'Biological Perspectives on Human Conflict' in Gurr, T.R. (ed.) *Handbook of Political Conflict*, New York: The Free Press, 19–68.
13. MacLean, P.D. (1972) 'Cerebral Evolution and Emotional Processes', *Annals of the New York Academy of Sciences*, 193, 137–49.
14. The inductivist model of science is discussed in Chapter 5. Basically, for the

present, we can typify inductivism as the practice of inferring generalizations from past occurrences which then shape expectations for the future.

15. Sorokin, 1962, op. cit.; and Wright, 1965, op. cit., 116–17.
16. Small, Melvin and Singer, J. David (eds) (1989) *International War: an Anthology*, Chicago: Dorsey Press, p. v.
17. Trigg, R. (1985) *Understanding Social Science*, Oxford: Basil Blackwell, p. 165.
18. Passmore, J.A. (1966) 'The Objectivity of History' in Dray, W.H. (ed.) *Philosophical Analysis and History*, New York: Harper and Row, 75–94.
19. Chagnon, N.A. (1968) 'Yanomamo Social Organisation and Warfare' in Fried, M., Harris, M. and Murphy, R. (eds) *War: the Anthropology of Armed Conflict and Aggression*, New York: Natural History Press, 109–59.
20. Howard, M. (1983) *The Causes of War and Other Essays*, London: Temple Smith, 171–72.
21. Lakatos, I. (1970) 'Falsification and the Methodology of Scientific Research Programmes' in Lakatos, I. and Musgrave, A. (eds) *Criticism and the Growth of Knowledge*, London: Cambridge University Press, p. 118.
22. Chagnon, N.A. (1968) 'Yanomamo Social Organisation and Warfare' in Fried, M., Harris, M. and Murphy, R. (eds) *War: the Anthropology of Armed Conflict and Aggression*, New York: Natural History Press, 109–59.
23. Waltz, K. (1982) 'The Myth of National Interdependence' in Maghoori, R. and Ramberg, B. (eds) *Globalism Versus Realism: International Relations' Third Great Debate*, Boulder: Westview Press, 81–96.
24. Lorenz, op. cit., p. 164.
25. Mowat, F. (1963) *Never Cry Wolf*, New York: Dell Books, p. 59.
26. Ardrey, 1961, op. cit., p. 44.
27. Sack, R.D. (1986) *Human Territoriality: its Theory and History*, Cambridge: Cambridge University Press.
28. Ibid., p. 2.
29. op. cit., 40–5.
30. Morris, D. (1967) *The Naked Ape: a Zoologist's View of the Human Animal*, London: Cape.
31. MacLean, P.D. (1967) 'The Brain in Relation to Empathy and Medical Education', *Journal of Nervous and Mental Disease*, 144, 374–82.
32. Harlow, H. (1969) 'Love in Infant Monkeys', *Scientific American*, June; Byrne, R. and Whiten, A. (1987) 'A Thinking Primate's Guide to Deception' *New Scientist*, 1589, December, 54–9.
33. Trivers, R.L. (1972) 'Parental Investment and Sexual Selection' in Campbell, B. (ed.) *Sexual Selection and the Descent of Man 1871–1971*, Chicago: Aldene. According to some versions of this theory, the sexual strategies of men and women are fundamentally different. From a biological point of view it is to the advantage of a man to impregnate promiscuously as many women as possible, while, because of the dependency of a woman with young children over a long time on a man, her best genetic strategy is faithfulness and care. This is, of course, merely a scientistic affirmation of certain sexual stereotypes.

2
THE PROBLEM OF RELATIVITY

Introduction

Relativity in social science is one the most basic problems confronting it. Stated simply, the relativity thesis suggests that social objects will be perceived in different ways depending on the social position of the observer. The social world is perceived from a 'point of view' that is dependent on the socialization, experiences, or beliefs of the individual or, more usually, the group. Hence, someone coming from a working-class background will see the social world in a different way than someone coming from an upper-class background. Or, an individual from a Third World culture will see a different world to someone from the developed and industrialized countries. Historically different 'types' of relativity have been recognized such as class or cultural relativity.

It is possible to distinguish between two broad schools of relativity, the 'strong' thesis and the 'weak' thesis. According to the strong version of relativity, there is and can be no such thing as 'objective' social perception, where there is a description of social reality that is independent of the social position of the observer, but merely many relative points of view each congruent with the social position of the observer. According to a weaker version of the thesis, cross-cultural understanding is possible, but because of social conditioning and interests many people are biased in their perception and see the social world only from the point of view of their own culture or class.

The problem of social relativity has repercussions in numerous other areas. If it is the case that it is the business of social science to be a *generalizing* activity, so that the propositions it makes about people or societies have relevance beyond a particular society, then an assumption is being made that in at least some ways societies and peoples have something in common over and above their cultural, linguistic, class, historical or religious differences. Hence a statement like 'The fundamental cause of violent human conflict is the frustration of human needs' would as a social scientific statement be held to be applicable whether we are talking about Uganda, Kalihari Bushmen, Bosnia or the Gulf War. If, however, societies are sufficiently different in their essentials so that there can be no generalization across different societies, then the pretensions of social science to be a generalizing activity are misplaced.

At best, and if then, social science can only occur within and have relevance to a limited social context. Further, social science is a product of the Enlightenment and the 'advanced' and 'developed' world, and social scientists will often claim to have a superior understanding of social reality to that of the people they are observing or describing. Hence developmental economists may make statements about the 'best' means to develop; sociologists may make statements about the 'functions' of religion; or political scientists argue for democracy as the 'best' form of government. All of these theories or theses will involve values. Maybe the developmental economist will argue that by improving and stabilizing the means of production, longevity will increase and child mortality decrease. But the participants in the situation may see the world from an entirely different point of view. The flora and fauna have spirits; man lives in a symbiotic rather than exploitative relationship with nature; and the rituals and practices of the tribe are hallowed by tradition and the spirits of ancestors. Their experience and construal of social reality is very different from that of the social scientist. Who is right? Are they both right but from different points of view? In what sense, from this perspective, can social science claim to have a superior understanding of the world?

It is perhaps important early in the discussion to distinguish between subjectivity and relativity, for they are not the same thing. Often, however, they are conflated in such a way as to justify anarchic proliferation of opinions and beliefs. If the perception of the world is essentially relativistic, then my opinion or your opinion is as good as any other opinion. Perhaps the argument could be supported (as a *reductio ad absurdum* of the general relativist thesis?) by suggesting that in the last analysis every individual has a unique constellation of experiences and hence will see the world in a unique way. Such a view would seem to lead, however, to some form of solipsism which is hardly justified by experience but which seems to be implied by some forms of extreme postmodernism. In general relativism has been related to *group* perceptions, on the basis that it is within the group that commonality between people is developed. It is through shared experiences, history, language, etc. that a particular view of the world is developed. Hence a relative view of the world is not the same as a subjective opinion. Thus we distinguish between groups, castes, disciplines, orders, etc. on the basis of their commonality while recognizing that within particular collectivities there is room for individual variation. Within such collectivities, except for the odd historical passage, there are usually well-agreed criteria; it is between collectivities separated by time, culture, or belief that the real problem arises.

The idea that the social background of the observer could affect perception is hardly new. Plato, for example, believed that by adjusting the background and circumstances of individuals and groups certain kinds of people could be produced; hence his interest in manipulating the education of the guardians.[1] Francis Bacon, in his discussion of the idols of the tribe, the den, and the market-place, also argued that the background of individuals affected the manner in which they perceived the world.[2] Neither is the idea of relativity in the sense used here necessarily limited to the social world. Bishop Berkeley argued that perception of the natural world was dependent upon the situation of the observer.[3] How big is an elephant? Directly in front of me it is over two metres high while three miles away its 'real' size is a mere centimetre. The colour of something will depend on the light in which it is viewed, and the structure of matter appears different dependent upon the level of magnification. Or, to give an example used by Bishop Berkeley, if there are three bowls of water, one hot, one lukewarm, and one cold, the temperature of the lukewarm bowl of water will appear to be hot or cold depending on whether your hand has been in the hot or cold bowl of water first. Bishop Berkeley had great fun with arguments of this sort in the eighteenth century world of emerging natural science.

To the natural scientist this did not pose too great a problem. It merely demanded a consensual agreement as to what conditions were to be considered as standard. Hence a 'metre' was initially the length of a platinum–iridium bar kept at a certain temperature in Paris and, later, for greater accuracy, was based on the wavelength of light. Similarly, temperature was measured by a column of mercury under certain conditions or, later, by the kinetic energy of atoms or molecules. Hence, it is frequently the case, due to the standardization of conditions, the relative immutability of their subject matter, and the unconscious nature of that subject matter that the natural scientist can ignore many of the philosophical problems of the nature of reality. However, for the social scientist the adoption of standard conditions would not appear to be a way out of the problem of relativity as it was for the natural scientist. There is no obvious standard position from which to observe social reality, and the development of such standardized perceptions can come about only in a limited number of ways. For example, as a result of the communications revolution the variety of perspectives found globally may decrease because of cultural universalization. Or, due to the economic or political domination of a small number of states, a dominant if not universal perspective may be imposed. Or, social science may develop its own consensus about the nature of social reality, a solution that may have utility for social science but would not solve the wider problem of social relativity.

The ambiguous status of relativity in social science

We should also note the peculiar status of relativity in social science and the assumptions (frequently unrecognized) that lie behind it. For social science both uses relativity as a mode of explanation and in the main implicitly denies that it is itself relativistic. Social relativity, as defined here, is the thesis that people's perspectives on the world are a consequence of their social (and particularly group) existence. While this is a critique of the possibility of social science, it is, nevertheless, a common mode of explanation in social science, which can be demonstrated by looking at two typical examples of social scientific explanations. Frank Parkin, seeking to give an explanation of working-class Conservatism turns the traditional modes of explanation on their heads[4] by looking not at why working-class voters voted Conservative against their apparent self-interest, but rather why they voted Labour against the prevailing normative social ethos.[5] In this approach, which utilized the ideas of Edward Shils regarding the presence of a central value system, radicalized members of the working class were seen to be deviants.[6] The core notion of Parkin's attack was the idea of the 'structural barrier' that insulated the individual from the prevailing and dominant social norms. Hence living in a working-class area, or being a member of a trade union insulated the individual from core system values. The model was predictive in the sense that it could empirically explain variations in allegiance to deviant norms. The argument is that the social conditions of a group affect the way they see the world and subsequently their behaviour.

Just as Parkin uses the idea of structure to explain political deviance, so does Rokkan with cleavage analysis.[7] According to this perspective the major explanatory cleavages in Western European polities — occupational, rural/urban, linguistic/ethnic, and religious — emerged during the joint processes of statebuilding and industrialization. These cleavages were laid down and persist in their effect to the present day and can be used to explain a great deal of political behaviour. The cleavages can be overlapping and reinforcing or they can lead to increased differentiation. The point is, again, that the nature of the social structure is used to explain the beliefs, perceptions and behaviour of individuals. There is systematic variation in the beliefs that people hold and the way they behave politically which is congruent with their position in the social structure, which also affects what kinds of social experience they have.

While only two examples are given here to illustrate the point, this type of explanation is used throughout social science. The underlying argument being that the social conditions and the social grouping that this gives rise to can explain the behaviour of individuals. There are a number of intervening steps (often assumptions) in the explanatory schema that are taken as given — such as congruent patterns of socialization — that we shall not discuss here. But there is also an important assumption being made here which is often unarticulated: the observing social scientist can in some sense stand aside (above? apart?) from his subject and evaluate the beliefs and the consequences of those beliefs of other social actors and groups. For, if their beliefs are the consequence of a particular structural social–environmental exposure, are not the perceptions and interpretations of the social scientist also subject to similar influences? On what epistemological basis has the social scientist the right to consider his/her interpretation of social reality to be privileged? Further, where there are disputes in social science over interpretations of social reality, as there are in all the social sciences, stemming from apparently irreconcilable paradigmatic or theoretical differences, in what sense can the statements of social science be considered as items of 'knowledge'? Seen in this way the ambiguous nature of relativity, as both a mode of explanation and a critique of the activity, in social science is clearly seen.

Two classical relativists

Two relativists who have exerted a considerable influence on the development of social science are Karl Marx and Karl Mannheim. Marx's views on what he termed 'ideology' were never fully articulated,[8] especially in terms of their epistemological significance, even though the social determination of ideas plays a fundamental role in the dynamics of his theory of history.[9] According to Marx — simplifying his ideas considerably — social and political life is 'driven' by the economic mode of production, and the manner in which people view their existence is strongly affected by the economic circumstances of their lives.[10] The developing capitalist industrial society of the nineteenth century was having the effect of simplifying the social structure, with the consequent emergence of two 'great' classes: the bourgeoisie — as the owners of the means of production — and the proletariat, the exploited and ownerless class who sold their labour. These two classes would develop their own normative belief systems about the world congruent with their position and interests in the economic system. The bourgeoisie would attempt to 'universalize' their beliefs and to persuade the proletariat of their view, and to the extent that they succeeded the proletariat would be suffering from 'false consciousness' in that they would hold beliefs which were inimical to their 'real' interests. As the capitalist economic system developed, the intense competition would drive the less efficient to bankruptcy with a consequence of reducing the size of the bourgeoisie and increasing the size of the proletariat. The drive for efficiency would also lead to increasing mechanization, with increases in both unemployment and the meaninglessness of labour for those still employed. The nature of the economic system would lead to booms and slumps, but the net result would be 'emiserization', or the progressive impoverishment of the working classes. Under these pressures the proletariat would begin to organize, recognize their true interests, and would eventually take over the system through revolution.

This is very much a simplification of what is a very complex theory. In many ways it is undoubtedly wrong, and at different stages of his long and illustrious literary career Marx expressed himself in different ways, and later theorists from the same genre have attempted to rescue his theory in a number of ways. It was also the foundation of one of the major ideologies of the twentieth century. What is important to note here, however, is the role that ideas play. They are a consequence of the material conditions of life and a cause of behaviour. People (the proletariat or the bourgeoisie) see the world in particular ways because of their situation in the world.

There are several problems with Marx's view of ideas. The first is that while recognizing the relativity of ideas, he also maintains that one view of the world (the emerging proletarian view) is the historically correct perspective in that it is that view that will be manifested universally in the world. It is thus a 'restrictive' view of ideology; while the relativity of ideas is recognized, one belief system is held to be true while all others are distorted.[11] Opposed to this is the 'inclusive' conception, where all belief systems are held to be equally determined and equally true or false. Second, there are problems with the position of the observer: if ideas are determined by the material circumstances of life, how can they be articulated or developed by someone who has not experienced those conditions? Third, it is unclear as to what ideas are or are not 'determined' by lifestyle. Is it all ideas or just some? To what extent are ideas about mathematics or science influenced by the material conditions of life? This is a problem that was recognized by Marx's collaborator, Engels. He softens the mono-determinism of Marx's thought and sees 'the economic relations' as a 'red thread that runs through all other relations and enabling us to understand them'.[12]

Karl Mannheim was a much more sophisticated thinker about belief systems than Marx, and the description of his work here is again a simplification.[13] Partly his greater sophistication was because ideology was the central focus of his work while for Marx it was a much more peripheral factor. He accepted some of the central tenets of Marx's work, particularly with respect to the social and group determination of beliefs. However, he rejects the view (in the main) that some belief systems are correct and others are false. He also rejects the idea that it is only classes that produce ideology; many other groups such as sects, status groups, and generations can produce their own particular way of thinking.[14] This in itself raises an interesting question. If a particular individual is a member of several groups — generational, ethnic, religious, class, etc. — then presumably beliefs would be drawn from different sources. With increasing degrees of social complexity, we may expect the individual to be less determined by any particular group to which he or she may belong, and hence be more autonomous. The argument here would then be that the social determination of ideas is contingent rather than necessary; whether an individual's ideas are determined by group membership will depend on circumstances rather than necessarily being determined.

This is not, however, the conclusion drawn by Mannheim. For him the ideas of the individual are determined by group membership.[15] 'Strictly speaking it is incorrect to say that the individual thinks. Rather it is more correct to insist that he participates in thinking further what other men have thought before him' and 'we belong to a group not only because we are born into it . . . but primarily because we see the world in the way that it does.' Not every person in the group will experience the whole ideology, only fragments. The whole structure is something that is discovered by the analyst, i.e., Mannheim, whose aim is the 'reconstruction of the systematic theoretical basis underlying the single judgements of the individual.'[16] In other words, the 'ideology' is a construct developed by the analyst which is not actually held by anyone.

Mannheim is also confusing (or confused) about the various levels of ideology, ranging from 'particular' conceptions which relate to only some aspects of experience, to 'total' ideology (which encompasses the whole of experience). It is only the latter which is of any real interest, for with the former there can be bridges between different kinds of experience. He also makes a distinction between 'relativism' and 'relationism'. Relativism is where the belief systems constructed through the experiences and thought of social groups have no point of contact; they are quite literally different ideational worlds. Relationism, on the other hand, is where there is one social world, but different groups see different aspects. It is as if several blind people were examining an elephant; each one from their perspective would have a different view of what an elephant was, even though there is only one elephant. This distinction is important, for while he is often talking about radical relativism, he uses relationism as the basis for his own 'great escape'.

The great escapes

It is plausible to suggest that relativism is a psychologically debilitating position. It is great fun to destroy the position of other thinkers by showing that they are merely a function of the time, culture, class, or place from which they originated. But what of the relativist writers themselves? Are they not also trapped in time, place or group as well as the people they are writing about? Why should anyone read them if their thinking is so limited? It is possible that others would read their works merely through interest, much as one might read a detective thriller or watch a good film, to enjoy the works for their inherent interest alone. But many of these writers *want* to have more universality and applicability than the relativistic position into which they have locked themselves. There is the earnest (and in most cases unattainable) desire for literary or philosophical immortality, to create something that has significance beyond the commonplace and singular position of the writer. It is an easy and superficially destructive intellectual position to take but psychologically difficult to apply to one's own work.

There is another problem. If it is the case that there are no universal statements that transcend the social group, whether this be class, culture, or whatever, what is the status of the statement, 'All social points of view are relative to the social position of the observer'? If this is put forward as a universal statement, then there must be at least one non-relative statement that transcends groups; but if the statement is true then there cannot be any statements that are universal and transcend group judgements.[17] The strong relativist position is thus self-contradictory and cannot with certainty be demonstrated. Further, if it cannot logically be demonstrated that there are no universal statements about people or societies that transcend particular groups, then the possibility exists that there *are* such statements.

Thus relativists will often seek to escape, to demonstrate why *their* work should not be considered relativistic in the same way as everyone else's. The most recent example of this are the contemporary post-modernists. Having engaged in radical deconstruction of all positions pretending to generality or universality, they find themselves in a limbo with no firm intellectual ground to stand on, and at least some of them — for example, some of the postmodernist feminists — do want to say something positive about society.[18] They wish to '. . . move from deconstruction to reconstruction to construction, despite the intellectual logical contradiction involved in denying modern foundations and then positing one's own vision as in some ways "better".'[19] But in order to do so, they must find a way of justifying why their own views are not subject to the same critiques that they have made of the work of other writers and in so doing are implicitly arguing that there are criteria that have more general relevance. In this desire to be positive, they are following a long historical tradition. Plato, for example, having demonstrated that social perception is a function of education, training, and position in society, brings forward the theory of the 'ideal forms'. By training, education and thought these can be known, and thus the true and undistorted nature of the world will be seen. Auguste Comte, a towering figure in the nineteenth century, sees systematic distortion in the way that the world has been historically perceived. Through the advent of science — in his terms positive or positivist thought — the true view of the social and physical world will become clear. Hegel sees the Spirit moving through history, moving ever closer to its absolute realization, while Marx sees the universalization of truth following the establishment of a classless society after the communist revolution. If ideological distortion is a function of class, and after the revolution there is only one class, then there cannot be ideological distortion and relativity. It is also an amazing coincidence that all these thinkers see the undistorted truth as being on the threshold of revelation, with their own theories being an important element in bringing about this historical realization. Typically, modesty is not characteristic of such thinkers.

Mannheim's own way out relies — in contradiction to some of his other writings — on the notion of relationism.[20] The assumption here is that there is only 'one world', but different societies and groups are experiencing different aspects of it such that it appears as a number of different worlds. The answer, according to Mannheim, is to bring all these perspectives together, to 'subsume' them in the 'floating intelligentsia', which is a collection of individuals from different classes, groups, sects, etc., and out of the interaction between all these perspectives a 'true' vision of the world would emerge. One can see what Mannheim is getting at here; out of argument and debate we often see things more clearly, especially the weaknesses in our own views. But it really does not solve his problem. How would we know that the emergent perspective *is* like the 'real world' unless we knew what that world looked like? It is like being shown a photograph of someone we have never seen and being asked if it is a good likeness.

In general, we might suggest that the great escapes don't work if at one and the same time relativism is maintained with respect to others but denied in one's own case. Logically relativism cannot be demonstrated, but neither can it be wholly denied. In order to demonstrate thoroughly the non-existence of relativism, criteria of judgement are necessary that transcend group differences. This is a matter of intense debate that we will come back to later.

Other responses to the problem of relativism

While some writers have argued that all perception is relative, others have denied this and asserted either that there are constants in human behaviour that transcend the limitations of the group or that through the human agency of learning such differences as exist are no barrier to understanding someone from another culture. Hence it would not matter if one person were a millionaire American entrepreneur and the other a working-class Mongolian priest, there are sufficient similarities between them to reduce the problem of relativity from insurmountability to a mere difficulty.

It is not necessarily the case, however, that even if universals were discovered that they would be an absolute refutation of relativism. Three examples may demonstrate this. Almond and Verba in one of their works argue that *all* human societies have to perform certain functions, such as socialization, articulation, and aggregation of demands etc., merely in order to *be* societies.[21] Therefore there are essential similarities between all societies that allow them to be compared and contrasted and thus understood. But the level of analysis is rarified and the categories contentless; what is important is what goes into the categories. Can that be compared and understood in similar terms? Second, Fantz argues that when shown the picture of a face children in any culture will respond in a similar favourable manner but not when shown a picture with the same marks not organized as a face.[22] This may well be true, but what is important for cultural relativity is the form of cultural learning that occurs thereafter. No one need deny that a Yanomamo child reared in Germany would perceive the world as a German rather than as a Peruvian Indian. Third, Noam Chomsky argues that in spite of the apparent diversities between languages, they all have an underlying similarity or 'deep structure' that reflects the capacity and structure of the human brain with respect to language acquisition and formation.[23] This may again be true, but given the flexibility of human language a great many different meanings and understandings are possible at the practical level of use.

Thus, in order for the human universal argument to successfully counter relativity, it must refer to some concrete aspect of humans or societies rather than a category or capacity. Both of the latter can be 'filled' or 'manifested' in very different ways. There are a number of contenders here that if correct might act as refutations of relativity. Kluckholm and Strodtbeck, for example, argue as follows.[24] There are a number of problems that have to be solved by all societies such as production, distribution, reproduction, socialization, etc. There is variation in both particular societal answers to these problems and variation in the mixes between different solutions. But there is not an infinite variation of solutions. There are only so many ways that even human ingenuity can discover to manage the problems of reproduction and socialization. Thus there is a limitation on the range of variation. The next stage of their argument is important, for they then suggest that in all complex cultures there are ranges of responses to particular problems that are differentially preferred. A couple of simple or trivial examples may demonstrate what they are getting at. In British culture we have two proverbs, 'Many hands make light work' and 'Too many cooks spoil the broth'. These are giving precisely opposite advice, yet they are not confusing because they will apply and be relevant to different situations. Similarly, with the proscription on killing. In general killing another individual is forbidden, but there are cases where it is prescribed (as in war), or where it is condoned (as in self-defence), or where intentionality plays a large part in the judgement of the act (manslaughter). What there is here is a range of applicable values to the simple act of killing, and which one is relevant is dependent on the social rules applicable to a particular situation. These will vary between societies. For example, in some societies it is considered condonable for a man to kill someone who has seduced his wife. The fact that in Britain it is not considered condonable — different social rules apply — does not mean that it is beyond comprehension, because there are 'condonable' killings in British society. Understanding is achieved by a fairly simple extrapolation.

There are four further implications of this approach. First, just as the presence of human universals does not necessarily refute relativism — as was noted earlier — neither does the absence of universals imply relativism. In the approach outlined above, societal and group variation was admitted and yet cross-group understanding is seen as possible. Second, in such an approach there is an important role for human agency. Whether cross-cultural understanding is possible depends very much on the willingness of the observer to learn. The argument is that there are bridges across all cultures and groups, but like all bridges to get anywhere they have to be crossed. Unless the effort to understand differences is made, understanding will not occur. It is not an automatic process. Third, while the above argument may establish that cross-cultural understanding is possible, it does not and cannot establish which perspective or view is 'right' or 'correct'. It merely suggests that we are not forever locked into a nexus of ideas determined by our own cultural or group background. Finally, we might take into account the change in communications that has occurred over the past century and the effect of this on inter-group understanding. There are very few groups or cultures that are not penetrated by a cosmopolitan consciousness — emanating largely from Western society — and thus able to maintain complete group insularity. This may be seen as cultural imperialism, but the invention and dissemination of the transister radio probably signalled the death knell of cultural isolation. Even those cultures and groups that are reacting against such value incursions by emphasizing religious or cultural distinctiveness are still, none the less, victims of cultural penetration. To the extent that this is true, more bridges are in place than previously.

A further and venerable approach to human universals has come through arguments about 'human nature'.[25] The general argument here is that if human nature is everywhere the same, then from that one fact, with appropriate cultural modifications, different human societies and their behaviour can be understood and explained. Some, such as Thomas Hobbes, Sigmund Freud, Konrad Lorenz or Hans Morgenthau, argue gloomily that the human creature is selfish, egocentric and violent. Such a pessimistic view is modified somewhat in the writings of the socio-biologists, who point to important differences with respect to in-group and out-group behaviour but with the emphasis still on the violent and group-egocentric nature of human beings.[26] Other theorists, such as Maslow or Burton, have an entirely different view of human nature.[27] They see human nature as composed of 'needs', although they present different lists of human needs. Conflict, violence, and selfishness comes through the frustration of human needs. Yet other theorists see human nature as wholly neutral; what counts here is the learning processes that the individual or society goes through.[28] According to this view there is no human nature as such; it is merely a function of the responses of individuals to the experiences they have. In general, the variation in views regarding human nature, and the seeming impossibility of ever establishing a common view, would seem to make this unpromising ground for the discovery of human universals, whatever the various protagonists may maintain.

A further denial of relativism comes through the argument that human experience is essentially *translatable*. Two examples may demonstrate this argument. Aristotle, the Greek philosopher, wrote his work in the fourth century BC. He wrote in Greek and within a culture that was very different from mine. Thomas Aquinas was a late medieval theologian who read Aristotle in Latin and wrote his comments in the context of a culture very different from either Aristotle's or mine. I read Arisotle in English translated from the Greek and Aquinas on Aristotle in English translated from Latin. If I, in the late twentieth century, perceive Aquinas to have a similar understanding of Aristotle to my own, then the problem of language and culture cannot be sufficiently problematic as to obscure meaning. Hence relativism is not an important problem as far as understanding is concerned. The second example is more contemporary. Books published in one language are, as a common practice, translated into a myriad of other languages. The Bible probably leads the field in this respect, but many others are not far behind. Some would argue that there are things that can be said in one language that are unsayable in other languages and that a language is a unique phenomenon with respect to its internal references and nuances. There is undoubtedly some truth in this; some things are perhaps said better in one language than another. On the other hand, language is a very flexible instrument, full of alternative expressions and circumlocutory ways of saying things, and it may well be the case that while something said in one language may not be said *exactly* the same in another language, the dissimilarities are so small as to render the loss in meaning irrelevant for all practical purposes. I can thus read *War and Peace* or *The Brothers Karamatzov*, or even the wonderful novels of Georges Simenon, translated from the Russian and the French, without too much loss of meaning or understanding. If this is true then there *must* be a translatability of human experience between societies or cultures with the implication that while there are differences between cultures and groups, the uniqueness of these differences has been grossly over-estimated.

Conclusion

According to one notable theorist, there is a basic and fundamental dichotomy in our thinking.[29] Bernstein contrasts 'relativism' with 'objectivism' which is 'the basic conviction that there is or must be some permanent, ahistorical matrix or framework to which we can ultimately appeal in determining the nature of rationality, knowledge, truth, reality, goodness, or rightness' while 'relativism is the basic conviction that when we turn to the analysis of those concepts tht philosophers have taken to be most fundamental . . . we are forced to recognise that in the final analysis all such concepts must be understood as relative to a specific conceptual scheme, theoretical framework, paradigm, form of life, society, or culture'. This is a description of the 'strong' view of relativity, noted in the introduction to this chapter. And, were the relativity thesis to be true it would undoubtedly lead to the 'Cartesian anxiety' noted by Bernstein.

The stark dichotomy posed above is probably too sharp. A distinction needs to be made between relativity as a problem of *understanding* and relativity as an epistemological problem regarding knowledge. With respect to understanding, relativity is better seen as a contingent feature, that is, it is conditonal rather than absolute. Throughout history scholars have studied other cultures, religions, languages, or societies and have believed that they do understand them. They *could* be wrong, but it is unlikely that self-deception could occur on such a massive scale. It is also probably the case that there are limitations on understanding. For example, however much comparative knowledge of separatist movements I accumulated, together with detailed historical and ethnographic knowledge of particular cases, I still would not understand the Kurdish, Eritrean or Bosnian situations in precisely the *same* way that the actors in those situations do. But that is not to say that 'understanding' is not possible or that I have not understood. It is just that there is a limitation, a limitation that extends to some degree to relations between separate individuals within one society as well as between individuals from different societies.

There is another aspect to 'understanding'. If it is the case that it is indeed possible to understand other societies, even if not perfectly, across time and space, then it must be possible to make comparisons between them which means that the ability to detect similarities and differences must exist. We only understand in so far as the object of our understanding reflects some aspect of our own experience. Later we will refer to explanation as 'the reduction of the unfamiliar to the familiar'.

With regard to relativism as a basis for epistemological uncertainty and the consequent quest for some form of absolute certainty, with respect to either knowledge or values, over and above human constructions and understandings of the world, we can only agree that there can be no such certainty. But is this a problem? If one leaves aside religious belief and revelation, the only things which we are left with are human construals and understandings that will vary in time and space. There can be nothing else. Often social science is contrasted with natural science in this respect, in that natural science is believed to have discovered natural laws that are invariable in time and space. Natural science, however, is as much a human construct as any other mental production and, as such, is subject to change and revision. Who has ever seen a quark, let alone six different kinds of quark? Or a black hole? These are merely mathematically and imaginatively deduced descriptions and inferences from certain kinds of indirect evidence. Similarly with social science, the theories and models we use to understand and describe 'reality' are human constructs and can only be evaluated according to criteria (see Chapter 5) that we know to be contentious and imperfect. To suggest that 'social inequality in the distribution of social goods tends to occur when there there is surplus value to be distributed' is a human construal of evidence that may or may not be true and may or may not be universal. It is certainly open to criticism and revision. To worry about the absolute certainty of human productions, rather than better or worse interpretations, is to seek a perfection of the human condition that cannot possibly exist. Rather than seeking to tilt at the imaginary windmill of absolute certainty, we should be looking at the management of uncertainty or how we as social scientists respond to such problems.

Notes

1. See Plato, *The Republic of Plato* (Trans. F.M. Cornford) (1936), London: Oxford University Press.

2. See Bacon, Francis (1901) *The Dignity and Advancement of Learning*, London: George Bell, 207–11.
3. Berkeley, G., (1967), *The Principles of Human Knowledge and Three Diologues Between Hylas and Philonous*, London and Glasgow: William Collins.
4. See, for example, McKenzie, R. and Silver, A. (1968) *Angels in Marble: Working Class Conservatives in Urban England*, London: Heinemann Educational; and Nordlinger, E.A. (1967) *The Working Class Tories: Authority, Deference, and Stable Democracy*, London: MacGibbon and Kee.
5. Parkin, F. (1967) 'Working-class Conservatives: A Theory of Political Deviance', *British Journal of Sociology*, 18, 279–90.
6. Shils, E. (1965) 'Charisma, Order, and Status', *American Sociological Review*, 30, 199–213; and (1975) *Centre and Periphery: Essays in Macro-Sociology*, Chicago: University of Chicago Press, 3–16.
7. Rokkan, Stein and Urwin, D.W. (1983) *Economy, Territory, Identity: the Politics of Western European Peripheries*, London: Sage Publications. See also Rose, R., and Urwin, D.W. (1969) 'Social Cohesion, Political Parties and Strains in Regimes.' *Comparative Political Studies*, 2, 7–67.
8. See McLellan, D. (1986) *Ideology*, Milton Keynes: The Open University Press, p. 10. 'Indeed, as with so many of his central concepts, that of ideology is far from completely clear in Marx; his comments on ideology tend to be *obiter dicta* and he never produced a coherent account.'
9. See, for example, 'It is not the consciousness of men that determines existence, on the contrary, their social existence determines their consciousness'; Marx, K. (1970) *A Contribution to a Critique of Political Economy*, Moscow: Progress Books, p. 21, and: 'The production of ideas, of conceptions, of history, is at first directly interwoven with the material activity and the material intercourse of men, the language of real life. Conceiving, thinking, the mental intercourse of men, appear at this stage as the direct efflux of their material behaviour. The same applies to mental production as expressed in the language of politics, morality, religion, metaphysics, etc., of a people'; Marx, K., (ed. C.J. Arthur) (1970) *The German Ideology*, London: Lawrence and Wishart, p. 47.
10. There is dispute, partly caused by Marx's own unclarity on the point, as to whether the relationship is causal and deterministic or merely an influence relationship resulting in a tendency. For further comment on Marx see Engels' letter to Hans Starkenburg in Hook, S. (1933) *Towards an Understanding of Karl Marx*, London: Victor Gollancz, p. 279; Plamenatz, J. (1971) *Ideology*, London: Macmillan, p. 47.
11. See Seliger, M. (1975) *Ideology and Politics*, London: George Allen and Unwin Ltd, 14–15; and (1977) *The Marxist Conception of Ideology: a Critical Essay*, Cambridge: Cambridge University Press, p. 1.
12. See Engels' letter to Hans Starkenburg in Hook, S. (1933) *Towards an Understanding of Karl Marx*, London: Victor Gollancz, p. 279. Robert Merton (1967) commenting in *Social Theory and Social Structure*, New York: The Free Press, p. 479, suggests that if a move such as this towards mere heuristic utility is allowed, then through such flexibility anything can be explained away.
13. It should be noted that *Ideology and Utopia*, a seminal book and perhaps the most important work in the field, was not written as a unitary work but is a compilation of essays over a number years. Hence, within the work there are contradictions which are in part a reflection and a consequence of the

development of Mannheim's thought. *Ideology and Utopia*, however, stands as one of those works that raises important and significant questions with which contemporary scholars are still struggling. This assessment of the centrality of Mannhiem's work is by no means universally shared. Maurice Cranston (1968) in 'Ideology and Mr. Lichtheim', *Encounter*, 13, refers to Mannheim as 'an inferior thinker', while McLellan (1986) op. cit., p. 49, suggests that he is 'vague and ambiguous'.

14. Mannheim, Karl (1936) *Ideology and Utopia*, London: Routledge and Kegan Paul, 247–48.
15. Mannheim, ibid., p. 3; p. 19, p. 186.
16. Mannheim, ibid., p. 52.
17. See Parsons, Talcott (1936) 'Review of Alexander von Scheltung's Max Weber's Wissenschaftlich' in *American Sociological Review*, 1, 675–81.
18. See Rosenau, P. (1992) *Post-modernism in the Social Sciences: Insights, Inroads and Intrusions*, Princeton: Princeton University Press, 144–55.
19. Ibid., p. 145.
20. He attempts to escape in various other ways, but this is the most interesting attempt.
21. Almond, G. and Verba, S. (1957) *The Civic Culture*, Washington: Little Brown.
22. Fantz, R.L. (1961) 'The Origin of Form Perception' in *Scientific American*, 204, 5, 66–72.
23. Chomsky N. (1968) *Language and Mind*, New York: Harcourt Brace.
24. Kluckholm, F.R. and Strodtbeck, F.L. (1961) *Variations in Value Orientations*, Evanston, Ill: Row, Peterson, 1–48.
25. Berry, C.J. (1986) *Human Nature*, London: Macmillan.
26. Shaw, R. Paul and Wong, Y. (1989) *The Genetic Seeds of Warfare: Evolution, Nationalism, and Patriotism*, London: Unwin Hyman.
27. Maslow, A.H. (1970) *Motivation and Personality*, London: Harper and Row; and Burton, J.W. (ed.) (1990) *Conflict: Human Needs Theory*, London: Macmillan.
28. Skinner B.F. (1971) *About Behaviorism*, London: Jonathan Cape; and Watson, J.B. (1924) *Behaviorism*, Chicago: University of Chicago Press.
29. Bernstein, R.J. (1983) *Beyond Objectivism and Relativism: Science, Hermeneutics and Praxis*, Philadelphia: University of Philadelphia Press, p. 18.

3
LANGUAGE IN SOCIAL SCIENCE

Introduction

Language has always been a matter of prime concern in social science and in recent years has become an even more contested area. At one end of the spectrum is the school of thought that believes that by precise definition and classification social science can build rigorous and useful models and theories about the world. At this end of the spectrum, there would tend to be a close identification of social science with natural science. At the other end of the spectrum are those who see language as infinitely flexible and precise meaning as forever unobtainable. Any attempt to 'capture' the world theoretically is doomed to failure. Here social science is seen as being closer to literary interpretation.

It is, of course, impossible most of the time *not* to use language in description and communication.[1] Even mathematics is a language, though one with much more precisely specified rules than natural language. And, at the base of all language, is the presumption that the emitter and the receiver share similar meanings. At times, of course, they may not, and confusion and misunderstanding (the basis of much comedy and sometimes tragedy) will occur. Most of the time everyday communication occurs with little problem, partly because hints as to the specific meanings of words are indicated by the context in which they are used. The word 'game', to use a famous example, has many meanings, but which one is relevant is usually determined by context.[2]

Language is important in another way. Words in themselves are merely artificial symbols, conventions established, usually within historical groups, as to how those symbols should be used. They may be auditory or graphical, and meaning may even be conveyed in culturally specific 'body language'. They are not *arbitrary* symbols, however, since there exists in most cases agreement on how they should be used. A language is a store of such symbols and agreements. Since a living language is in constant development and change, new symbols will be brought into the language and old symbols dropped or develop new meanings. A symbol — a word or a phrase — will usually be related to a concept but will always be less rich or complex than the concept it is indicating. The word 'football', for example, indicates a game, but the thought or the concept of the game will in the mind be much more complex than the simple word itself. It will trigger images and emotions in the mind of the receiver (boring, Saturday afternoon, broken leg, sweeper system) that are not intended or known by the emitter. There is, therefore, always a 'gap' between the word and the concept that is a possible source of confusion. In most cases this does not matter too much because we use words in complex and subtle combinations to reduce areas of possible confusion. But the gap will, none the less, always be there.

It is also the case that the language we have will influence what we think. In the past some thinkers believed that there was an identity between thought and language. This is clearly wrong. Music and art, for example, are ways of thinking that involve no verbalization, and we sometimes have an idea and 'search' for the best word or words to express it, sometimes being driven to use new words or old words in new ways. But while language and thought are not the same thing, it is none the less true that we are *influenced* in what we say by the language, concepts, and theories that we have. Indeed, part of learning a discipline is to master its range of terms and theories and their applications. This may represent the store of disciplinary wisdom that the student is expected to master. Once having demonstrated this mastery through performance in examinations and dissertations, the student becomes 'qualified' in that area. Another way of looking at it is to see such learning as the imposition of a conceptual straightjacket, where tradition and hierarchy are hallowed and creativity and novelty are stifled. It is for this reason that some postmodernists encourage us to look at the 'margins' or the 'silences' of theory, or, in more accessible language, at what a theory is *not* saying or what questions it is *not* attempting to answer. This is good advice, but is saying little more than that the student (in the widest sense) should be open and critical, should not accept disciplinary impositions without good reason, and should be constantly questioning.

Some formal characteristics of definition

Right at the beginning of most research activities, words in the form of definitions are important. These may change as the research progresses, but what is being studied is defined as a means of specifying an area as precisely as possible. A definition is always a specification of a limited number of attributes of a phenomenon. It is an attempt to identify a phenomenon as distinct from all other phenomena. What this means is that while it is always possible to give a long list of the features of any existing object or set of objects, this is rarely very useful. What is normally sought in a definition — particularly a technical disciplinary definition — is a specification of the essential characteristics by which a thing is to be recognized. Hence, while there are a myriad of ideas associated with the notion of 'crime', a definition might be used which identifies only essential characteristics, ie, 'an act which is prohibited by law'. Such an approach is undoubtedly an aid to clarity, communication, and generalization — since it is applicable across cultures — but it also impoverishes the idea by stripping it of the richness of its associations.

These linguistic and conceptual associations are built into the normal meanings of words, and it is doubtful whether any amount of careful definition will successfully rid technical terms in social science of their associations. For example, the term 'economic man' as someone who in the market-place is a 'self-interested and rational' actor will be viewed normatively and emotionally very differently by a Marxist and a monetarist economist. Broadly, we can think of words normally carrying three kinds of meaning: denotative, connotative, and indexical. By 'denotative' we refer to the descriptive element of a word; hence by 'man' we might mean 'a *homo sapiens* of the male sex'. By 'connotative' we refer to the emotional, normative, or evaluative components of meaning. Thus 'man' might carry different kinds of emotional baggage to a radical feminist, a Yanomamo warrior, or an advertising executive. By 'indexical' we refer to the *linkages* that words have, what a word is associated with in the mind. We might make reference to 'the Cold War', which leads, depending on the individual, to an immediate thought of nuclear weapons, the USA and the USSR, and the Cuban Missile Crisis. The meanings that words carry, therefore, are complex and made more so by the fact that these different sorts of meanings can change independently. For example, the connotative meaning of 'father' will vary somewhat depending on the childhood experiences of the individual, while the denotative component remains stable. In another case, that of 'democracy', the approbationary connotative meaning remains stable (who could deny that democracy is a 'good thing'?) while the denotative element (what *is* democracy?) varies enormously.[3] In general, social science definitions will seek, without complete success, to reduce the role of connotative and indexical meaning in favour of maximizing descriptive meaning. Can one *ever*, though, however defined, use words like 'war' or 'poverty' without some emotional overtones?

A further point to be borne in mind when discussing definitions is to remember that all we are talking about is the *use* of words. We are *not* talking about the 'real' world, although what we decide may well have implications for how we study the world. Definitions, generally, are neither right nor wrong but only more or less useful. Hence, someone may define 'rabbit' as 'a large grey animal with tusks and a trunk'. So long as that person used the word 'rabbit' consistently in that sense, there would be nothing wrong with the definition though we may question the usefulness of it. Thus, if the word 'war' is defined as 'a conflict with at least 1,000 battle deaths where one of the parties is a member of the state system', this tells you only about how I am using the word and says little about anything else. I *could* define 'war' in numerous other ways but choose to use the word in this particular way. This means, of course, that words do not have a 'real' meaning but only the meaning that we assign to them. Hence, every time the word 'war' is used, the term 'a conflict with at least 1,000 battle deaths where one of the parties is a member of the state sytem' should be substitutable.

There are also various types of definition, only the more important of which — conventional, etymological, ostensive, and stipulative — will be discussed here. *Conventional* definitions refer to well-understood meanings; there is no need to define because what is meant is understood by the audience. Most of our communication employs conventional meanings most of the time. However, once we start moving into specialist fields, conventional understanding may break down. For example, two people may be having a discussion about democracy, with one assuming that the term refers to direct democracy, while the other assumes a representative democracy model. The conversation would be somewhat confused unless the term was more precisely specified. *Etymological* definition refers to the roots of a word or to its dictionary meaning. Hence, the meaning of 'democracy' might be established by reference to the Greek origins of the term. The problem is, of course, that in time and situations usage changes, and the origin or dictionary definition may be inadequate where new or special meanings have been developed. *Ostensive* definition is where the experience is substituted for verbal description. For example, it is difficult to define the colour 'red'. Reference might be made to wavelengths of light (approximate wavelength range of 740–620 nanometres), but this may not correspond to the subjective experiences of the observer. The only way of conveying exact meaning might be by example.

The most important type of definition, however, is *stipulative* definition. This is where a word is given a special meaning in order to increase the precision of use. All specialist fields will develop stipulative meanings, whether we are talking about sport, business, or academic disciplines. Computer specialists, for example, will talk about 'bytes', 'RAM', 'ROM', 'hard disk', 'floppy disk', 'modem', 'operating system', 'wimp', 'wysiwyg', etc., etc. with the consequence that those who are not part of that community have little comprehension of what they are talking about. In just the same way in cricket there are 'long legs', 'short legs', 'bouncers', 'sweeps', etc., etc. The creation of special words, or assigning new meaning to old words, may on occasion be unnecessary, leading to what is sometimes referred to as 'jargon', but in most cases it is a way of communicating with greater economy and precision to an audience which shares those meanings. Consequently, those desiring to join that specialist field will often have to undergo a lengthy period of socialization in order to learn the range of special meanings. Thus a student studying international relations will have to come to grips with 'realism', neo-realism', 'consociationalism', 'complex interdependence', 'idealism', 'spillover', 'regimes', 'saddle points', 'functionalism', 'neo-functionalism', etc., etc. Without such a vocabulary, the student would be incapable of taking part in the disciplinary discourse.

The role and limits of definition

Traditionally definition and classification have played an important part in social scientific discourse because it is difficult even to begin research without some fairly clear idea of what it is that is being studied. While in everyday speech it is not often necessay to define the words one uses since the context will usually indicate the usage, in social science greater precision is sought. Hence social scientists will normally not use terms like 'democracy', 'power', or 'crime' without specifying their usage. This is by no means a new activity. Philosophers through the ages have sought to be precise in their use of terms, both as an aid to clarity and to ensure that they are not misunderstood. There was, indeed, a school of thought that argued (optimistically) that if we used words correctly there would not be any real philosophical problems.[4]

Many studies will thus begin with defining the objects or subject matter of that study. This can in itself be very contentious. Three examples may demonstrate this. One scholar may identify 'politics' as that activity that happens at Westminster, or that which concerns the activities of political parties in a polity, while another may have a very much wider perspective, seeing politics as concerned with the distribution of power and resources.[5] Or, one scholar may define 'international relations' as the interactions that occur between states, while another will see it as *all* interactions that occur across state boundaries.[6] The point about these two examples is that while the same words are being used ('politics', 'international relations') completely different sets of objects are being identified. Third, if one were to engage in a study of the causes of war, it is necessary to say what a war is. According to Small and Singer, a war is where there are 1,000 battle deaths among all the system members.[7] Zacher, however, sees war as occuring where at least 500 persons enter a state with the purpose of changing the government or its policies,[8] while for Glossop war is 'large scale violent conflict between organised groups that are or aim to establish governments'.[9]

The point about these examples is that very different types of objects will be the subject of research, with the consequence that comparability between studies will be low and the cumulation of knowledge limited. Given this kind of definitional variability, a number of responses are possible. One response would be to condemn those who continually redefine concepts and hence add to the number of studies which are non-comparable and thus non-cumulative. The spectre of a disciplinary thought-police arises, where those who don't research within an accepted framework either don't get contracts or don't get published. This somewhat authoritarian approach ignores the fact that there are within all the social science disciplines different 'schools' (theories, approaches, paradigms etc.) between which there are very great theoretical chasms. It also leaves out of contention the question of values; social science has a strong normative as well as descriptive content, and since social scientists will hold different values they will define things in different ways. Further, were such conceptual uniformity imposed, there would be a heavy constraint on creativity. The introduction of a new term or the use of an old term in a new way *can* lead to new insights and new ways of seeing things. A further response, given this latter point, is to accept and encourage disciplinary conceptual anarchy. While this would emphasize creativity and innovation, there would be costs as far as communication and cumulation are concerned.

Within these two extremes there is, perhaps, a middle way that both avoids conceptual authoritarianism and conceptual anarchy. This is through the adoption of a number of guiding rules. The first is the *rule of historical usage*. Before a new term is introduced full cognizance should be given to the way the term has been used in the past by earlier scholars. This will attune the user to the range of uses and the functions of those uses and encourage the new use to be relatable to past usage. The second is the *rule of peculiar reference*. This states that a technical term should be so defined that it clearly demarcates it subject from all other subjects. For example, Raymond Aron defines 'ideology' as 'all ideas or bodies of ideas accepted by individuals or peoples, without regard to their origin or nature'.[10] This definition is not, as previously noted, *wrong*, but is so broad that it conflates many things that might be better kept separate (physics, philosophy, Communism, religion etc.). Similarly, 'structural violence' defined as 'damage done to people through the normal operation of the social system' is almost indistinguishable from inequality and its effects.[11] The third is the *rule of parsimony*. This states that a definition should use as few elements as possible to delineate its subject adequately. The reason for this is simple: the more elements (phrases, terms) that are used to define a word, the fewer things it is likely to apply to. Hence, a 'revolution' might be defined as 'the replacement of one regime by another'. This successfully delineates it from a *coup d'état* or an electoral change, where there is no regime change. However, if one adds 'violent change', and 'dictatorship of the proletariat', then the number of revolutions to which it could refer would be dramatically reduced. If these guidelines are observed, then creativity can at least in part be combined with cumulation.

The problem of essential contestability

Since Gallie's 1956 paper, the notion of 'essentially contested concepts' (ECC) has taken root in social science as an argument against the positivistic use of definition.[12] The idea that by careful definition, one could 'build' a social science of shared and agreed concepts was lost forever. The argument is that there are some terms the meaning of which will, in principle, always be contestable. The idea of an essentially contested concept is outlined by Connolly thus:[13]

When the concept involved is appraisive in that the state of affairs it describes is a valued achievement, when the practice it described is internally complex in that its characterization involves reference to several dimensions, and when the agreed and contested rules are relatively open, enabling parties to interpret even those shared rules differently as new and unforeseen situations arise, then the concept in question is an 'essentially contested concept'. Such concepts 'essentially involve endless disputes about their proper uses on the part of their users'.

Thus an ECC has three components: it is appraisive, it is complex, and the rules for its use are open. It is immediately clear that many of our central concepts in the political and social sciences are contestable in this sense such as democracy, politics, ideology, liberty, power, egalitarianism, community, etc. It is also clear that ECCs are far from new, even though the term was only recently coined. Plato, for example, was implicitly recognizing the problem in his discussion of 'justice' and was seeking to convince others of the plausibility of his usage as against the usages of others.

The problem of ECCs is not their existence, which is undeniable, but whether that existence vitiates any serious and cumulative study of society. If it is the case that conceptual variability is such that discussion is rendered unviable, then there can be no 'social science' that can give an opinion on anything that is worth more than the personal opinion of the speaker. However, it is *not* the case that a term can be used legitimately in any way whatsoever; while there may be variation and contestation about the precise usages of terms, it is usually the case that there are ballpark posts that define the arena of the debate within which the contestation will take place. The term 'democracy', for example, has in the contemporary world enormous positive evaluative connotations. To be a democracy legitimizes a regime in the eyes of many observers. Yet the meaning of the term 'democracy' is very contestable. The problem of the ECC is reduced in two ways. First by increased levels of stipulation. Hence it makes, given the potential variability, little sense to speak of 'democracy' but very much more sense to speak of 'democratic centralism', 'direct democracy', 'liberal democracy', 'pluralist democracy', or 'liberal anti-pluralism'. We can thus have a reasonable discussion *about* democracy, even while using the term in different ways, because we are aware of the way in which the other party is using the term. Because something is an ECC does not mean that there is confusion about it but merely that its meaning is not agreed. Second, it is a feature of the social sciences that while they are disputacious, they are normally organized into schools or approaches within which the degree of disagreement is much less than between approaches. Thus, while some concepts are ECCs, there are islands where there is some degree of agreement and hence comparability and cumulation. This means, necessarily, that there is some inter-island warfare, but in general this leads all the participants to understand the strengths and weaknesses of their positions much better and may on occasions lead to a modification of positions.

One final point should be made about ECCs. Because a concept is contestable does *not* mean that it can mean anything that the user wants it to mean. As was noted earlier, words are not arbitrary symbols, and the way they are defined and used can be more or less useful. An ECC is contestable, but the range of its contestation is not infinite or unlimited, even though it may change over time. Let us again take the example of 'democracy'. 'Democracy' can have many meanings, but beyond some limit of its range of usage there are political practices such that we might want to say 'that in any sensible use of the term that cannot be called democracy'. Examples here might be Stroessner's brutal regime in Paraguay, termed as a 'selective democracy'; Franco's fascist regime in Spain, termed 'organic democracy'; or Sukarno's regime in Indonesia called a 'guided democracy'. The aim in all these cases is to hijack the positive normative connotations of 'democracy' and to legitimize regimes which were profoundly authoritarian in nature. This is usually done with an eye on foreign opinion and the possibility of military and economic support. *Logically,* we can have no argument with the re-definition of the term, but in every other sense we could argue that such uses fall outside the range and dimensions of contestation. We are thus justified on occasions in both admitting that a concept is essentially contestable and saying that it is being misused.

Definition and classification

Classification is an extension of the activity of definition and may be considered as the activity of grouping objects with a perceived similarity of attributes into two or more named classes. A definition will normally bifurcate reality into a differentiation based upon identity and non-identity. Hence 'socialism' may be defined as 'a political and economic theory according to which the means of production, distribution and exchange should be owned and controlled by the people, everyone should be given an equal opportunity to develop their talents, and the wealth of the community should be fairly distributed'.[14] 'Socialism' is identified, but the world of ideologies of which socialism is a part is left unidentified, as is the world of things which are not ideologies. We may thus consider definition to be a primitive form of classification, in that the naming process is limited to one class, but also as something which is presupposed by classification.

Classification rests basically on the recognition of similarities and differences and the ability to group these into sets. No two objects are ever wholly alike — this follows from Leibniz's 'principle of indiscernibles' which states that if two objects shared all the same attributes they would be the same object — but they may share some attributes or characteristics that make them suitable for grouping under the same name as belonging to the same class of things.

Classification inevitably involves information loss but, equally inevitably, cannot be dispensed with. Thought itself is unimaginable without classification since were everything undifferentiated there would be nothing to think about. However, while necessary for the most primitive cogitation, costs are involved in that the inherent richness of phenomena is lost. Hence, to classify a group into 'catholics' and 'protestants' loses information about individuals' colour of hair, their hobbies, type of work, or the nature of their sexual perversions.

The preservation of richness cannot be achieved by a refusal to classify, but rather is related to the number of classificatory schemas taken into thought simultaneously and the complexity of the relationships between those schemas. Similarly, creativity or intelligence may be thought of as the ability to see new and useful forms of classification as well as the ability to manipulate and relate known classifications.

Classification, as we have said, involves definition and is itself an extended form of definition. Every classificatory schema involves at least an implied definition of each class within the schema plus a definition of the dimension along which the classified phenomena are ranged. The dimensions of classifications and the nature of the classes within a dimension have the ability to structure the way we see the world, and changes in the nature of classes have the ability to

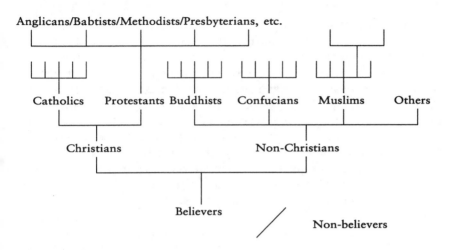

Anglicans/Babtists/Methodists/Presbyterians, etc.

Figure 3.1 Collapsing categories and information loss

restructure our perceptions with effects that stretch far beyond a mere linguistic change.

Two examples taken from conflict theory should make this clear. The first example used here for purposes of exposition is Adam Curle's book *Making Peace*, largely because he is himself clear, though other examples of the same type of redefinition could also be used.[15] Curle rejects the traditional dichotomy between conflict and peace; he rejects the notion that where there is not conflict there is, therefore, peace. Between the categories of conflict and peace he interposes a third category, that of 'unpeacefulness'. Conflict is an overt incompatibility of interests which when pursued with behavioural violence may become war;[16] peace is harmonious and constructive collaboration with a strong element of mutual development included;[17] while 'unpeacefulness is a situation in which human beings are impeded from achieving full development either because of their own internal relations or because of the types of relations that exist between themselves . . . and other persons or groups'.[18] This seemingly innocent reclassification — which involves the definition of the categories — occurs because there appeared to be an area of experience which was not adequately encapsulated by the classification; the classification was not held to be exhaustive (see below). From the reclassification (but also partly the reason for it) follows the notion of 'structural violence' (which marks an unpeaceful relationship) and the development of the 'objective' school of conflict research,[19] which concludes with the proposition that the peacemaker must on occasions, to ensure peace, foment conflict.[20] This conclusion, which is in part normatively based, is 'embedded' in the structure of the classification; to see social relations through this set of classificatory spectacles will strongly influence the conclusion reached both with respect to the nature of society and the range of preferred action.

The second example comes from Konrad Lorenz.[21] In his influential book *On Aggression*, Lorenz identifies through the observation of non-human (and non-primate) animal behaviour, two kinds of animal. There are those predators that are born with highly evolved killing apparatus and those without such apparatus. In order to minimize intra-specific killing, animals with lethal weaponry have also evolved inhibitions about killing which are brought into play in response to the appropriate submission gestures. Animals without lethal weaponry have no such inhibitions and in the appropriate circumstances will kill the other animal. In most cases, however, death will not result from such conflicts because the weaker animal will flee. A classification is thus established, and mankind is slotted into the non-lethal category: that is, as an animal with no inhibitions against intra-specific killing. Unfortunately man has developed intelligence which enables him to make and use lethal weapons but without the inhibitions that have evolved for lethal weapon holders. The depressing consequences for mankind are clear and do not require further elaboration. However, these two examples demonstrate how the change or establishment of classifications can fundamentally change the manner in which the world is analysed.[22]

Classification, and hence definition, underlie our conceptions of reality, although most of the time we do not realize this. Partly this is due to the fact that our perceptions are shaped by habit and custom, and partly it is due to the fact that the process of identifying and classifying is an automatic and natural process in the human animal. In a field of scholarship, however, attempts are made to make explicit that which is accepted implicitly. All theory, for example, involves a classification, in that what is considered relevant and what irrelevant is specified. Part of the activity of scholarship is an investigation of our concepts of reality and is an ongoing development and critique of these conceptions. Where there are self-conscious attempts of this sort, there are three criteria which should be borne in mind; again, rules which are useful but should not be slavishly adhered to. The first criterion is *usefulness*. A classification can be useful even if it does not conform strictly to the other criteria. For example, a commonly held classification of religiosity in Northern Ireland uses only the categories of Catholic and Protestant which would for many scholars appear inadequate. Yet it is useful for many purposes. Hence the notion of 'usefulness' has to be related to the purpose or function of the classification and cannot be established independently of any particular classification. In this sense 'usefulness' is an empirical evaluation, while 'exclusiveness' and 'exhaustiveness' are logical conditions (see below).

The idea of 'usefulness' in this context cannot be separated from the notion of 'explanation'. A classification is useful to the extent that it aids or facilitates an explanation. Indeed, given that many of the classificatory schemas we use in everyday life are deeply embedded in the unconscious and are used habitually without any reflection whatsoever, it is sometimes difficult to separate the explanatory function of a classification from the classification itself. To accept the dichotomy of 'aryan' and 'non-aryan' in the context of German Fascism is also to begin to explain the aetiology of Nazi ideas of racial supremacy. The world may divide into facts, but the manner of the division is a human construct for human reasons.

In general we might suggest that the usefulness of a classification is a function of the number and/or significance of the subsumptions or correlates associated with it. An example may clarify this. Historians, conflict theorists, those interested in ethnicity, and constitutionalists, among others, have found that one of the most useful dimensions to concentrate on in Belgium is the communal divide, particularly the Flemish–Walloon split, but also sometimes including the Bruxellois as a third category.[23] This is because historically communalism is also associated with the nature of politics, religious affiliation, discrimination, changing patterns of wealth, occupational structure, investment, struggles over legal and educational rights, and patterns of domination. Thus, to use a classification based on the communal structure helps to explain a great many other things about Belgian history, while to use a different fundamental classification would produce a different history but one which may not be as significant because fewer associated factors are called into attention.

The criterion of *exclusiveness* is far easier to deal with. It derives from Aristotle's 'principle of the excluded middle' which states that something cannot be both A and not-A at the same time. While this principle has been challenged, in the Hegelian dialectic for example and some Eastern philosophies, it has considerable utility as far as classification is concerned. Were it the case that individuals could fall into more than one defined class, then the classification loses its explanatory power in proportion to the amount of incorporated ambiguity. And, while ambiguity may be a source of intriguing pleasure and mystery in literature, it becomes a source of confusion in many other contexts. In so far as the task of scholarship is to increase understanding and clarity within a field of study by the delineation of objects and the relations between them, classificatory exclusivity would appear to be a necessity. Exclusiveness, however, must be sought, for there are many cases where it is not self-evident. Where there is obvious ambiguity and uncertainty in a schema, the usual way of overcoming it is either to reclassify and create new categories to incorporate the ambiguous cases or to redefine one or more classes to exclude ambiguity. For convenience we shall take the Belgian case already cited to clarify this point. The simple communal classification of Flemish, Walloon, and Bruxellois might appear to the sophisticated political or ethnic analyst to be inadequate, particularly with respect to the category 'Bruxellois'. Leaving aside non-Belgian migrants, European Community officials, etc., the vast majority of Belgians living in Brussels will derive from either Flemish or Walloon stock and will retain some of the characteristics of their communal origin, particularly language. Some Bruxellois will be second, third, or fourth generation inhabitants of Brussels whose communal links will have been much weakened, while others will be first-generation migrants with strong affiliations with their ethnic origins. For the purposes of a study of political allegiance and party identification, the explanatory power of the schema would be weakened if the first-generation migrants were included as Bruxellois. In this case the analyst might redefine the meaning of 'Bruxellois' to exclude first-generation migrants, portioning them out into the Flemish and Walloon categories. Or, alternatively, new categories might be created to deal with these ambiguous individuals with the consequence of maintaining exclusivity. Again, though, it should be noted that the raw social material has not changed its configurations but only the prism through which we view it. It is the prism that gives meaning to social phenomena.

The third criterion of good classification is *exhaustiveness*. This refers to whether the dimension which the classification is subdividing into classes adequately covers the entire range of cases of that dimension. To milk our Belgian example again, there is a small population of around 60,000 German-speaking Belgians who are not covered by the three-category classification previously discussed. For the purposes of party identification and the distribution of parliamentary political power flowing from the ballot box, this would probably not be a significant omission; for an advertiser seeking to target potential purchasers it might be a highly significant omission given the differences in language, newspaper reading, and television viewing.

The last two examples drawn from the Belgian case do make an important point. While classifications will often appear 'natural' because they are part of the social and conceptual furniture that we carry with us, they are always open to change and adjustment. There is no obvious or uncontentious limit to the change or creation of classifications, and classifications are always related to function or purpose. Thus with a change in purpose, which may be socially or politically constructed[24] or constructed in the process of scholarship, new classifications can emerge in a relatively unconstrained manner. Since the consequence of new classification is often dramatic in that fresh and unconventional aspects of the world are revealed, the impact of such an activity can be considerable.

Conclusion

Definition, classification, and identification underlie many of our ordinary activities as students of society, and our attempts to achieve precision are sometimes thwarted by the fact that we have to use words according to rules that are themselves, if not arbitrary, at least amenable to adjustment. There is, however, no choice. An attempt to mathematicize or make more precise the language of social analysis would merely hide the problems behind symbols rather than solve them. The best defence against the confusion that can arise from the use and misuse of terms is to be aware of the nature of the words we use and the difficulties we shall undoubtedly encounter. It is the case that the linguistic basis of social science is a source of uncertainty at the very start of the research endeavour and will inhibit comparison and cumulation. From this there is no escape other than authoritarian imposition of usage which given the structure of social science is unlikely to occur and would in any case merely produce an artificial unity. However, while there is variation in definition and classification, this variation is to some extent structured by the paradigmatic nature of social science and need not lead to confusion even while it inhibits cumulation. The other side of the coin, however, is to recognize that we live in a changing world, and the concepts, definitions, and classifications we employ must necessarily evolve to match the mobility of the phenomenon we study. Social science, while it attempts to build models, create theories, and discover generalizations that cross time and place, is a running interpretation and re-interpretation of social phenomena. In addition, the internal dynamics of individual disciplines within social science will, through debate and criticism, lead to autonomous conceptual and theoretical change. Seen from this point of view, the indefiniteness of language and the flexibility of our conceptual tools are necessary for a reasonable understanding of society.

Notes

1. It is possible some of the time, as for example, with music and the visual arts.
2. See Wittgenstein, L. (1958) *Philosophical Investigations*, Oxford: Blackwell, p. 71.
3. See Benn, S.I. and Peters, R.S. (1959) *Social Principles and the Democratic State*, London: George Allen & Unwin, 332–33.
4. See, for example, Ayer, A.J. (1967) *Language, Truth and Logic*, London: Victor Gollancz, p. 133.
5. See Pateman, C. (1970) *Participation and Democratic Theory*, Cambridge: Cambridge University Press.

6. Banks, M. (1984) 'The Evolution of International Relations Theory' in Banks, M. (ed.) *Conflict in World Society: a New Perspective on International Relations*, Brighton: Wheatsheaf, 3–21.
7. Small, M. and Singer, J. David (1982) *Resort to Arms: International and Civil Wars 1860–1980*, Beverly Hills: Sage, p. 55.
8. Zacher, M.W. (1979) *International Disputes and Collective Security*, New York: Praeger, p. 21.
9. Glossop, R.J. (1987) *Confronting War: an Examination of Humanity's most Pressing Problem*, Jefferson: McFarland & Co., p. 7.
10. Aron, Raymond (1953) 'The Diffusion of Ideologies', *Confluence*, 2, p. 4.
11. Mitchell, C.R. (1981) *Peacemaking and the Consultant's Role*, New York: Nichols Publishing Company, and Farnborough: Gower, 12–42.
12. Gallie, W.B. (1955–6) 'Essentially Contested Concepts', *Proceedings of the Aristotelian Society*, 56.
13. Connolly, W.E. (1983) *The Terms of Political Discourse*, Boston: D.C. Heath, 10–44.
14. Elliott, F. and Summerskill, M. (1957) *A Dictionary of Politics*, Harmondsworth: Penguin, p. 287.
15. Curle, A. (1971) *Making Peace*, London: Tavistock Publications Ltd. See also for related approaches Schmid, H. (1968) 'Peace Research and Politics', *Journal of Peace Research*, 5, 3, 217–232; Hoivik, T. (1971) 'Social Inequality: The Main Issues', *Journal of Peace Research*, 8, 119–42; Kohler, G. and Alcock, N. (1976) 'An Empirical Table of Structural Violence', *Journal of Peace Research*, 13, 343–56.
16. Ibid., 3–4.
17. Ibid., p. 15.
18. Ibid., p. 1.
19. See Webb, K. (1986) 'Structural Violence and the Definition of Conflict', *International Encyclopedia of Peace*, Volume II, Oxford: Pergamon Press. For an excellent discussion of the debate between the objective and subjective approaches to conflict see Mitchell, C.R. (1981) op. cit.
20. This conclusion is stated most forthrightly in Schmid, op. cit.
21. Lorenz, K. (1966) *On Aggression*, New York: Harcourt Brace and World Inc.
22. It should perhaps be noted that on empirical grounds Lorenz has been refuted. There are numerous species of animals with killing weapons who engage in intra-specific killing.
23. See, for example, Clough, S.B. (1930) *A History of the Flemish Movement in Belgium: a Study in Nationalism*, New York: Richard R. Smith.
24. An example of this would be the reclassification of Commonwealth immigrants in the 1962 Commonwealth Immigration Act into 'New Commonwealth' and 'Old Commonwealth' immigrants through the emphasis on 'patrials'. The classification was used to avoid using colour as a criterion of acceptance even though the purpose of the Act was to limit coloured immigration. See Peach, G.C.K. (1968) *West Indian Migration to Britain*, London: Oxford University Press.

4
SOCIAL SCIENCE AND IDEOLOGY

··

Social science as an ideology

One of the problems with social science is that in all the disciplines there are theorists and writers coming from many different points of view and advocating many different things. Hence there are Marxist sociologists of a radical bent and monetarist economists with conservative tendencies. It is clear that social science theories do have values, and they do, at least implicitly, advocate policies and social action. It is reasonable to ask, therefore, whether social science is not just a collection of ideologies and social scientists a bunch of ideologists, selling their wares under a false label.

It is the aim of this chapter to argue that social science and ideology are in fact very different things. To suggest this is not to imply that social science is better or worse than ideology in a normative sense: ideology performs political and social functions that are incapable of being performed by social science, and social science comments on social life in ways that cannot be emulated by ideology.[1] The dry and abstract formulations of Talcott Parsons would be unlikely to mobilize many people; even Karl Marx and his followers had to popularize his radical ideas before they could become a basis for mobilization. Neither does the argument here suggest that social science is more 'objective' than ideology and thus to be preferred on those grounds. Further, to suggest that 'social science' is not 'ideology' does not mean that it is a science; it merely means that it is a different kind of thing to ideology.

To discover whether social science is an ideological perception along with other ideologies, we must first establish what we *mean* by an ideology. This follows from an application of Passmore's principle of non-vacuous comparison.[2] Passmore comments: 'A striking feature of philosophical words, however, is that it is very easy to fall into the trap of so defining them as to make them vacuous in either of two directions: they may become vacuous through applying to nothing at all, or through applying to everything, thereby losing their usefulness as modes of distinguishing.'

In order to say whether social science is or is not an ideology it has to be *compared* with those things that we call 'ideologies'. A couple of examples may clarify this philosophical fork. If we were to define 'ideology' as a 'logical and deductive interrelated set of political beliefs held by social groups', since there are no such sets, the definition would be valueless for all practical purposes. Or, if it is maintained that *all* possible systems or modes of thought are 'ideologies', as indeed Raymond Aron argues, then the term 'ideology' loses any usefulness in distinguishing among types of thought. The term 'ideology' only has meaning in so far as there are things which are 'non-ideological' that can serve as relevant comparisons.

As this principle is described by Passmore, it is a plea that when using comparison the relevant comparative category should not be empty. More generally, however, it can be suggested that the perception of an observation or circumstance is radically affected by the frame of reference within which it is located, that is by the comparative categories by which it is judged and compared. Thus, to suggest that social science is 'merely' or 'only' an ideological perception would only make sense in so far as there is no or little distinction between ideology and social science. In this chapter it will be suggested that there are very great similarities but that there are also important dissimilarities. It is an important part of the argument here that ideology and social science do have things in common but that the criticism of social science that it is merely ideology on the basis of the common elements that they share is wholly misplaced. This form of 'merely/only' argument, which is usually a form of reductionism, is quite common but is usually misleading, for it will often extend the usefulness of an analogy beyond permissible limits by conflating the fact of possession of common characteristics with the idea of identity. For example, a widely held view is that man is *merely* a 'naked ape'. The reductionism utilized here is that while the higher primates and man do share certain characteristics, what is important is what differentiates them not what they have in common. Thus the importance of culture in the life of man, his capacity for rational thought, his ability to engage in complex planning, his possession of language all make him a very different creature to the higher primates let alone the rest of the animal kingdom. To only stress the commonality between man and the apes is to miss the point. Similarly, we would not want to say that Concorde is merely a flying wheelbarrow just because a wheelbarrow and Concorde are both means of transport. Thus, to stress the commonality of ideology and social science is again to miss the point of what it is that makes social science different.

A conception of 'ideology'

The specification of 'ideology' is not an easy matter. It is probably impossible to get to an incontestable view of ideology, but it is necessary precisely to identify the concept in order to sustain the argument.[3] The fact that incontestability is not attainable does not vitiate the activity of attempting to achieve a non-arbitrary and plausible conception. Were this not the case then there would be little point in any social analysis whatsoever. A related aspect needs to be borne in mind. The concept must be identified fairly and with care so that the subsequent argument does not become true by definition.

The concept of 'ideology' is far from new: for example, Francis Bacon talked about the 'idols of the market-place'.[4] The word 'ideology' was first coined by Destutt de Tracy during the enlightenment to describe a new 'science', the derivation of ideas from biology. It was subsequently used pejoratively as a term of abuse by Napoleon; this sense of the word remains with us in that to call someone an 'ideologist' is often used to describe a mode of dogmatic and doctrinaire thinking. Later, particularly through the work of Marx and Mannheim, 'ideology' came to be seen in the context of the social group. Looking at the various usages of the term, however, the following main themes emerge.

Ideology as:

- systematic; coherent; quasi-logical; congruent; constrained beliefs;
- beliefs referring specifically to social and/or political structure;
- beliefs demanding high affective identification; loyalty; commitment;
- beliefs held by a group;
- being quasi-scientific; distorted thinking;
- incorporating a philosophy of history; social theory;
- futuristic beliefs;
- being a myth;
- being dogmatic; closed; rigid manner of thinking;
- being an artifact of organization;
- including specific reference to the nature of man;
- referring to function for the individual;
- referring to function for the group;
- incorporating a reference to values; morality; ethics;
- referring to any ideas whatsoever;
- specific reference to individual beliefs;
- referring to ideas which are held with certainty;
- referring to abstract principles;
- intolerant; against compromise;
- functional in the conduct of conflict both within and without the group;
- being explanatory; defining the situation; orientating function;
- demanding action;
- persistence through time.

Perhaps the clearest message demonstrated by this list is what we knew already, that there is little overall agreement on what is meant by the term 'ideology'; what exists is a plethora of stipulative definitions leading to the problems of comparison and cumulation noted in the previous chapter. One reason for the variation in usage is that 'ideology' is an essentially contestable term *par excellence*. To say that a term is essentially contestable, however, is merely to describe it; a more interesting and illuminating exercise is to say why it is so contestable. Here attention is briefly drawn to four reasons for the contestable nature of ideology, the problems of levels and disciplines, functions, different emphases, and politics.

One problem with the academic usage of ideology is that it is used at various levels in different disciplines or even within the same discipline. Hence, ideology has been used as an explanatory variable at the international level, the national and group level, and at the individual level. It is asking rather a lot of a single concept to work this hard and to remain useful or maintain the same precise meaning across such a range of phenomena. It is, of course, not unusual for the same concept to appear within different disciplines and at different levels, but the effects of such transfers are not always as marked as with the case of ideology. Second, the term ideology is used to explain markedly different things, and it would be surprising if the same concept could be effectively applied to the explanation of revolutions, voting behaviour, and the international stance of nations. Third, even while scholars may be defining ideology in different ways for the purposes of different studies, they *may* not be talking about wholly different concepts but merely drawing attention to different aspects of a very complex phenomenon. Finally, throughout the history of the term it has been politicized which has led to confusion. It has been used both descriptively (Afrikaaner ideology, Communist ideology, the ideology of nationalism, etc.), and as a term of political abuse. Bearing these variations and the reasons for the variation in mind, the usage of 'ideology' adopted here is as follows:

Ideology is a body of ideas held by a group that contains values relating to political action and the distribution of public goods.

There are many other things that can be said about ideology, as has been demonstrated, but for the purposes of identification, this usage is sufficient. In the previous chapter rules of effective stipulation were given with justifications for the adoption of those rules. The first principle enjoins us to note the way in which a concept has been used and what it has sought to explain. The second principle suggests that the definition adopted should not be subject to easy conflation. And the last notes that definition is best when kept parsimonious. The usage adopted here fulfils these criteria as well as conforming to the logical criteria also noted in Chapter 3. Thus, while the concept of ideology remains contestable, this usage is not arbitrary and can therefore properly be used as a basis for the subsequent argument.

The structural non-differentiation of ideology and social science

It was suggested previously that according to many perspectives ideology is the product of a social group. Such a suggestion conformed both to a range of historical and contemporary usage. If social science, therefore, is to be typified as ideology, it is also the case that a social grouping must exist to support those ideological beliefs. It may be remembered (Chapter 2) that Karl Mannheim attempted to circumvent the linkage between ideology and social grouping with respect to the intelligentsia by positing the idea of the 'floating intelligentsia'. This group was 'between classes' and 'subsumed' other groups with the consequence that it was not a group in the same way that other groups are. In reality, however, it can be argued that the intelligentsia — if in the contemporary world of scholarship this is at least partly identified with the academic profession — is very much a social group. A distinction can be maintained on the nature and kind of views held but not on the 'groupness' or the structural position of the group.

The definition of 'group' is a somewhat contentious matter. Rather than enter into a discussion which would not help in the present argument, I shall uncritically accept Sherif's well-known and widely used definition.[5]

We define a group as a social unit that consists of a number of individuals (1) who, at a particular time, have role and status relations with one another, stabilised in some degree, and (2) possess a set of values or norms regulating the behaviour of individual members, at least in the matters of importance to them.

There is little doubt that according to this definition the world of academia and scholarship is very much a group. Perhaps it is possible to go further and suggest that it is an overarching group with subgroups within it partly defined by paradigmatic, disciplinary, and national boundaries. There are role and status relations of a very high order such as chancellors, vice-chancellors, deans, professors, readers, senior lecturers, lecturers, senior research fellows, research fellows, teaching assistants, research assistants, advanced and less advanced graduate students, and undergraduates. Consonant with the hierarchy there is a reward structure which is articulated in monetary, prestige and patronage terms. In addition, there is a differentially and disproportionately held capacity to determine both excellence and advancement; a relatively few number of people with prestige and reputation are able to control the shape of a discipline, at least in the short term, in so far as their perspectives are the ones that are recommended and read. As with most groups, there are conditions of entry. The more valued is group membership, then the higher the tendency of those in the group to limit entry. Knowledge of the appropriate norms and language are needed together with evidence of competence. The weight of calling cards is measured in several ways. There is the possession of appropriate degrees, and these may be gradated, not only by the level of degree attainment, but also by the origin of the degree; a doctorate from Harvard or Oxford will usually be worth more in the academic market-place than a doctorate from a minor Third World university. Publications are important, with distinctions not only being made between books and journals but also between which publisher and which journal. There is even a citation index which reveals how much any one author is cited by others and thus (implicitly) what their prestige is within the profession. Finally, anyone attempting to join the profession needs referees to attest to their excellence and their chances are much enhanced by having referees with high status and reputation. There are also certain expected behaviours that accompany group membership that regulate aspects of the communal life. Examples would be the implicit and explicit norms regarding relations between undergraduates and staff, the acceptance of hierarchy, the maintenance of the right to intellectual independence, the sanctity of the examination, or the aversion to plagiarism.

According, then, to Sherif's definition, it is reasonable to suggest that the social science community is a group or, at least, a series of inter-locking and overlapping groups. It is, however, possible to go further than this and suggest that this group possesses a particular structural location of dependence which, in a simple determinist framework, might be expected to flavour the kind of views that are held. Within most developed societies this group is extremely dependent upon the largesse of the state. With the twentieth-century growth and penetration of the state into society came the institutionalization of intellect and an increase in the perceived value of intellectual goods. The tradition of the scholar-gentleman, or the linkage between religion and scholarship, was broken with the professionalization of scholarship. However, a consequence of this institutionalization was dependency, a relationship which is sometimes obscured by the sometimes close links between the state and academia. Thus, in addition to being a group, professional scholars are frequently also structurally located in a situation of dependency on the state.

The problem here is, however, that while we can typify the social scientific community as a group, and can make a reasonable case for structural location and dependency, at least in many countries, in fact social scientists are found on every side of every question. Thus within macro-economics there are at least three major substantive schools — monetarist, Keynesian, and Marxist — each with subdivisions and schisms within them. Similarly, within international relations there are realists, structuralists, and pluralists, again with significant schisms within each school. Or, within psychology, there are behavioorists, Freudians, clinical psychologists, social psychologists, and Gestalt psychologists. Not only are there paradigmatic differences between social scientists within the same discipline, but there are also differences of political persuasion: within the social scientific community there will be found radicals, reformists and conservatives of every hue and colour. While there is a tendency for there to be a degree of congruence between social scientific beliefs of social scientists and their political positions, there is no straightforward connection. This is due to the position and training of social scientists. Ideologies come to us in their social context as 'baskets' of ideas that are experienced as congruent and coherent; the social scientist will often not accept the congruence and thus hold what would in other contexts be seen as an anomalous juxtaposition of ideas. This can be related to the critical function of social science. Even the most conservative of social scientists, by holding his/her views in a manifest and forensic manner, will be performing a critical function through making explicit that which relies for its appeal on the naturalness of the implicit. It cannot, therefore, be true that either 'groupness' or structural location importantly influences the substantive beliefs of social scientists.

At this point a further argument might be used to rebut this conclusion. It could be asserted that the argument as made concentrates on the wrong level of conceptual analysis, that the ideological features of this group are to be found not at the level of substantive matters but in the nature of the assumptions necessary about the nature of society and the state in order to maintain a degree of investigative freedom and plurality of opinion. That is, an ideology of pluralist liberal-democratic society of some kind is assumed as part of the atmosphere within which social science can flourish. Ideology resides, therefore, not in the substantive outputs of social science but in the acceptance of the conditions that guarantee the ability to produce those outputs.

This is a far more significant argument, for it seems to be the case that for social scientific scholarship to flourish institutionally, particular social conditions of freedom would seem to be necessary. Since the conditions of social science would seem to be those conditions of liberal-democracy, and liberal-democracy is largely supportive of capitalistic economic organization, implicitly social science is an advocate for a particular form of economic and social organization, even though individual social

scientists may be advocates for a very different form of social organization. Further, as has already been suggested, social science cannot help
but be a critical discipline, not in the sense of being an overt critique of
any particular regime or social formation but in the sense of reformu-
lating the perception of the natural into considered choice. Thus for
social science to operate, the social and political tolerance typical of
liberal-democracy is necessary.

The problem with this kind of argument is that in one sense all ideas
need a social context in which to be expressed. There can be no
disembodied proposition without a proposer, and all proposers derive
from a social context. And, if 'knowledge' is only knowledge within a
particular social context, it becomes more difficult to validate it outside
that context. However, merely to suggest that certain sorts of ideas have
an affinity with a particular social environment is not sufficient to dismiss
the validity of those ideas unless it can also be shown that the environment in question has some kind of determining effect upon the formation
or shape of those ideas. This argument, then, could be attacked through
the use of what is sometimes called the 'fallacy of origin'. Accordingly,
we could argue that the validity attributed to a set of ideas can be
unrelated (but need not be) to the source or social origins of those ideas
and that ideas or beliefs have to be judged on their own merits not on
who said them in what context.

This argument, however, while acceptable within an empiricist
philosophy, is unacceptable within the tradition of ideology and the
sociology of knowledge that derives from Marx and Mannheim. According to this view, 'knowledge' (or what is believed to be knowledge) is
always related to the social context in which it emerges. Thus, from this
point of view, by accepting the fallacy of origin argument, a philosophical position is assumed that necessarily prejudges the argument in
that knowledge and its social context are de-linked. A more significant
response is to note the incoherence within the sociology of knowledge
argument itself, whereby the statement invalidates itself. If it is the case
that all social propositions are related to the social position of the
proposer, and this invalidates the proposition, then this proposition must
itself be so related. If it *is* accepted as a reasonable generalization, then
there is no necessity to deny the possibility of a similar status to at least
some other propositions or bodies of propositions. If we are to accept
that there does exist at least some possibility of social statements that are
not determined by social context — while admitting that there are some
that are — then we are driven to the consideration of other and
independent means of deciding between bodies of propositions, i.e., to
the use of criteria of validity (see Chapter 5). Thus, within either an
empiricist or a sociology of knowledge framework, the same conclusion
is reached if incoherence in the latter is to be avoided.

One further argument may be adduced here, one that accepts that ideas have social origins but draws very different conclusions. There is no contradiction involved between the statement that particular social conditions are necessary for the emergence of a particular analysis and the statement that the analysis has a validity beyond the social context within which it emerged. Thus we can accept the notion that particular social conditions exert a social influence on ideas without denying validity to those ideas. It can be argued, for example, that natural science could not have emerged in the form in which it did unless there was an increased complexity of society, a level of technological development both to support and exploit the new knowledge, a decline in the ideational hegemony of religion, and a sufficient accumulation of wealth to support and institutionalize the new activity. But a process that leads to knowledge enabling the virtual eradication of smallpox or a spaceship to Neptune cannot merely be dismissed because a certain form of social organization was necessary for its emergence.

These arguments suggest that we do not have to dismiss the findings of social science merely because of the structural position of social science. Social science is not ideology merely because of the 'groupness' of social scientists or the structural location of that group. However, the arguments derived from the sociology of knowledge are not entirely without merit for they serve as a perpetual reminder that some social science could be ideology or that social science itself could become ideological advocacy. This, indeed, was the case with much social science in the Soviet Union prior to the accession of Gorbachev. The continued restatement and challenge of this position leads to continual self-assessment of the status and value of social science and is thus of permanent value.

Values in ideology and social science

One of the major overlaps between ideology and social science circles around the question of values such as the nature of human nature, the nature of the social world, and prescription and advocacy. Both social science and ideology are infused with values at base, but because they are both value laden does not mean that they are the same thing. As noted previously, the possession of shared characteristics does not imply identity.

It is the case that theories of social science do make value assumptions about the nature of the world some of which are quite similar to those of ideology. Theories of social science, for example, frequently make assumptions about human nature, sometimes very openly. This argument may be taken further, for ideas about human nature will overlap with both advocacy and views about the nature of the world. If it is believed that human nature is largely biologically determined in terms of either group performance or individual behaviour, then at least some expectation of constancy in human responses to situations in the world is presumed, and certain kinds of controls and management procedures are advocated. If human nature is opportunistic, self-interested, and ego-centric, then domestic control and international realism are the normal prescriptions; while if human nature is malleable and responsive to environmental change, then reform and the satisfaction of desires both domestically and internationally are more likely to be prescribed.

The views in social science about the nature of the social world are likewise variable, the dimensions ranging from the phenomenological interpretation which suggests that the world is constructed through the interactions and perceptions of man himself, to the environmentalist determinist position where the nature of the social world is a consequence of the material conditions of life, to the perception of the social world as fundamentally unchanging. Each of these views of the world are likely to produce a different sort of social science, the first an interpretive ethnomethodologically- or phenomenologically-based social science, the second a Marxist change-orientated or structuralist social science, and the third a positivistic social science that seeks to find laws and generalizations in history and society. In addition, the situation is made more complex in that there is no regular overlap or functional constraint between perceptions of human nature and perceptions about the nature of the world. Thus various combinations can emerge.

The third aspect of value comes into advocacy. Whether the individual social scientist likes it or not, his/her theories are linked to policy advocacy; there are no — or at least very few — theories of social science that have not at heart some degree of policy relevance. Even something as abstract as Axelrod's iterative games and the reciprocated strategy has immediate relevance for bargaining and conflict.[6] Similarly, abstractions at the level of catastrophe theory and chaos theory are soon expressed in political terms with implied political consequences.[7] At times, of course, social science theories take the very centre of the political stage: the Keynsian revolution and the monetarist response were both cases of theories of economics coming to dominate. Similarly, the 'short, sharp, shock' juvenile crime deterrence policy had its roots in the belief that such crime was the result of poor training and a lack of discipline. Thus while a piece of academic work may be, in the mind of the researcher, pure research, it will always tend to have some prescription within it. Social science research, like research in natural science, is undertaken to clarify some aspect of the world about which there is a problem, confusion, or a lack of knowledge. In such clarification the world is defined either in terms of reinforcing held images of the world or challenging held images. In natural science the relationship between discovery and social effect may be very variable; the discovery of quarks with left-handed charm is interesting theoretically but has little immediate practical import, while the discovery of cold fusion (if indeed this was a discovery), or the development of the hydrogen engine threaten to revolutionize the economy of the world. Social research of any kind, however, while it may not always have any immediate effect on the social world, none the less has in general a very much more direct relationship to the social world. A change in the definition of poverty, the discovery of increased trade flows between countries, or a statement about the economic effects of the removal of oppression in developing countries has an immediate prescriptive possibility that is not always present with natural science discovery.

For the social scientist who believes in the aim of value-freedom, the role of values in social science is to be deplored as an obstacle to objectivity and clarity. An argument can be made, however, to the effect that it is values that at base give meaning to social science. It could also be argued in this context that even if it were possible that a social science discipline *could* be value-free, it would be arid and sterile. Values are necessary to identify what is perceived as significant for study in social affairs and that study can in turn help to define what is significant. Values give meaning and significance to social science. Max Weber, an advocate for value-freedom, noted that values must come into the selection of topics for study; there is no such thing as value-free selection. Weber writes:[8] 'Order is brought into this chaos only on the condition that in every case only a part of concrete reality is interesting and significant to us, because only it is related to the cultural values with which we approach reality.'

He believed, however, that thereafter the process could be largely value-free in the sense that the procedures could be replicated by others to reach the same conclusions. However, while this may be a laudable aim and may have utility in natural science, in social science the selection of a topic for study is also a statement of importance and significance; choice of topic is not an insignificant or largely irrelevant part of the research process but part of the process of structuring, defining, and re-defining social reality. The hope expressed by Weber, therefore, that once this aspect of value input is past, value-free social science can begin, is fatally flawed in that the entire process of social research throughout its entirety is predicated on value.

The values that are involved in the selection of topics for social scientific study can come from several sources. These may be categorized as social values, personal values, and disciplinary values. These are not mutually exclusive. Social values may be defined in terms of the definition of importance stemming primarily from the concerns of society or a significant section of society. Such values may be either pro-status quo, anti-status quo, or relatively indifferent. Issues are thrown up by the process of social change, that are socially defined as important, and which are then defined as research topics. Thus, with the penetration of the state into society, the increased levels of interdependency within and between states, the growth of mobility, and changes in technology, domestic and international terrorism as a mode of dissent became defined as a social and political problem leading to an enormous growth of research in this area. We can, in the context of the definition of social problems such as this, on occasion make reference to the 'amplification spiral'; an amplification spiral exists where research both responds to and creates yet further emphasis upon a social problem.

Similarly, personal values can influence the definition of importance and hence the selection of research topics. These may or may not be congruent with social values or with disciplinary values. For example, it is reasonable to suggest that often people go into the study of politics as an academic subject because of some personal political values they hold. There are problems that they perceive as needing clarification and resolution. Similarly, many students are drawn to study international relations because of an abhorrence of war or Third World poverty. Personal values would also include such factors as ambition or the desire for professional standing.

It is also the case that disciplines in social science will specify what are important and significant problems and that this selection will be influenced both by changes in the external world and by changes in the perception of the external world by additions to scholarship. To take international relations as an example of the process of defining what is important, there have been a number of 'great debates' that have dominated the discipline. Or, within the field of domestic political science, due to the growth of state penetration into society, attention was diverted to the problem of government overload.[9] When the discipline defines an area of research as important, there is an increase in research in that area because of the rewards that potentially accrue in terms of the career structure within the discipline.

If the above arguments are accepted, the conclusion must follow that ideology and social science cannot be distinguished by the fact that one purveys values and the other does not. However, while we cannot separate ideology and social science on the simple grounds of the presence or absence of values, a distinction can none the less be made on two further grounds. These are, first, the presence of additional values in social science not found in ideology; it is not that social science has fewer values than ideology but that it has some crucial values in addition to ideology. Second, the role and function of values in ideology and social science are fundamentally different.

The additional values referred to in social science are those of openness and the acceptance of challenge and dispute as a legitimate and proper activity. That is, in so far as social science makes claims to the establishment of knowledge, such claims are validated by reference to criteria of validity. These will be discussed in more depth in the next chapter. This does not mean that there is any lack of contestation through the use of undisputed criteria but that because there is such contestation the status of social knowledge is held to be more tentative. The awareness of the conditions of knowledge preclude the degree of certainty that is more typical of ideology.

In all the social sciences there are debates which are sometimes referred to as theoretical disputes, sometimes as paradigmatic differences, sometimes as competing perspectives or research programmes. There is no social science discipline that is not marked by divisions of this kind. The legitimacy of challenge is a characteristic of the disciplines *per se*; to be a social scientist is necessarily to engage in debate. The process of engaging in debate begins at a very early stage of induction into a discipline, for learning a discipline is not merely learning the facts of that discipline but also the organization and structuring of those facts by theoretical frameworks. Different theoretical frameworks not only organize the facts in different ways to provide alternative explanations of phenomena but will also call into significance different kinds of facts, and will even create facts, to support and justify the theory. Hence at the very base of a social science discipline is dispute about conflicting interpretations of the world.

We can go even further than this, for while the divisions within social science disciplines will lead to the formation of schools, sometimes marked by separate journals and academic organizations, within the schools the process of change, challenge, and theoretical fragmentation and reformulation will continue. Thus within Marxist social science there is debate and dispute about the fundamental ideas on which the Marxist analysis is based — the nature of capital — with some maintaining the notion of the homogeneity of capital and the dependency of the state while others argue for the fragmentation of capital and the relative automony of the state.[10] The idea of schools within a social science discipline cannot, therefore, be easily and directly likened to that of party, since the principles of openness and competition of opinion apply within schools as well as between them. Indeed, the successful articulation and prosecution of a schismatic (new) interpretation in the marketplace of opinion is the basis for many a successful career. The encouragement of schism and differentiation is thus built into the very structure of academia as well as being supported by the aforementioned values. To merely re-articulate a point of view, or to lack originality in thought, is to be categorized as a disciplinary hack; to follow the 'party-line' is not an exercise in loyalty but a display of dullness.

A further point noted above was that the function of values in social science and ideology was very different. In social science values are to be explored with respect to their limits. They are placed in juxtaposition with other values to discover potential contradictions. For example, while we may indeed believe that development is a desired objective — with the notion of growth and change built into the very nature of the capitalist economic system — further development has implications for resource depletion; it will lead to lateral· expansion and potentially dangerous patterns of intersection; it will have effects on pollution and the ozone layer; and will affect commodity prices and thus inhibit development in the poorer nations of the world. Or, to take two of the fundamental problems of liberal-democratic theory, tension constantly exists between the right to express and protest and the necessity to maintain social order and between the notion of liberty and the quest for relative equality. Questions will arise not only with respect to the optimization of competing values but of the means to achieve those values; different means may enhance or inhibit the possibility of achieving a goal. In debate the very idea of development and what we mean by development is questioned. In the course of the examination of a belief — which is a disciplinary rather than an individual activity — there is a general movement to complexity that is reflected in a body of 'literature' that has to be mastered before someone can claim to 'know' the subject. While individual scholars may adopt and advocate particular positions with respect to an issue, they cannot claim expertise or knowledge unless they also know and can cope with the competing perspectives to their view in terms that satisfy the criteria of scholarship accepted by their peers.

The function of values in the realm of ideology is very different, for while the individual social scientist will struggle for coherence in his thought, an ideology will attempt in varying degrees to be itself coherent but more importantly will address itself to the maintenance of coherence and unity of action of a group. The first function of ideology is to promote a persuasive view of the world. A further purpose of an ideology is to exclude divisiveness, which will often manifest itself in a lack of openness. It is not the case, however, that ideology is in fact always without schism; it is the aim of ideology to achieve that but an aim which is not always attained. For example, if we look at either the extreme left or the extreme right in Britain we would find ideological fragmentation of a high order. The same would also be true of many peripheral nationalist movements. Ideological fragmentation at this level, however, is not evidence of openness, but rather is evidence of competitive struggle within the group or movement. Typically, each ideological formulation is struggling for the supremacy of its interpretation of the world with the aim of denying or limiting the articulation of alternative formulations. Ideology is thus concerned with power, with defining a situation or circumstance in a particular and conclusive manner.[11] To describe ideology in this way, however, is not to be pejorative about ideology; it could readily be argued that without the presence of unifying beliefs among aggregated populations, social achievement would be difficult to attain.

There is, however, a consequence of this point of view which, if not logically entailed, is none the less related. If it is the nature of ideology to attempt to define the social universe in such a way as to achieve closure and naturalness, and as a corollary of this to be an advocate for particular policies and prescriptions, and it is the nature of social science to be open and tentative, then does this not place a limit on the degree of advocacy as a practical activity that can be legitimately engaged in by the social scientist? This, then, leads to something of a paradox that can only be resolved by the recognition of a continual tension in the thought and activity of the social scientist. It is clearly the case that the social scientist cannot be a political and social neuter, that he or she cannot entirely avoid avocacy and prescription. However, to engage in advocacy to any great extent is to endanger the openness that characterizes social science debate (see Chapter 9). Still greater are the difficulties when the social scientist not only engages in advocacy but also becomes a practitioner in the social and political arena, an actor claiming 'expertise' based on openness and the tentative acceptance of knowledge.

Conclusion

Significant differences have been claimed here to exist between social science and ideology even though there are also similarities. The most important difference resides in the nature of the beliefs held and how they are held: social science is open and disputatious and marked by tentatively held beliefs. To engage overmuch in political debate and policy advocacy, as a social scientist, is to negate the strengths of social science as a purveyor of a multitude of rich insights and interpretations of the social world. Further, functionally social science and ideology are very different. Without ideology many of the great (desirable as well as undesirable) changes in the world would not happen. Shared belief systems help to mobilize individuals for collective social action and are thus of great value. However, while social science and ideology do have some similarities, they are very different creatures.

Notes

1. This is not a dismissive point of either ideology or social science. While we may often 'blame' ideology for different states of the world that may be

repellant to us, it is none the less also true that many of the great achievements of the world are only brought about by large numbers of people working in concert to attain a desired end. Thus the increasing emancipation of women, or the growth of a 'green' consciousness are both examples of the process of mobilization.

2. Passmore, J.A. (1966) 'The Objectivity of History' in Dray, W.H. (ed.) *Philosophical Analysis and History*, New York: Harper and Row, 75–94.

3. See Adams, James Luther (1955/6) 'Religion and the Ideologies', *Confluence*, 4, 72–84; Apter, D.E. (ed.) (1964) 'Introduction', *Ideology and Discontent*, New York: The Free Press, 16–17; Aron, Raymond (1953) 'The Diffusion of Ideologies', *Confluence*, 2, p. 4; Bell, Daniel (1961) *The End of Ideology in the West*, New York: The Free Press, 'Epilogue'; Barnes, S.H. (1966) 'Ideology and the Organisation of Conflict: On the Relationship Between Political Thought and Behaviour', *Journal of Politics*, 28, 513–30; Bergman, Gustave (1951) 'Ideology', *Ethics*, 61, 205–18; Birnbaum, N. (1960) 'The Sociological Study of Ideology (1940–1960): A Trend Report and a Bibliography', *Current Sociology*, IX, 2, 89–172; Borg, Olavi (1966) 'Basic Dimensions of Finnish Party Ideologies: A Factor Analytical Study', *Scandinavian Political Studies*, 1, 94–117; Converse, P.E. (1964) 'The Nature of Belief Systems in Mass Publics', in Apter, D.E. (ed.) op. cit., p. 207; Corbett, P. (1965) *Ideologies*, London: Hutchinson, p. 12; Dahrendorf, R. (1959) *Class and Class Conflict in Industrial Society*, London: Routledge and Kegan Paul, p. 186; *Economist Brief Books*, (1970) London: The Economist, No. 20; Elliott, W.Y. (1953) 'Ideas and Ideologies: Diffusion, Seepage, or Overflow', *Confluence*, 2; Gerschenkron, Alexander (1961) 'Reflections on Ideology as a Methodological and Historical Problem' in Hegeland, Hugo (ed.) *Money, Growth, and Methodology*, Berlinska, Boktnyckeriet, Lund: C.W.K. Publishers; Harris, N. (1971) *Beliefs in Society*, London: Pelican Books, p. 43; Huntingdon, Samuel P. (1957) 'Conservatism as an Ideology', *American Political Science Review*, 51, 454–73; Ladd, E. C. (1969) *Ideology in America*, Ithaca: Cornell University Press, p. 7; Lane, Robert (1962) *Political Ideology*, New York: The Free Press, 14–15; la Palombara, Joseph (1966) 'Decline of Ideology: A Dissent and an Interpretation', *American Political Science Review*, 55, 5–16; MacRae, Donald G. (1958) 'Class Relationships and Ideology', *Sociological Review*, 6, 261–72; Merelman, Richard M. (1969) 'The Development of Political Ideology: A Framework for the Analysis of Political Socialisation, *American Political Science Review*, 63; Parsons, Talcott (1959) *The Social System*, Glencoe, Ill: The Free Press, 349–50; Plamenatz, John (1971) *Ideology*, London: MacMillan, p. 15; Putman, Robert D. (1971) 'Studying Elite Political Culture: The Case of Ideology', *American Political Science Review*, 60, 651–81; Rokeach, Milton (1960) *The Open and Closed Mind*, New York: Basic Books, p. 35; Roucek, Joseph S. (1944) 'A History of the Concept of Ideology', *Journal of the History of Ideas*, 5, 479–88; Sartori, Giovanni (1969) 'Politics, Ideology, and Belief Systems', *American Political Science Review*, 63, 398–411; Schurman, Franz (1971) *Ideology and Organisation in Communist China*, California: University of California Press, p. 18; Spengler, Joseph J. (1961) 'Theory, Ideology, Non-economic Values, and Politico-Economic Development', in Braibanti, R. and Spengler, J.J. (eds.) *Tradition, Values, and Socio-economic Development*, London: Cambridge University Press, p. 32; Tomkins, Sylvan (1963) 'Left and Right: A Basic Dimension of Ideology and Personality' in White, Robert W. (ed.)

The Study of Lives, New York: Atherton Press, p. 389; Walsby, Harold (1947) *The Domain of Ideologies*, Glasgow: William MacLellen, p. 17.

4. Bacon, Francis (1901) *The Dignity and Advancement of Learning*, London: George Bell, 207–11.

5. Sherif, M. (1966) *Group Conflict and Cooperation: their Social Psychology*, London: Routledge & Kegan Paul, p. 12.

6. Axelrod, R. (1984) *The Evolution of Cooperation*, New York: Basic Books.

7. See, for example, Nicholson, M. (1989) *Formal Theories in International Relations*, Cambridge: Cambridge University Press, 167–85.

8. Max Weber (1968) '"Objectivity" in Social Science', reprinted in Brodbeck, M. (ed.) *Readings in the Philosophy of the Social Sciences*, New York: Macmillan, 85–97.

9. See, for example, King, A. (ed.) (1976) *Why Britain is Becoming Harder to Govern*, London: BBC Publications; Birch, A. (1984) 'Overload, Ungovernability and Delegitimation: The Theories and the British Case', *Journal of Political Science*, 14, 135–60.

10. See, for example, Held, D. (1983) 'Central Perspectives on the Modern State' in Held, David *et al.* (eds) *States and Societies*, Oxford: Basil Blackwell, 1–59; Jessop, B. (1982) *The Capitalist State: Marxist Theories and Methods*, Oxford: Martin Robertson; Jessop, B. (1980) 'The Transformation of the State in Post-War Britain', in Scase, Richard (ed.) *The State in Western Europe*, London: Croom-Helm, 23–93; Poulantzas, N. (1973) *Political Power and Social Classes*, London: New Left Books, 1973.

11. In this context the recent work of Michael Mann is of interest in that ideology is seen as one of the dimensions or aspects of power. See Mann, M. (1986) *The Sources of Social Power*, Vol. 1., Cambridge: Cambridge University Press, 22–4. The same point is made but in a much more radical manner and as a central theme in the later poststructuralist work of Michel Foucault. The production of knowledge is itself the consequence of the ability to decide on the rules according to which knowledge is to be evaluated. Knowledge is thus a consequence of power, and power the ability to construct the rules pertaining to what is to be considered as knowledge. See Philp, M. (1985) 'Michel Foucault' in Skinner, Q. (ed.) *The Return of Grand Theory in the Human Sciences*, Cambridge: Cambridge University Press, 65–81; Foucault, Michel (edited by Lawrence D. Kritzman) (1988) *Politics, Philosophy, Culture: Interviews and Other Writings 1977–1984*, London: Routledge.

5
WHAT SCIENCE AND SOCIAL SCIENCE?

Introduction

Alan Ryan writes that 'there is only one central methodological question about the social sciences, and that is whether they are sciences at all'.[1] A presupposition here, however, is that there is such a thing as 'science' on which social science can realistically be modelled. One of the aims of this chapter is to demonstrate that the idea of a 'scientific *method*' is as debatable as the notion of social *science*. Thus, the simple belief that there can be a unity of method between science and social science — and hence social science can be a *science* — has first to answer the question 'which science?' or, more correctly, 'which conception of science?' Social scientists in general (although there are many exceptions) have been rather naïve in their beliefs about science.

A second aspect in Ryan's statement which can also be questioned relates to the level of analysis. The science/non-science question is only of importance in so far as the assertion of science is able to guarantee some degree of certainty regarding the output of social science. There is no other significant justification for the debate about science in social science. The option remains open, therefore, that there may be other means of justifying social scientific claims to knowledge that do not make explicit recourse to doctrines of science. The argument here will be that there are embedded in the various theories of science 'criteria of validity' that are routinely used in social science to justify claims to knowledge. The problem is that these criteria of validity, which will be extracted in the discussion of models of science in this chapter, are not always additive and in particular cases may well point in different directions. However, while such criteria will forever be the subject of contestation — since there is no obvious criterion of selection regarding the prioritization of criteria — it is reasonable to argue that such criteria can be used and are used outside of the context of particular models of science.

Thus, while the criteria of validity are to be extracted from the models of science, which are primarily epistemological models, they can thereafter be used as independent criteria unrelated to any particular model of science. It thus becomes possible to argue that social science is not a branch of interpretive literature, nor a science, but is *social science*, a thing in itself. Its justifications thus derive from the nature of the activity itself rather than being validated by reference to external standards and practices which are not appropriate to it. In this chapter, therefore, five 'models of science' will be described and discussed in terms of their utility for an understanding of social science.[2]

The inductivist model of science

The inductivist model of science was the first of the models of science to be clearly articulated.[3] It is certainly implicit in the ideas of Bacon and explicit in the work of John Stuart Mill.[4] It is also the case that at least since the famous critique of David Hume, the status of induction as a basis for science has remained problematic.[5] Yet, while the critiques of induction are trenchant and telling, induction as a mode of generating knowledge remains attractive.[6] There is, for example, little doubt that in everyday life we do all the time generalize from the past to the present and the future and that the past considerably structures our expectations regarding the future.[7] However, much of the literature on induction has been primarily of a philosophical nature which has been centrally concerned with the establishment of certainty with respect to knowledge. It could, therefore, be argued that the application of philosophical doubt or scepticism to the realm of science and social science is inappropriate; what we seek is not, perhaps, certainty but rather good and justifiable reasons for belief.

Induction has been defined as 'the process by which the scientist forms a theory to explain the observed facts';[8] it is an extrapolation from the past to the future in the expectation that the future will continue to behave in the same manner as in the past. Thus the fact that gravity has operated to the best of our knowledge universally in the past gives us cause to believe that it will operate in such a way in the future. The problem is, of course, that we have not observed all the operations of gravity but merely a miniscule number of past events as a proportion of all events and have obviously not observed those events that have yet to happen. The logical grounds for extrapolating to all events are dubious. Yet, while the logical grounds may be questionable, Hume is undoubtedly right in suggesting that sometimes we have little option in practice but to proceed inductively, a point that Russell recognizes when noting that in cases such as this we approach certainty without limit.[9] An important consequence of this point is that even the most general of natural laws can logically only be considered as probabilistic. Thus, while linguistically they may be formulated in universal terms, and given mathematical constructions that enable them to be used in a deductive fashion (e.g., $E=MC^2$), none the less they remain in essence only probabilistic statements of greater or lesser certainty. The model demonstrating the cyclical process of science according to this view was schematized thus by Kemeny, quoting Einstein that 'science begins and ends with facts':[10]

The inductive model of science

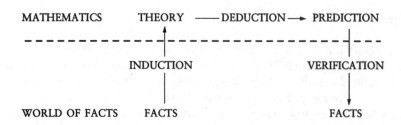

Over the years a great deal of effort has gone into attempting to formulate rules of induction; if there is forever a degree of philosophical uncertainty about the status of inductive knowledge, and yet we cannot help but use induction, are there any rules that can aid us in deciding what is or what is not acceptable as a piece of knowledge?[11] Chalmers lists three conditions that had historically emerged to justify acceptance of an inductive statement.[12] The first of these was that the number of observations should be very large; the second that the observations must be repeated under a wide variety of conditions; and the third that no observation should conflict with the derived generalization. At first glance these rules seem quite straightforward, but in reality they do little to solve the problem of induction as a practical problem.[13] There have, of course, been other attempts to circumvent the problem. John Stuart Mill, for example, justified the belief in induction on the grounds of the uniformity of nature, though recognizing that such a belief was itself an inductive generalization. If it were the case that nature everywhere was the same, then the future would be the same as the past. But, having made that one inductive leap, other inductions were acceptable. Another approach was theological. If God was perfect and rational, then so also would be nature.[14] Yet another approach makes recourse to probability theory.[15]

In the end, of course, there is no way around the problem of induction, and hence there remains a continuing central problem for any model of science that is based purely upon induction; it is difficult to see any methodology or logic that could go from the known to the unknown. Inductivism by its necessary emphasis upon the continuity of discovered trends has to assume a certain type of reality which has a high degree of permanence. This is an assumption that may be made in natural science but which cannot under any circumstances be justified as a primary epistemological principle in social science where such continuities as exist do so due to the perceptions, feelings, and motives of human actors; if these should change, then so also will social reality.

While as a general model of science, the inductive view is ultimately unsuccessful as a guarantor of knowledge, none the less, it is difficult to ignore entirely the criteria of validity which are embedded in induction. These are the three 'conditions of induction' which were, it will be recalled, that the number of observations should be very large, that the observations must be repeated under a wide variety of conditions, and that no observation should conflict with the derived generalization. For example, the widespread belief that there is a biological basis to human aggression is partially founded on the frequency of human aggressive behaviour;[16] similarly, the idea that war is somehow embedded in the human psyche is strengthened by the belief that 'there always has been and always will be war'.[17] When Lenski asserts that 'societies beyond the hunting and gathering stage develop a greater capacity to engage in war' on the basis of large numbers of observations, it is difficult to treat the proposition as being other than of some significance.[18] Or, when Quincy Wright isolates four very different kinds of society — animal, primitive, historic, and modern — and suggests that the disturbance of 'equilibrium' is the common factor regarding the onset of war, the variety of conditions under which this is asserted to be true is persuasive.[19] The fact that something has occurred frequently and in a wide range of circumstances *does* often lead us to believe that some kind of law or plausible generalization is involved. The third of the conditions is more problematic and will be dealt with in the next section.

The central point to be made here, however, is that while we cannot accept inductivism as a model of science or as a mode of practice to be adopted in social science, for the reasons given here and in the next section, it is nevertheless true that the criteria of validity embedded in such a model can and do influence whether we accept or reject propositions within social science, particularly when allied to other criteria of validity.

Falsificationism

The philosophical problem of induction has proved an insuperable barrier to the construction of a coherent philosophy of science based solely upon induction. It was in this context that falsificationism was introduced by Karl Popper. The rejection of an inductively based science, however, was not merely a simple change in the criteria of validity but was also a major epistemological change regarding the nature of knowledge, for it introduced the notion of 'fallibalism'.[20] Whereas the hope of nineteenth century science had been the search for certainty, the new approach abandoned any such grandiose ideas and held all knowledge to be tentative. Thus, while the scientist is bound always to seek the truth, she/he can never know with certainty when it has been achieved. In a sense, therefore, rather than repairing the imperfections of an inductivist model of science with respect to certainty, falsificationism accepts the limitations and proposes a mode of thinking that handles or copes with uncertainty.

The doctrine of falsification, therefore, while accepting that we can never with certainty know what is true, suggests that we can know what is *false*. The process of science, therefore, is the progressive elimination of what is false, with what is left unfalsified representing that which is nearer the truth.[21] According to Popper, this is an 'evolutionary' theory of knowledge, which sees human knowledge as developing through trial and error, conjecture and refutation, although the development may not be even and there may be many evolutionary blind alleys.[22] It has, though, to be considered as an optimistic theory of knowledge, in the sense that there is the possibility of improvement in our state of knowledge. Popper is thus rejecting any notion of epistemological relativism; improvement of knowledge is possible, and not all knowledge statements are equally right or equally arbitrary.[23] Through falsification and the 'crucial experiment' we can often decide among them.

A further aspect of the critique of induction lies in the notion that 'facts' are in some sense 'lying around' waiting to be picked up. Popper distinguishes between what he terms the 'bucket' theory of knowledge and the 'searchlight' theory of knowledge.[24] The heart of this critique lies in the argument that there can be no perception without a prior theoretical 'expectation'; it is the theory or the expectation that guides the perception and hence the observation. Popper writes, from a lecture given in 1961:[25] 'My experiment consists of asking you to observe, here and now. I hope that you are cooperating and observing! However I fear that at least some of you, instead of observing, will feel a strong urge to ask: "WHAT do you want me to observe?"'

Popper is here not necessarily referring to theory in a formal sense — indeed, at one point he asserts that all languages are theory impregnated — but to theory in the sense of a principle of selectivity with respect to the real world. This can perhaps be illustrated by noting that we are all the time assailed by a myriad of sense impressions, the vast majority of which are unnoticed and unretained; it is only those which have some significance to us from a point of view that become perceptions. Those perceptions that are self-consciously sought on the basis of some prior articulated theoretical expectation we might properly refer to as 'observations'.

A corollary of this point of view is that unlike the inductivists such as J.S. Mill, Popper argues that there can be no method of discovery, nor a method of verification, but only a method of falsification. Progress, or the evolution of science, occurs through the scientist having ideas, or making 'conjectures', which she/he will then attempt to demonstrate as false. The progress of science is, as is the development of a child, a matter of trial and error, with the difference being that in science error should be self-consciously sought in a methodical manner. To the extent that any idea or theory is not able to be falsified, we may have a tentative confidence in that theory, while always realizing that it may later be demonstrated to be erroneous. Scientific knowledge, therefore, is not the same as truth, even though it is truth which is the aim, but is a basket of scientific theories which to date have failed to be falsified. We can, however, according to this perspective, suggest that science is moving ever closer to the truth, and may in parts already have achieved truth, but we will never know that truth has actually been attained.

Since it is the case that all perception is dependent on selection according to a point of view or theory, how then are scientific theories to be distinguished from other kinds of theory? This brings us back to the 'criteria of demarcation' introduced by Popper, that is, the notion of falsification. The essence of a scientific theory, then, is its potential for falsification. A theory which is not falsifiable may be a perfectly good theory, but it is not a *scientific* theory. A scientific theory must not only describe and explain some aspect of the world but either implicitly or explicitly also give rise to a known set of conditions which if they were to exist would act as a falsification or refutation of that theory. Thus a theory that has the capacity to explain all sets of alternative conditions is not, in fact, a scientific theory. Thus Popper's stringent critique of Marxism (among other social theories) is primarily based on the unfalsifiability of that theory.[26] As he points out, terming it the 'conventionalist strategy', it is always possible to 'immunise' a theory against criticism or falsification.[27] Thus the theory of imperialism tacked on to Marxism by Hobson and Lenin effectively deferred the testing of Marxist predictions to an indefinite future while explaining why past predictions had not come to pass.[28] A further example of the conventionalist strategy at work can be taken from frustration–aggression theory.[29] The two primary hypotheses of the frustration–aggression theory are first, that all aggression is the result of frustration, and second, that all frustration leads to aggression. Frustration is defined as 'interference with goal directed activity' and aggression as 'behaviour intended to hurt or damage another'. Initial testing revealed that the two basic hypotheses of the theory were wrong — which stimulated two responses. One response was to limit the scope of the hypothesis and to specify conditions where it would not pertain, while the other changed the meaning of frustration which was then extended so that it covered *all* possible motivations. For example, fighting to preserve life when attacked becomes an example of frustration–aggression because the goal (the maintenance of life) is being frustrated by an attacker. Similarly utilitarian aggression, or socially organized aggression, or conformist aggression can be redefined. The result is that the frustration–aggression theory is no longer really testable because all possible outcomes will merely confirm the theory. Popper would then say that, however plausible it may seem, it is not a scientific theory.

There is a beautiful simplicity about Popper's views of science, and there is no doubt that his framework of trial and error, conjecture, and refutation has left a deep mark in the philosophy of science. For what he provides is an apparently clear criterion of validity that makes a great deal of intuitive sense. However, while falsification will always one of the criteria of validity in the social scientist's toolbag — and is implied by the third criterion in the inductivist model — the clarity of the criterion is actually more apparent than real.

One of the problems with the Popperian approach is that in order to make tests, whether these are crucial or not, an hypothesis has to be clearly stated with the criterion of its falsification known in advance. Thus while Popper is always talking about understanding the world in terms of theories, testing is actually done at the level of the hypothesis. The question then arises as to whether the falsification of a particular hypothesis represents the effective falsification of the entire theory. Consider, for example, the theory of classical political realism. This is a basket of ideas tied together in a non-deductive but plausible manner. Some of the central ideas are the separation of domestic and international politics, the eternal struggle for power among states, the notion of the national interest, the inevitability of emergence of balances of power, the idea of an anarchic international community, and the absence of morality in international politics. Does the discovery of elements of morality as influences in the formation of foreign policies of some states either entirely invalidate that hypothesis or, more importantly, invalidate the entire theory of political realism? Similarly, Smelser's theory of collective behaviour involves six internally complex determinants: structural conduciveness, structural strain, growth and spread of a generalized belief, precipitating factors, mobilization of participants for action, and the operation of social control.[30] Would the absence of an apparent structural strain necessarily invalidate the entire theory?

According to Popper, it does invalidate the entire theory.[31] This does not mean that Popper means that the whole theory is to be abandoned (as is frequently thought by commentators on Popper) but that it should be adapted through further bold conjectures.[32] The problem remains as to what precisely is being falsified when an hypothesis which is embedded in a complex theory is falsified. Certainly, the theory is not abandoned; good theories are far too valuable to be thrown away because of simple falsification, and, as we shall see, there are reasonable grounds for living with falsification in social science.

The history of science indicates that theories are not born or created in a pristine state. They take time to develop. This can be demonstrated by taking the heliocentric view of the solar system as an example. The heliocentric perspective has its roots in Greek philosophy, having been articulated in crude form by Aristarchus of Samos. His ideas were, however, ignored for some two thousand years, partly due to the massive authority of Aristotle who rejected them. With the fall of Constantinople and the beginning of the unravelling of the 'Catholic synthesis', other Greek philosophers became known in the original rather than at second hand. Copernicus, the 'timid monk', reformulated the heliocentric view in 1453 but in such a way that many of the features of the geocentric theory were retained, particularly the use of epicycles as time-lagging devices, since it was assumed that the planets went around the sun in circular orbits rather than ellipses. It was not until 1609, with the publication of Kepler's three laws of planetary motion that the elliptical nature of orbits was accepted, but even then the theory was not fully formed until Galileo's dynamics and Newton's three laws explained why there should be ellipses. It took something like two hundred years for the heliocentric view of the solar system to emerge as a developed and coherent theory.[33] At any point in that period the theory could have been considered as falsified by the incoherences and contradictions within it, as well as the erroneous predictions derived from it. Clearly, though, as Kuhn points out (see below), there are other factors and other criteria of importance apart from falsification that influence scientists then as now. The same story of lengthy development could be repeated in many other areas of science, and the message is clear. We do not take falsification too seriously. Thus, the fact that social science theories can be falsified in particulars does not in itself constitute adequate grounds for rejecting particular theories. Thus the continual reformulations of Marxism or political realism can be seen as the normal process of adjustment and change rather than as grounds for scepticism.

It is also the case that if social scientists followed the advice of Karl Popper and considered falsification as the decisive criterion of demarcation, there would be remarkably few, if any, theories in social science. This would mean, therefore, that there would be no social science, since we use theories to highlight aspects of reality that are deemed important with respect to the production of a particular phenomenon. The situation is perhaps rather more complex in social science than is usually the case in natural science, as it is usually the case that there are several contending and contemporaneous interpretations of any particular case, depending on the theoretical perspectives adopted. More importantly, however, it is the case in social science that there is greater difficulty in specifying the limiting conditions within which any particular theory will apply. Thus in natural science, a theory, law, or hypothesis is stated in such a way that the conditions under which it will operate are specified. Galileo's Law of Falling Bodies, for example, where bodies are said to fall at 32 ft/sec^2, is true only in a vacuum. In social science the identity of cases is far more difficult to establish and hence the conditions under which a theory may be said to be applicable or not applicable are much more difficult to establish. Since the identity of cases, that is, the similarity of phenomenon, that can properly be brought under a common theoretical explanation is not only dependent on the physical characteristics of the situation but is also conditioned by the consciousness and perception of actors (which are highly variable factors), the variability between cases is greater and hence the need for a greater number of theoretical explanatory frameworks. Hence the act of aggression, behaviour designed to injure or harm another, may be very physically similar between cases but may arise through frustration, conformism, utilitarian use, or be socially organized. Thus, there can be four explanations of the 'same' piece of behaviour dependent on the motives and perceptions of the actors. To make 'bold conjectures' regarding the causes of aggression and posit universal causes is to lay oneself open to instant refutation; there is a case to be made for a degree of causal modesty — sometimes it is because of this and sometimes because of that.

As a criterion of validity the idea of falsification cannot be entirely neglected. But, even in the amended form of the later Popper, it cannot be considered as the sole criterion of demarcation on whether to accept or reject a theory. However, the Popperian prescription (for it is a prescription of how scientists ought to behave rather than a description of how they do behave) cannot be wholly rejected; the injunction to seek disconfirmation can in the long run only be beneficial. In the short term it is unlikely, however, that social scientists do engage in this activity as a primary quest. Rather, the critical *structures* of the various disciplines comprising social science will engage in falsification behaviour, with greater or lesser success, rather than the individual constantly behaving in this way in respect to his/her own speculations.

The structural criterion of science

The work and views of Thomas Kuhn are often seen as a critique of Popper. But, as Kuhn himself points out, there are large areas of agreement as well as disagreement.[34] Hypothesis falsification within an agreed paradigmatic structure is not contrary to Kuhnian views and is indeed part of the process leading to the discovery of anomalies and eventual revolution. Neither Popper nor Kuhn would espouse any inductivist view of science, though their rejection of inductivism would be on somewhat different grounds: for Popper the scientist is much more of a free-floating rational intellect, while for Kuhn the ideas of the scientist are highly constrained by scientific socialization to the discipline within which he or she is working. Further, Kuhn is sometimes perceived by his readers as launching an attack on the authority of science, while by others he is seen merely as giving a naturalistic account of science.[35] Perhaps an essential difference between Popper and Kuhn is the direction from which they are coming. It would be a grave injustice to Popper to suggest that he not historically aware, but while he draws all the time on the history of science to demonstrate his thesis, he approaches the history and structure of science as a philosopher. Kuhn, on the other hand, is an historian first and foremost, and his philosophical analysis of science emerges out of his historical work. Kuhn, like Lakatos, is concerned to describe science 'as she is' rather than how it might or should be.

The central concept of Kuhn's philosophy of science is the 'paradigm'.[36] The notion of the paradigm is somewhat complex and made more so by Kuhn's use of the term to describe different things; according to Margaret Masterman he uses the term in twenty-one different ways in *The Structure of Scientific Revolutions*.[37] Masterman reduces the number of usages to three overlapping concepts, the 'metaphysical' paradigm, the 'sociological' paradigm, and the 'artefact' or construct paradigm.[38] The metaphysical paradigm refers to the extra-theoretic aspects of a scientific theory which affect the way in which man views the world and his place in it. Thus the Copernican revolution, the Darwinian theory of evolution, Einstein's theory of relativity, or the theory of the altruistic gene were not merely scientific statements but had and continue to have metaphysical consequences for man's view of himself. The sociological paradigm, which is the pertinent usage for this chapter, refers to a concrete scientific achievement which acts as a model or framework within which scientific research is conducted. Thus Newtonian mechanics 'set' the framework and the agenda for generations within that particular field. Finally, the artefact paradigm refers to a particular set of tools, techniques, or instrumentation that are held relevant to the validation of scientific knowledge.

A scientific discipline, according to Kuhn, is characterized by agreement on the fundamentals of that discipline. When such agreement pertains, the discipline is enjoying a period of normal as opposed to extraordinary or revolutionary science. The activity of the scientist is constrained to work within the framework of the paradigm and to engage in the activity of problem-solving; the paradigm is largely unquestioned and a research failure is the consequence of a lack of ingenuity on the part of the individual scientist. Through the process of developing (and amending) the paradigm, increasing complexity occurs. As the paradigm is developed into new areas and used to solve new problems, an increasing number of *ad hoc* hypotheses become incorporated as measures to 'save' the paradigm. It thus becomes increasingly unwieldy. Eventually a challenger arises, an alternative perspective, which is marked by greater simplicity, in the sense that what were problems or anomalies in the old paradigm are expectations within the new. A period of revolutionary science ensues, where there is conflict between the adherents of the old and the new. Some scientists will experience a *Gestalt* switch through which they will see the reality of their discipline in a different way, while others will not make such a switch but will eventually die or retire. A paradigm will never be replaced unless there is a competitor. The period of revolutionary science ends with the establishment of the new paradigm as the unquestioned framework within which problem-solving occurs.

Within this general scenario of the development of science — whether it can be termed 'progress' is a moot point — Kuhn stresses the importance of the scientific community. While science is communicated to new entrants through textbooks and university courses that teach the paradigm as the prevailing and unquestioned version of the truth, the activity of science resides in the beliefs, practices, and problem-perception of the community of scientists themselves. Science *per se* would cease to exist if there were the sudden demise of the scientific community; the textbooks would not communicate the culture of science that is an essential part of the practice and activity of science. A fundamental adjunct to the notions of community, culture, and the transmission of knowledge is the idea of authority; the paradigm is the authoritative version of truth and only those working within its purview are conducting real science.[39]

Emerging from this discussion we have a further criterion of validity, which we may term as *congruence*. An item of proposed knowledge gains in plausibility and acceptability to the extent that it is congruent with the received wisdom of the discipline. This does not imply mere replication but merely that an explanation has to be constructed and be congruent with the accepted disciplinary explanatory mode.[40] Indeed, we may define 'explanation' as the 'reduction of the unfamiliar to the familiar', and in so far as something is seen to be explicable in terms of the known and accepted paradigm, it is held to have been explained. However, according to Kuhn, social science is not a science if only because there is no agreement on fundamentals. This is not a very important issue in itself; what is more important is whether the logic of paradigms applies within the multi-paradigmatic social sciences with respect to the congruence criterion.

Further, Kuhn lays great stress on the idea of community in under-standing science. Can we reasonably speak of a 'social science community' in the same sorts of terms that Kuhn uses with respect to natural science? In general we can in six different ways. First, just as in natural science one cannot legitimately speak of the scientific community, but only of scientific communities broadly identified by disciplinary specialisations, so one can only speak of social scientific communities. The explanatory frameworks of economics are very different from those of psychology. Second, a particular social science has a special language for communication: in so far as the boundary of a community is marked by a communication disjuncture a discipline might be defined by the reach of its language. This might be termed as 'jargon' but is properly to be seen as stipulative usage for economical communication. Even practitioners from different 'schools' within a discipline will generally understand the usage of other schools, while not necessarily agreeing with the perspective espoused by those other schools. Third, there are controlling structures in all disciplines, and these are often themselves divided into schools. These will reflect the ability to publish and where to publish. Where a new school develops the controlling structure may be unsympathetic, leading to the establishment of new journals devoted to a particular perspective. Control will also be apparent in hiring and firing. The doyens of the profession will attempt to use their patronage to 'seed' their perspective elsewhere. Fourth, there exists a judgemental audience of peers who will communally decide on the pecking order in disciplines. This will partly be reflected in promotions but also in funding, conference invitations and expenses, and the definition of core books. The reputation bestowed by the audience of peers will also affect ease of publication. Fifth, the community will decide what constitutes the current significant debates. Different issue areas or problems will assume importance at particular times, and then fade as they are resolved or something else is defined as intellectually 'sexy'. Finally, there are qualifications for entry. Not anyone can be a social scientist (i.e., a psychologist, an economist, etc.). Qualification can be seen in two ways. There must be an acquaintance with the core works in the field, both historical and contemporary. There must also be qualification in terms of academic attainment: to gain entry the calling card of at least a master's degree is needed and more normally a doctorate.

We can, therefore, reasonably suggest that the social scientific disciplines do constitute communities in a Kuhnian sense. We can also suggest that they are marked by the presence of paradigms but not precisely in the sense specified by Kuhn; later we will use the term 'research programme' to describe these communal projects. The difference is that social science is in a state of what Kuhn might refer to as 'permanent revolution' in that there is always debate over fundamentals in the argument between different theoretical perspectives within a discipline although not necessarily marked by debate over fundamentals within a theoretical perspective or paradigm. The congruence criterion referred to earlier will thus tend to apply within theoretical perspectives rather than to widely accepted disciplinary perspectives as would be the case in natural science. Hence, in psychology the debate between a Freudian and a behaviourist perspective will be fundamental, but within each perspective contributions will be evaluated according to canons prevailing within that perspective. Similarly, within economics there will be fundamental debate over the cause of economic crisis between the monetarist, Keynesian, and Marxist schools, with the congruence criterion applying to validate contributions within each school.

What has excited many commentators on Kuhn's work is the manner in which he identifies science as a culture and a process with assumptions that go largely unchallenged most of the time. And, while Kuhn denies that his approach is necessarily relativistic, in that later scientific theories are better than their predecessors in several ways,[41] at the same time he wants to relate scientific knowledge to the beliefs of a group and at times refers to these beliefs as ideological.[42] What is important for this work, however, is not Kuhn's relativism but his identification of a significant criterion of validity, that is, congruence. We will return to this later.

Imre Lakatos and the 'fruitfulness' of theories

Lakatos is primarily regarded as a philosopher of science who attempted a reconciliation of the Popperian and Kuhnian perspectives.[43] He introduced the notion of 'sophisticated falsificationism' into the discourse on the nature of science. The difference between 'naïve' and 'sophisticated' falsification lies in the more rigid rules of acceptance or demarcation criterion of the latter.[44] Lakatos is thus recognizing the point made by Kuhn that scientists do not in fact falsify theories unless a better alternative is available and is attempting to provide rationalist criteria for making such choices. At the level of the hypothesis Popperian naïve falsification may operate,[45] but at the level of theory-choice additional criteria are needed. While, therefore, modifying Popper, Lakatos at the same time downgrades the significance of extra-scientific factors which are so important in the ideas of Kuhn.

While for Karl Popper it is the 'theory' which is the basic unit of analysis, and for Kuhn it is the 'paradigm', Lakatos prefers to write in terms of 'research programmes'.[46] A research programme directs the scientist as to what to research (the positive heuristic) and what to avoid (the negative heuristic). The research programme is composed of a 'hard core' and 'auxillary hypotheses'. The hard core is essentially untestable; it is a given which must at all costs be 'protected' by the ingenuity of the auxillary hypotheses. An auxillary hypothesis can be overthrown without necessarily rejecting the hard core.

Whereas Popper sees progress towards truth occurring through falsification, and, notwithstanding the critique of relativism, Kuhn asserts development occurs through the extension and eventual overthrow of paradigms, Lakatos sees progress as leading from the competition between research programmes.[47] Social science, from this perspective, is not disbarred from being 'scientific' through the possession of too many research programmes; if anything, it is to the benefit of social science that there are multiple research programmes. This is a theme that we will return to.

Given that there are multiple research programmes, and that there always have been in science, on what grounds do we either initially or ultimately choose among research programmes? Lakatos has already noted the three conditions necessary for sophisticated falsificationism (see Note 44) but deepens this view in his discussion of 'progressive' and 'degenerative' research programmes. A research programme is 'theoretically progressive' if it predicts some 'novel, hitherto unexpected fact'; and it is 'empirically progressive' if 'each new theory leads us to the discovery of some new fact'. Lakatos is, therefore, drawing our attention to a further criterion of validity, the idea of 'fruitfulness'. Our theories should not only be assessed according to where they have been and what they have explained but also in terms of where they are going and what they are stimulating. An example may help to illustrate this. A recent debate occurred in the law courts in the United States with Christian fundamentalists arguing that fundamentalist views of evolution and the message of the geological record should be taught as well as the conventional scientific Darwinian and Neo-Darwinian accounts. It is clear that fundamentalist accounts can, with appropriate 'conventionalist strategems', explain more or less the same empirical domain as can more normal scientific accounts. However, having done this there is nothing more to be done. The perspective leads nowhere and cannot advance knowledge, while the conventional scientific approach is forever throwing up new ideas and stimulating further research. The one approach is 'fruitful', while the other is not.

The abandonment of the search for method

The spread of postmodernist thinking stemming from structuralist and poststructuralist perspectives, accepts uncertainty as a given. Relativism and the uncertainty associated with it are a fact of life, and any search for a definitive epistemological base to knowledge is seen to be doomed to failure. The optimism of nineteenth-century views of science, or the belief in the evolution of knowledge advanced by Karl Popper, is rejected. Paul Feyerabend, as a representative of this school, denies that there can be a philosophy of science that can successfully capture the essence of science.[48] He is not, however, in spite of the title of his most renowned publication (*Against Method*), wholly denying the relevance of method for the scientist but insists instead that all methodologies have their limitations. Methodology cannot provide clear-cut rules of choice for the scientist. Like Lakatos and Kuhn, he roots his analysis in the history of science, attempting to demonstrate that scientists in action will frequently ignore epistemological rules and in so doing make advances. The scientist, in this view, is not a conscientious methodologist; rather he is an 'unscrupulous opportunist' who adopts a pluralistic methodology. In these circumstances, Feyerabend argues, there can be only one methodological rule, and that is that 'anything goes'.[49] To hold fast to a strict methodology is to engage in a mindless conformism which, writes Feyerabend citing J.S.Mill, 'maims by compression like the Chinese lady's foot'.[50] This mindless conformism, however, applies not only to the practice of science itself but also to the training and teaching of science. Hence, embedded in Feyerabend's thinking is also a theory of education and scientific training.

Feyerabend's thinking, while within a postmodern framework, draws also on liberal thinking, particularly that of John Stuart Mill. He argues that the Kuhnian view of science as the communal acceptance of fundamentals is profoundly wrong and asserts instead the principle of 'counter-induction'. Counter-induction involves the assertion of difference; it is always worth while to assert difference because this will lead to a deeper understanding of what is known.

Unanimity of opinion may be fitting for a church, for the frightened or greedy victims of some (ancient, or modern) myth, or for the weak and willing followers of some tyrant. Variety of opinion is necessary for objective knowledge. And a method that encourages variety is also the only method that is compatible with a humanitarian outlook.

Coming from a postmodernist direction, it appears strange to see Feyerabend writing of the possibility of 'objective knowledge'. However, knowledge is defined in such a way as to incorporate variety and difference; in a sense, the more variety and difference that can coexist, the more 'objective' is the perception of the world.

Knowledge so conceived is not a series of self-consistent theories that converges towards an ideal view; it is not a gradual approach to the truth. It is rather an ever increasing *ocean of mutually incompatible (and perhaps even incommensurable) alternatives*, each single theory, each fairy tale, each myth that is part of the collection forcing the others into greater articulation and all of them contributing, via this process of competition, to the development of our consciousness.

Consonant with this unusual but interesting idea of objectivity is Feyerabend's assessment of the role and place of science in contemporary society. There are many ways of understanding the world and there is no good reason to privilege the scientific view.

In one respect, while launching an attack on the idea of falsification, Feyerabend is in agreement with Popper about the creative aspects of the scientist's work. He places great emphasis on what Popper would call conjecture. Ultimately, the assessment of any one theory or perspective cannot be adequately done from within that perspective but only from alternative and perhaps competing perspectives. In this sense, for Feyerabend science should be in perpetual revolution, and, agreeing with Lakatos, progress is more likely to be achieved where there are competing theories or research programmes. He suggests that it is in the nature of a scientific theory to tend towards self-confirmation; the theory specifies what are the significant explanatory variables and data is collected and analysed on that basis with the consequence that the facts will tend to confirm the theory. Where a 'conventionalist strategem' is also adopted (that is, *ad hoc* modification to rectify anomaly), which is a frequent and normal procedure, the potential for self-confirmation increases further. To avoid an endless process of self-confirmation, alternative perspectives are needed.

There is another reason why alternative and competing theories are to be welcomed, even though this may lead to a degree of angst regarding uncertainty and theory choice. This is that the more theories (paradigms, research programmes, etc) there are in a discipline, the greater the empirical content considered relevant in that discipline. A theory, by its nature, abstracts from the environment a limited number of features that are considered relevant for a particular purpose. Different theories will draw attention to different aspects of the environment, with the consequence that the empirical content of a discipline will be greater the more theories there are. Theoretical pluralism thus not only adds to empirical understanding in a particular discipline but also, as Feyerabend points out, through the clash of perspectives which increases understanding of particular theories. From this point of view, rather than being a weakness of social science, as Kuhn would maintain, theoretical pluralism is a source of strength and richness.

Attractive though Feyerabend's anarchistic perspective is, and even on occasion demonstrably correct, it could be argued that as a general doctrine, complete methodological *laissez-faire* really cannot work.

Chalmers, quoting Krige, puts this very succinctly: 'if anything goes, then everything stays'.[51] The brunt of this argument is that without some generally accepted decisional criteria, nothing could ever be rejected; the storehouse of scientific knowledge would increasingly resemble a lumber room as accumulated and unrejected theories multiplied. And a consequence of this would not be the humanitarian ends sought by Feyerabend but an increasing authoritarianism; since there are no rational or scientific criteria to decide between theories they would thus be decided by power.

This criticism is achieved by Chalmer's acceptance of some of Feyerabend's more lurid passages without taking sufficient account of the more cautious caveats in Feyerabend's work. In a sense, Feyerabend is almost a party to his own misinterpretation through his love and perhaps over-use of the striking phrase and the purple passage.[52] Chalmers is, of course, correct to say that everything cannot stay, and Feyerabend in his frequent historical analyses is demonstrably aware that everything has not stayed. In reality, when Feyerabend says 'anything goes', he means that in the last analysis there are often no rational criteria for choice among theories, not that scientists in their everyday work never follow methodological precepts. Feyerabend would not deny that blind tests in drug testing or mapping and sampling in epidemiology are not useful methodologies and techniques, nor that deepening and extending existing theoretical insights is not a useful and necessary task — this is implied by the asserted consequences of alternative articulations — but that, first, there is no especially privileged methodology; second, that there is competition between criteria and hence methodological pluralism; and, finally, that the abandonment of methodological purity is a necessary part of scientific progress. It is with these thoughts in mind that we return to social science.

Method, science, and social science

This chapter was predicated on the belief that the adoption of the idea of science by the social scientist was naïve in that it was based on the supposition that there was a 'thing' called scientific method. It was also assumed that science was in some sense linearly progressive and less controversial than in fact it is. This discussion of the analyses of science has demonstrated these suppositions to be questionable. The resort to science as a means of avoiding the uncertainties of relativism with all the associated angst is demonstrably inadequate and ineffective. In many ways, however, science is like social science. But science itself is not like science in the way imagined by many social scientists; rather social science is like science in the sense that it is marked by constant debate and dispute over fact, theory, and method. The argument over the unity of method in science and the social sciences can be sustained only to the extent that it is recognized that in both method is a matter of controversy. In this sense Lakatos and Feyerabend are right and the inductivists and Kuhn wrong.

However, the examination conducted here does more than merely demonstrate the limitations of a unity of method in science and social science theses; it has also *en passant* disaggregated the question of whether social science is a science or not through the identification of criteria of validity embedded in different versions of science. These different versions of science can be considered as competing versions or rationalizations of the process of assessing or evaluating knowledge in the empirical realm; they can thus be considered as epistemological doctrines. The reason for engaging in this decomposition was, it may be remembered, that it was argued that the important question was not whether social science was or was not a science but whether there were means for judging or evaluating social science output. These criteria can be referred to as frequency and regularity of occurrence, falsification, congruence, and fruitfulness. To these might be added theoretical scope and theoretical coherence. The latter are important as developed criteria of validity but are often ignored in the early stages of a research programme in favour of a perceived fruitfulness of approach. In natural science, as in social science, if coherence was taken to be a central criterion, most theories would be strangled at birth; development takes time.

The picture of social science developed here is one of contestation and conflict between groups of scholars and theories of a subject. Epistemological certainty is a casualty in this war. Individuals may have their own certainties, but these are merely psychological beliefs; disciplines are not marked by such agreements. And, while we can properly argue that such diversity adds to the empirical understanding of the world, does it in any sense solve or answer the question posed by the radical relativist? In one sense the view adopted here suggests that knowledge is always in flux, always inconstant, unstable, and mutable. Clearly, our analysis of the nature of social science as an activity does not support the objectivist hope, in that uncertainty and debate are typical of both science and social science. But neither does it support the radical relativist position, in that it is not the case that 'anything goes'; within social science there are limitations on the range and scope of belief established by the contesting research programmes of a discipline, the contest between these structured by the criteria of validity which are the weapons with which the battle is fought. Further, the implication is that disciplinary knowledge is not knowing truth *per se* but knowing and understanding the nature of the arguments within a discipline of what the proposed variants of the truth are. The consequence of this is that there are certain things that *cannot* be said; the range of permissable arguments is limited. Thus, while there is indisputably uncertainty and contestation, the radical relativist conclusion does not follow.

An additional consequence follows from this argument. Since knowing in a disciplinary sense is awareness and understanding of the competing research programmes and perspectives, the social scientist who is *too* wedded to any perspective begins to approach the ideological end of the spectrum as opposed to the social scientific end. As noted previously, values are an ineluctable part of social science and preference a necessary component for participation in a research programme. But values, like conjectural knowledge, must be held tentatively lest the social scientist becomes an advocate, thus losing the dispassion, distance, and detachment that is necessary for comprehensive disciplinary understanding.

Notes

1. Ryan, Alan (1981) 'Is the Study of Society a Science?' in Potter, D. *et al.* *Society and the Social Sciences*, London: Routledge and Kegan Paul, 8–33.
2. For an excellent and accessible introduction to this literature see Chalmers, A.F. (1982) *What is This Thing Called Science?*, Milton Keynes: The Open University Press.
3. 'Induction' is the practice of deriving generalizations about the present or future from the observation of past facts. Still one of the best introductions is in Russell, B. (1912) *The Problems of Philosophy*, London: Oxford University Press, Chapter 6.
4. Mill writes:

   We have found that all Inference, consequently all Proof, and all discovery of truths not self-evident, consists of inductions, and the interpretations of inductions: that all our knowledge, not intuitive, comes to us exclusively from that source. What Induction is, therefore, and what conditions render it legitimate, cannot but be deemed the main question of the science of logic — the question which includes all others.

   See Mill, J.S. (1973) *Collected Works of John Stuart Mill*, Vol. VII, London: Routledge and Kegan Paul, p. 283.
5. Hume writes with characteristic brevity and lucidity:

   As to past experience, it can be allowed to give direct and certain information of those precise objects only, and that period of time which fell under its cognizance: But why this experience should be extended to future times and to other objects which, for ought we know, may be only in appearance similar, this is the main question on which I would insist. [p. 48] Let the course of things be allowed hitherto ever so regular; that alone without some new argument or inference, proves not that, for the future, it will continue so. In vain do you pretend to have learned the nature of bodies from your past experience. [51–2]

   See Hume, D. (1955) *An Inquiry Concerning Human Understanding*, Section IV, Pt.II, New York: Bobbs-Merill, 46–53.

6. Caws breaks the problem of induction down into three separate but related problems:

> Inductive inferences are problematic in three ways. The first problem is to account for their happening at all, and this may be called the psychologocal problem of induction ... The second is to describe the logical relationship between protocol sentences and the generalizations and hypotheses to which they lead; this may be called the logical problem of induction ... The third is to justify our confidence in inductive inferences ... It may be called the metaphysical problem of induction, or Hume's problem.

See Caws, P. (1965) *The Philosophy of Science: a Systematic Account*, Princeton: Van Nostrand, 195–6.

7. Hume makes the distinction between philosophical certainty and human learning; he uses the example of a child learning to fear the flame having been burnt but maintains his philosophical 'skepticism' (p. 48, pp. 51–2), and then suggests that the ready human recourse to induction is a principle of human nature.

> This principle is custom or habit. For wherever the repetition of any particular act or operation produces a propensity to renew the same act or operation without being impelled by any reasoning or process of the understanding, we always say that this propensity is the effect of custom. By employing that word we pretend not to have given the ultimate reason for such a propensity. We only point out a principle of human nature which is universally acknowledged, and which is well known by its effects.

Hume, D. (1955) *An Inquiry Concerning Human Understanding*, Section V, Pt.I, New York: Bobbs-Merill, 56–7.

8. Kemeny, J.G. (1959) *A Philosopher Looks at Science*, Princeton: Van Nostrand, p. 93.

9. Russell, op. cit., p. 65.

10. From Kemeny, op. cit., p. 86.

11. Norman Campbell, however, is entirely dismissive of the problem of or the search for rules of induction:

> ... we can omit all reference to the 'Canons of Induction' which were supposed by an earlier generation to provide the one and only means for discovering scientific laws. They are futile, because the problem they profess to resolve is not one which has ever troubled an intelligent person.

See Campbell, N. (1952) *What is Science?*, New York: Dover Publications, p. 76.

12. Chalmers, op. cit., p. 4.

13. Pollock comments:

> Principles of induction seem simple until we try to formulate them precisely; then they become quite complicated and it is never clear whether we have got them quite right.

Pollock, J.L. (1986) *Contemporary Theories of Knowledge*, Savage: Rowman and Littlefield, p. 1.

14. For Spinoza science, or the investigation of nature, was coterminous with the investigation of the nature of God. Since God was infinite, nature could also be so considered. See Wild, J. (ed.) (1930), *Spinoza Selections*, Letter XXXII, Letter XXXV, New York: Charles Scribner's Sons, 440–6.

15. Summarising Sir Roy Harrod's view, Caws writes:

> ... Harrod's thesis amounts to this: If there are continuities, and if we traverse them uniformly, then we are always more likely to be somewhere in the beginning or middle

regions than very near the end of any one of them. And this is obviously true. The reason why this solution too ends in failure is that such a consideration is of no comfort to somebody who happens to be near the end.

See Caws, P. (1965) *The Philosophy of Science: a Systematic Account*, Princeton: Van Nostrand, 256–8.

16. See, for example, Shaw, R. Paul and Wong, Y. (1989) *Genetic Seeds of Warfare: Evolution, Nationalism, and Patriotism*, Winchester: Unwin Hyman, especially 3–5; and Reynolds. V. *et al.* (eds) (1987) *The Sociobiology of Ethnocentricism: Evolutionary Dimensions of Xenophobia, Discrimination, Racism and Nationalism*, London and Sydney: Croom Helm.

17. See, for example, the exemplar of the realist school of international relations, Morgenthau, H. (1954) *Politics Among Nations: The Struggle for Power and Peace*, New York: Knopf, p. 27; A further contribution with respect to the frequency argument is Sorokin, P. (1962) *Social and Cultural Dynamics*: Vol. III, 'Fluctuations in Social Relationships, War and Revolution', New York: Bedminster.

18. Lenski, Gerhard (1966) *Power and Privilege: a Theory of Stratification*, New York: McGraw-Hill, p. 122. Lenski initially lays out what is almost an axiomatic and deductive system and then justifies the propositions by a systematic examination of literature on historical distributive systems. But, and this is the important point, the justification for accepting these propositions is strengthened by multiple cases and examples.

19. Wright, Q. (1965: rev. ed.) *A Study of War*, Chicago: University of Chicago Press, p. 68, 743–4.

20. See Popper, K.R. (1962) *The Open Society and its Enemies*, Vol. II, 4th. rev. ed., London: Routledge and Kegan Paul, p. 375.

By 'fallibilism' I mean here the view, or the acceptance of the fact, that we may err, and that the quest for certainty (or even the quest for high probability) is a mistaken quest. But this does not imply that the quest for truth is mistaken. On the contrary, the idea of error implies that of truth as the standard of which we may fall short. It implies that, although we may seek for truth, and though we may even find truth (as I believe we do in many cases), we can never be quite certain that we have found it.

21. See Popper, K.R. (1979) *Objective Knowledge: an Evolutionary Approach*, Oxford: Oxford University Press, p. 58.

22. See Popper, K.R. (1974) 'Campbell on the Evolutionary Theory of Knowledge' in Schilpp, P.A. (ed.) *The Philosophy of Karl Popper*, Vol. II, La Salle, Ill: Open Court Publishing Company, 1061–5.

23. In the 'Addendum' to Popper, K.R. (1962) *The Open Society and its Enemies*, Vol. II, 4th. rev. ed., London: Routledge and Kegan Paul, p. 369, Popper writes that 'The main philosophical malady of our time is an intellectual and moral relativism' and a dose of Tarski and Popper goes a long way to curing this malady. See also Burke, T.E. (1983) *The Philosophy of Popper*, Manchester: Manchester University Press, 82–131.

24. See Appendix 1, 'The Bucket and the Searchlight: Two Theories of Knowledge' in Popper, K.R. (1979) op. cit., 341–61.

25. We can define a 'fact' as a 'situation or circumstance about which there does not seem to be valid reason for disagreement'. Since all facts are or can be expressed as propositions ('the cat is on the mat'), the total store of facts is the sum of such propositions that can be made. Since all objects can be propositionally related *ad infinitum* (e.g., this manuscript is being prepared

approximately 26 billion years after the formation of the Earth) the number of facts is therefore infinite. As we are completely uninterested in the vast majority of these facts, some principle of selectivity is needed to choose those in which to be interested. See Popper, K.R. (1979) op. cit., p. 259. Chalmers, op. cit., 28–9, gives a further telling if somewhat grisly example:

> Consider the simple sentence in commonsense language, 'Look out, the wind is blowing the baby's pram over the cliff edge!' Much low-level theory is presupposed here. It is implied that there is such a thing as wind, which has the property of being able to cause the motion of objects such as prams, which stand in its path . . . and it is further assumed that this will be deleterious for the baby.

26. See Popper, K.R. (1962) op. cit., p. 81 *passim*. For an attack on and rebuttal of Popper's critique see Cornforth, M.C. (1968) *The Open Philosophy and the Open Society: a Reply to Dr. Karl Popper's Refutation of Marxism*, London: Lawrence Wishart.
27. See Popper, K.R. (1974) 'The Problem of Demarcation' in Schilpp, P.A. (ed) op. cit., p. 983.
28. See Hobson, J.A. (1938) *Imperialism*, London: George Allen and Unwin; and Lenin, V.I. (1917) *Imperialism: the Last Stage of Capitalism*, Communist Party of Great Britain. A further example is Galileo's rejection of the argument that the moon was not covered by mountains and craters. His distinguished colleagues, when invited to observe the moon for the first time through a telescope, falsified Galileo's claim by the quite reasonable point that if the moon were covered by mountains and craters the edge of the moon would be crinkly. Galileo 'saves' the theory (or 'immunizes' it) by two alternative *ad hoc* hypotheses for which there was no evidence at all and which would not have made any difference if there had been any evidence. See Feyerabend, P. (1978), *Against Method*, London: Verso, 128–9.
29. Dollard, J. *et al.* (1944) *Frustration and Aggression*, London: K. Paul, Trench, Trubner; Berkowitz, L. (1962) *Aggression: a Social-psychological Anslysis*, New York, London: McGraw-Hill.
30. Smelser, N.J. (1963) *Theory of Collective Behavior*, New York: Free Press.
31. See Popper, K.R. (1974) 'The Problem of Demarcation' in Schilpp, P.A. (ed.) op. cit., p. 982.
32. Popper writes, ibid.:

> If we falsify it we falsify the whole system. We may perhaps put the blame on one of its laws or another. But this means only that we conjecture that a certain change in the system will free it from falsification; or in other words, that we conjecture that a certain alternative system will be an improvement, a better approximation to the truth.

33. For an excellent and accessible discussion of this development see Koestler, A. (1964) *The Sleepwalkers: a History of Man's Changing Vision of the Universe*, Harmondsworth: Penguin.
34. See Kuhn, T.S. (1970) 'Logic of Discovery or Psychology of Research?' in I. Lakatos and A. Musgrave (eds) *Criticism and the Growth of Knowledge*, Cambridge: Cambridge University Press, 2–3.
35. Barnes, B. (1982) *T.S. Kuhn and Social Science*, London: Macmillan, 11–15.
36. Kuhn, T.S, (1970) 2nd ed. (enlarged), *The Structure of Scientific Revolutions*, Chicago: Chicago University Press, 43–51.
37. See Masterman, Margaret (1970) 'The Nature of a Paradigm' in Lakatos, I. and Musgrave, A. (eds) op. cit., p. 61.
38. Ibid., p. 65.

39. This view is, of course, anathema to both Popper and Feyerabend. Popper writes in Popper, K.R. (1970) 'Normal Science and its Dangers' in Lakatos, I. and Musgrave, A. (eds) op. cit., 52–3: 'In my view the "normal" scientist, as Kuhn describes him, is a person one ought to feel sorry for . . . The "normal" scientist, in my view, has been badly taught . . . He has been taught in a dogmatic spirit: he is a victim of indoctrination.' Paul Feyerabend, drawing on J.S. Mill writes: 'The second reason is that a scientific education as described above (and as practised in our schools) cannot be reconciled with a humanitarian attitude. It is in conflict 'with the cultivation of individuality which alone produces, or can produce, well-developed human beings', it 'maims by compression, like a Chinese lady's foot, every part of human nature'. See Feyerabend, P. (1978), *Against Method*, London: Verso, p. 20. Kuhn's response to this would be to suggest that 'progress' as defined by the scientist can only occur where there is agreement on fundamentals. See Kuhn, T.S, (1970) op. cit., p. 52, p. 163.

40. For a social scientific argument of this kind see Sartori, G. (1969), 'From the Sociology of Politics to Political Sociology', in Lipset, S.M. (ed.), *Politics and the Social Sciences*, New York; Oxford University Press, 65–100.

41. See Kuhn, T.S, (1970) op. cit., p. 206.

42. Kuhn writes:

Already it should be clear that the explanation must, in the final analysis, be psychological or sociological. It must, that is, be a description of a value system, an ideology, together with an analysis of the institutions through which that system is transmitted and enforced. Knowing what scientists value, we may hope to understand what problems they will undertake and what choices they will make in particular circumstances of conflict. I doubt that there is another sort of answer to be found.

See Kuhn, T.S. (1970) 'Logic of Discovery or Psychology of Research?' in Lakatos, I. and Musgrave, A. (eds) op. cit., p. 21.

43. Lakatos, I. (1970) 'Falsification and the Methodology of Scientific Research Programmes' in Lakatos, I. and Musgrave, A. (eds) *Criticism and the Growth of Knowledge*, Cambridge: Cambridge University Press, 91–196. This interpretation of Lakatos is supported by Paul Feyerabend (1974) 'Consolations for the Specialist' in Lakatos, I. and Musgrave, A. (eds) when he writes:

This picture is a synthesis of the following two discoveries. First, it contains Popper's discovery that science is advanced by a critical discission of alternative views. Secondly, it contains Kuhn's discovery of the function of tenacity which he has expressed, mistakenly I think, by postulating tenacious periods. The synthesis consists in Lakatos's assertion (which is developed in his own comments on Kuhn) that proliferation and tenacity do not belong to successive periods of the history of science, but are always copresent (p. 211).

44. Lakatos writes:

For the naive falsificationist a theory is falsified by a ('fortified') 'observational' statement which conflicts with it (or which he decides to interpret as conflicting with it). For the sophisticated falsificationist a scientific theory T is falsified if and only if another theory T1 has been proposed with the following characteristics: (1) T1 has excess empirical content over T: that is, it predicts novel facts, that is, facts improbable in the light of, or even forbidden by T; (2) T1 explains the previous success of T, that is, all the unrefuted content of T is included (within the limits of observational error) in the content of T1; and (3) some of the excess content of T1 is corroborated.

See Lakatos, I. (1970) 'Falsification and the Methodology of Scientific Research Programmes' in Lakatos, I. and Musgrave, A. (eds) op. cit., p. 116.

45. Although to call Popper a naïve falsificationist is really to do him a grave injustice. As Lakatos points out, ibid., p. 181, Popper's thought evolved from the 1920s to the 1950s from naïve falsificationism to something close to sophisticated falsificationism.

46. Lakatos writes ibid., p. 132:

For one of the crucial features of sophisticated falsificationism is that it replaces the concept of theory as the basic concept in the logic of discovery by the concept of series of theories. It is a succession of theories and not one given theory which is appraised as scientific or psuedo-scientific. But the members of such series of theories are usually connected by a remarkable continuity which welds them into research programmes. This continuity — reminiscent of Kuhnian 'normal science' — plays a vital role in the history of science; the main problems of the logic of discovery cannot be satisfactorily discussed except in the framework of a methodology of research programmes.

47. Lakatos writes, ibid., p. 155:

The history of science has been and should be a history of competing research programmes (or, if you wish, 'paradigms'), but it has not been and must not become a succession of periods of normal science: the sooner competition starts, the better for progress. 'Theoretical pluralism' is better than 'theoretical monism': On this point Popper and Feyerabend are right and Kuhn is wrong.

48. Feyerabend writes:

The idea of a method that contains firm, unchanging, and absolutely binding principles for conducting the business of science meets considerable difficulty when confronted by the results of historical research. We find, then, that there is not a single rule, however plausible, and however firmly grounded in epistemology, that is not violated at some time or other . . . This liberal practice, I repeat, is not just a *fact* of the history of science. It is both reasonable and *absolutely necessary* for the growth of knowledge. More specifically, one can show the following: given any rule, however 'fundamental' or 'necessary' for science, there are always some circumstances when it is advisable not only to ignore the rule, but to adopt its opposite.

See Feyerabend, P. (1978), *Against Method*, London: Verso, p. 23.

49. Feyerabend, ibid., 27–8, writes with passion — his views on science are part of a general rejection of intellectual authoritarianism.

And my thesis is that anarchism helps to achieve progress in any one of the senses one cares to choose. Even a law-and-order science will succeed only if anarchistic moves are allowed to take place . . . To those who look at the rich material provided by history, and who are not intent on impoverishing it in order to please their lower instincts, their craving for intellectual security in the form of clarity, precision, 'objectivity', 'truth', it will become clear that there is only one principle that can be defended under all circumstances and in all stages of intellectual development. It is the principle: anything goes.

50. Feyerabend, ibid., p. 20.

51. Chalmers, A.F. (1982) op. cit., p. 144, suggests that far from leading to the type of intellectual freedom desired by Feyerabend, the opposite could be true. 'If this view is adopted, it is liable to lead to a situation in which those who have access to power will keep it. As John Krige has put it, in a way that I wish I had thought of myself, *"anything goes* . . . means that, in practice, *everything stays'*.

52. Feyerabend explains in the 'Preface' to *Against Method* that:

> This essay is the first part of a book on rationalism that was to be written by Imre Lakatos and myself. I was to attack the rationalist position and Imre was to restate it and to defend it . . . The origin explains the style of the essay: it is a long and rather personal letter to Imre and every wicked phrase it contains was written in anticipation of an even more wicked reply from the recipient.

6
THE MOVE TO SCIENCE

....

Introduction

The problem of uncertainty was one of the main instigations to adopt a scientific mode of analysis. In so far as the world could in some sense be viewed as 'the same' and relatively invariable — as the natural world was viewed by the scientist — then many of the uncertainties associated with social science evaporated. But the move to science was not *only* due to uncertainty; initially it was also due to the belief that in science there existed a powerful method for the discovery of new knowledge. At least part of the seductive pull of science was its ability to be a *model* for the developing social sciences. For not only did natural science provide knowledge which appeared to have the characteristics of indisputability and universality, but it also had applicability and predictability. Through the application of science the world could be changed. Disease could be conquered. Life could be made more productive and living easier. But, in addition, if the laws of nature could be understood, the homogeneity between explanation and prediction meant that the future could also be known.[1] It is but a short step to imagine the existence of social laws and their application in social engineering. Allied to the rise of science and its later institutionalization was a decline in the sway of theological belief; with the rise of a sophisticated technology the immutability of the physical world was challenged and with it accompanying fatalistic attitudes. With science came also belief in change, progress, growth, and development. The belief in science was not only about science but was also embedded in radical changes in thought about the nature of the world and man's place in it. It is little wonder, therefore, that a transference should occur from the natural to the social spheres of study.

The background to the contemporary debate

The adoption of the scientific mode in social description and explanation has been a complex process and one that has stretched at least from

Hobbes to the present day. It is reasonable to suggest that the empiricist cast of mind (the belief that knowledge comes from the observation of the world) — which if not identical to positivism and to the belief in science is at least a necessary condition for it — is a philosophical temperament as old as man himself. It is also reasonable to argue that the justification for the adoption of scientific modes of explanation emerged in advance of their full utilization; rather than the 'owl of Minerva flying at dusk', the philosophy anticipated its operationalization. One of the early 'scientific' expressions of this temperament was in the work of Francis Bacon who formalized and systematized a methodology based on induction and reduction.[2] Hobbes, under the twin influences of Euclidean geometry and Galileo's 'resolutive–compositive' method, adopted a view of political science that was heavily dependent on reductionism. By reducing the state to its constituent parts, as in a machine, the inter-connection and working of those parts becomes exposed.[3] The state can thus be analysed (and constructed) on scientific principles. Reductionism was also a major plank in the scientific beliefs of Auguste Comte who can, perhaps, be properly described as the progenitor of the modern scientific debate and the major originator of positivistic views. Indeed, Comte is credited with coining the term 'positivist', which in his vocabulary was synonymous with either 'scientific' or 'certain'.[4] A methodology was being created that, it was hoped, would yield unambiguous and definite knowledge. This was a theme to be taken up later by John Stuart Mill, though with much more modesty and circumspection regarding the differences between social and natural sciences, in his *System of Logic*, particularly with respect to experimental method.[5]

Emphasis is here placed on Comte's work for two reasons: that his was an early and clear statement of a position, and because he was very influential. Other early exponents of the scientific approach would be Marx,[6] Mill, and Spencer,[7] and later, Durkheim[8] and Weber,[9] the latter being particularly influential. The four central themes of Comte's work that are relevant to this concern are his reductionist beliefs, his idea that science was the highest stage of knowledge, his argument that only facts are real, and his rejection of certain kinds of question. These became reflected in the four central tenets of positivism, nominalism, phenom-enomalism, the fact-value distinction, and the idea of a unity of method.[10] His reductionist beliefs are indicated by the construction of a hierarchy of knowledge, broadly composed of the disciplines as they were conceived in his day. Hence:[11]

Any kind of knowledge reaches the positive [scientific] stage in proportion to its generality, simplicity and independence of other departments. Astronomical science, which is above all made up of facts that are general, simple, and independent of other sciences, arrived first; then terrestrial physics; then chemistry; and at length physiology ... Though involved with physiology, social phenomena demand a distinct classification, both on account of their importance and their difficulty. They are the most individual, the most complicated, the most dependent on all the others; and therefore they must be the latest.

Such a belief in extreme reductionism was not that unusual for the time.

Further, according to Comte, knowledge in all fields was not only to be explained through reduction, but also went through three stages:[12]

Seen in its full completeness the fundamental law of intellectual evolution consists in the necessary passage of all human theories through three successive stages: First, the Theological or fictional, which is provisional; secondly, the metaphysical or abstract, which is transitional; and thirdly the Positive or scientific, which alone is definitive.

Thus, only when the third stage is reached can we be truly said to have achieved the state of knowledge; all else is opinion. However, the social sciences would pass through these three stages last since they are the most complex and the most dependent on the other sciences. Comte's view of intellectual development is a trifle eccentric and perhaps a little flavoured with ethnocentricism, since the stages he identifies can be largely equated with pre-Christian, Christian/metaphysical, and Enlightenment beliefs. Like many other historical systemizers, the apogee of history is to be attained in his life. Similarly, his views of religion shared characteristics with others of his time, and in his later and increasingly eccentric writings he went on to describe a 'religion of humanity' based upon positivistic ideas.[13]

According to Comte, all knowledge was based on facts; 'all good intellects have repeated, since Bacon's time, that there is no real knowledge but that which is based on observed facts.'[14] Such a view, of course, excluded many types of question which hitherto philosophers had thought important. It laid the emphasis centrally on the question of *how* things happen and not *why*. The latter kind of question was thought by Comte to be forever unanswerable and thus not really worth asking. Thus, while there was an implicit teleology in his Law of Three Stages, any teleological questions were ruled out. While it may be possible to have some sympathy with Comte in his desire to confront the great metaphysicians of the past as well as the idealism of his present, his position here is entirely untenable. This will become clear later.

A further thrust towards a scientific mode of analysis came through a fusion of the enlightenment belief in progress and rationality together with the needs of the emerging and centralizing nation-state for instruments of coordination. The growth and bureaucratization of the nation-state led to a massive growth of new kinds of data which could not be dealt with by the traditional forms of analysis. As one scholar comments:[15]

it could only be systematically exploited through the use of techniques of statistical analysis, and it could only be meaningfully interpreted within the broader framework of the concepts and models of the generalising sciences of society . . . (p. 48) [Hence] with the accumulation of attempts to assemble parallel micro-tabulations across differing political systems has come an increasing concern with the logic of such comparisons and with it the 'grammar' of cross-national research. (p. 54).

It is no accident, therefore, that the growth of the belief in a *scientific* study of society was predated only minimally by the rise of the nation-state. Whatever differences the Manchester school of economics and Karl Marx had, they shared a similar belief that they were engaged in science and were discovering the universal laws of human behaviour. From this emerged the belief that there was a *universal* method — *the* scientific method — for the attainment of knowledge. Hence, it is often the case that the impetus for change within a discipline is as much due to factors external to that discipline as to factors within the discipline. One such external factor, the changing nature of the state, has already been noted. Along with the rise of a belief in a universal method for the attainment of knowledge, with the exemplar being the intellectual achievements of Newton, came an emphasis on the observable fact and a rejection of the metaphysical. Thus the deductive and systematizing approaches of a Spinoza or a Leibniz were cast aside, along with the dramatic idealism of a Hegel.[16] For the study of society this was reinforced by the atomizing forces of emerging industrialization. Ascriptive identity began to be replaced by identity based on achievement and socio-economic position, and the market became more important and competed with heredity status. The consequence of this was the emergence of the individual as the fundamental unit of analysis; the individual was a fact and all else merely a derivation.[17] In economics 'economic man' was discovered and market forces seen to be the effects of the rational choices of countless individuals, while in ethics individualism similarly became paramount in the influential theories of utilitarianism. Fed by the forces of the enlightenment belief in progress, obvious success in the application of science, and the need for coordinating the emerging and heterogeneous industrial society, the notion of social manipulability emerged. Knowledge is power, and if society could be understood in the same way that nature could, then the destiny of society could also be controlled. The emergence of positivism was a doctrine of optimism in the future of man and man's ability to control that future. Nowhere does this emerge more strongly than in the behaviouristic doctrines of Watson and Skinner.[18] In other fields, as in psychology, the manipulatory tendency emerged in structuralism, as in Marxism, or in functionalism or neo-functionalism in international relations, or, later, in Keynsian economics. However, while behaviouralism was a doctrine of manipulation and optimism, it carried with it a critique of the manner in which social science was then done; the established traditional, legalistic, historical (and in psychology introspective) modes of analysis were criticized for their loose relationship between facts and theory, the low level of generality achieved, and the low level of comparability. Kirkpatrick, for example, comments that: '. . . many of them [the behavioralists] accused the profession of dignifying sloppy, impressionistic, crudely empirical, and prejudiced research and writing with the name of science'. While Hoffman commenting on three political science texts in 1959 noted:[19] '. . . the need to separate political science from political philosophy, so that factual research will not continue to be the stepchild of normative reflections'.

Robert Dahl, in an influential article, noted that the later adoption of behavioural modes of inquiry was related to other external factors. He draws attention to the blending of traditions following the exodus of mid-European scholars in the 1930s, to the increasing availability of money for social science research, and to the importation or development of new tools and research methods for social scientific work. These led to a different kind of social science and the institutionalization of new methodologies. And, while there were differences and even a degree of unclarity — Eulau describes the movement as a 'persuasion', while Dahl is more specific in calling it a 'mood' or an 'approach' — the emphasis was upon the use of scientific methods.[20]

In this view the behavioural approach is an attempt to improve our under-standing of politics by seeking to explain the empirical aspects of political life by means of methods, theories, and criteria of proof that are acceptable according to the canons, conventions, and assumptions of modern empirical science.

A further consequence of the behaviouralist changes was that disciplinary boundaries in many cases became extended as more explanatory variables were incorporated. Scott Greer and Giovanni Sartori might argue over what constitutes a discipline,[21] but the reality was that disciplinary boundaries tended to dissolve. In international relations, for example, while the behavioural revolution began as an articulation of the realist perspective,[22] the use of the new empirical methods soon led to the incorporation of variables very different from the traditional explanatory variables. The reason for this was very simple; it was easy to do. If a machine was being used it was as easy to get out a correlation matrix as it was to get out a single correlation, or if a multiple regression or a stepwise regression was being done the additative explanatory properties of independent variables could be easily assessed. Thus came a growth of empirical complexity. Hence, for example, in studies such as Rudolf Rummel's field-attribute theory hundreds of variables were summarized by the use of factor analysis,[23] while in political science voting studies became far more complex and sophisticated.[24] More impressionistically, in addition to a change in scholarly style came a change of work ethic; this followed from optimism and the belief that the world could be changed through the utilization of the new methods. Not only did the number of social scientists increase dramatically[25] but also the new style encouraged publication. Once a data set had been 'set up', it was a comparatively easy matter to exploit it.

But all was not well and in all the social science disciplines a 'culture gap' developed between the new and the old.[26] In part this was a gap in communication. The new social science used methods which were not understood by scholars with a different academic heritage. To some, indeed, it was almost a foreign language. Congruent with the adoption of new methods came changes in teaching and training; it became in many universities necessary for students in social science to have a formal training in methodology. Some vocational professional associations, for example, stressed the need for a statistics component on all courses that they would validate to the extent of accepting graduating students for professional exemptions. Further, the research councils, government sponsored bodies, began to lay greater stress on the need for methodological awareness for postgraduate students.

The behaviouralist debate was not homogeneous throughout social science but was to some degree present everywhere. The homogeneity was also broken by different national patterns of acceptance. The United States, probably due to a greater cultural numeracy, accepted the new approach more readily as did social science in Germany and Scandinavia. French and British social science was more resistant, probably due to the prior dominance of historical, literary, and legal traditions. The influence of the United States in shaping and advocating a particular kind of social science was in part due to the sheer amount of work produced but was also aided by the frequency of postgraduate training for European scholars in the United States. The homogeneity was also broken by different patterns between and within disciplines. While debates did arise, in general it was with less ferocity in economics, psychology, and geography than, for example, in politics, international relations, and sociology. This variation was to be expected given the different degree of emphasis on normative matters within disciplines and the prior methodological history of disciplines.

The postulates of positivism

While positivism can be broadly described as the belief in the application
of natural scientific techniques to social science, it can, as previously
mentioned, be further broken down into four central ideas that support
the general belief. These are phenomenalism, nominalism, the fact-value
distinction, and the idea of the unity of method.[27]
   The idea of 'phenomenalism' broadly states that the only things that
are real are those that are observable. It is an injunction to base research
and theories about the world on facts observable in the 'real' world.
Thus, in psychology, the behaviourists attempted to remove 'mind' and
emphasize only what could be observed. However, the doctrine simply
stated is somewhat naïve about what constitutes a 'fact'. We may define a
'fact' as 'a situation or circumstance about which there does not seem to
be valid room for disagreement'. It is *not* the case that all facts are
epistemologically the same: some facts will rely on a direct or indirect
correspondence of experience and proposition, while others will depend
upon perceptual coherence for their confirmation. Thus 'I have a pain in
my knee' is very different from 'There are six kinds of quark'. If we
exclude lying, the former is always irrefutable while the latter is capable
of revision, yet at a given point of time and knowledge we would accord
both the status of facts. We can thus argue that rather than facts *per se*
providing certainty, there are gradations of certainty regarding facts. But,
if the argument above is accepted, and there are many 'facts' which
cannot be directly observed, verification of the truth of a factual statment
is necessarily indirect. In practice, the rules of verification are themselves
variable, and the verification principle becomes weakened to little more
than an injunction.[28] Further, given that there is an infinity of factual
propositions that can be made about any existent object, and hence an
infinity of facts, a principle of selection is needed for all observation. This
principle *cannot* be derived from the facts themselves but is external to
the facts.
   Not only can facts be brought into relevance by the nature of the
perception employed, they may also be *created* by that perception. That
is, it is not the case that facts are just lying around waiting to be picked
up and observed; we often 'make' our own facts. Thus ideology
conceived as 'a dogmatic perception of politics' calls into being a
technology (a tested questionnaire) that creates a set of facts (interpreted
answers to the questionnaire) which are constructs relevant to that
conception.[29]
   The notion that knowledge is to be only derived from facts receives a
further blow when related to the notion of the 'underdetermination' of
theory by facts.[30] Hence, the same facts can be used to support different
theories; the meaning of the facts is dependent on the theoretical

interpretation imposed upon them. For example, some Marxist theorists have seen elections as primarily pseudo-participatory with their *raison d'être* being the legitimation of the regime, while liberal-democratic writers see elections as being one means of controlling the power of political elites. The 'facts' are the same, but their meaning is wholly dependent on the theory through which they are viewed. The facts themselves do not determine the theory. Since the construction placed upon facts, and the perceived relationships between facts, fundamentally affects their status as pieces of knowledge, it cannot be the case that all we know or can know is that which is observable.

The emphasis on the purely factual nature of social science (or, indeed, of any study whatsoever) can also be questioned by a further consideration. The idea that either science or social science could exclude the 'Why?' questions, as asserted by Comte, is surely fallacious. Questions such as 'What *is* the Good Life?' or 'Why *should* women be treated as the equals of men?' are significant questions that will lead scholars to engage in research. Comte may well be right in believing that there cannot be any definitive answers to such questions — which is not the same as saying that they are unanswerable — but it is also true that such questions exercise an influence over what work is done. Similarly, while we can construct good practical and institutional reasons for the investigation of nature, the motives for orbiting Jupiter, discovering the fundamental building blocks of matter or the structure of the gene are more to be related to a conception of man's place in the universe. Thus, a social science that attempts to exclude intention and purpose cannot meaningfully interpret human behaviour since most human behaviour is purposive with respect to goals. It is the larger normative and metaphysical questions that give meaning to social science, and to attempt to exclude such questions in favour of a purely factual social science would render that activity arid and ultimately meaningless.

'Nominalism', the second central postulate of positivism, asserts that all general names are merely summary abbreviations for numerous objects in reality. Methodological individualism (the belief that all social explanation could be reduced to explanation of the behaviour of individuals) was asserted against methodological holism (the belief that social groups had an influence and existence beyond the mere interactions of individuals), and a long debate was begun marked chiefly by its sterility and lack of conclusion.[31] The idea that group names are merely abbreviations or shorthand for the interactions of numerous individuals was argued in opposition to the idea that the group had some ontological status of its own.[32] The debate was foolish because it sought to establish an ontological priority independent of the research questions asked, while in reality the question determined the appropriate level and unit of analysis. For example, if an explanation is sought for participation in political protest, it *may* be answered by reference to factors in the individual psyche, or equally, it *may* also be answered by looking at the fates of groups to which individuals belong. Both perspectives are equally valid and meaningful. Further, to assert methodological individualism as an *empirical* principle soon became as metaphysical as the doctrine it was seeking to supplant; the behaviour of the 'nation-state' cannot *in fact* be reduced to the consequences of the interactions of the persons comprising the nation-state. The mere volume and complexity of the data preclude it. The idea of methodological individualism therefore becomes stated in the form that *in principle* the behaviour of groups should be explicable in individualistic terms, a modification that effectively destroys the usefulness of the doctrine as a prescription for research.

The third postulate of the positivist school is the assertion that it is possible to distinguish between facts and values and therefore have a social science which is factual and devoid of values. The arguments presented in Chapter 4 were that social scientists make value assumptions about the nature of the world and human nature, and that there are inherent prescriptive and advocacy elements in social science, with a conclusion that social science cannot be considered as value free. The origins of the fact–value distinction lie deep in English empiricist philosophy, and particularly in the use of the syllogism to derive statements of value from statements of fact which marked a certain approach to a proof of God.[33] Perhaps the most famous argument along these lines comes from David Hume:[34]

In every system of morality, which I have hitherto met with I have always remarked, that the author proceeds for some time in the ordinary way of reasoning, and establishes the being of a God or makes observations concerning human affairs; when of a sudden I am surprised to find that, instead of the usual copulation of propositions, is and is not, I meet with no proposition that is not connected with an ought or an ought not.

Hume is pointing to the fact that a value (ie, an 'ought') cannot be derived from propositions of fact by the use of the syllogism since the conclusion is not contained in either the major or minor premise. The importance of this observation, however, lies not in the specific demonstration, but in the belief that the universe of 'facts' can be *separated* from the universe of 'values'. The mode of thought continued in linguistic philosophy where the distinction is made between analytic and synthetic statements, with the latter validated by reference to experience.[35] The use of Hume's argument to claim the possibility of value freedom depends on the ability to *describe* social reality in a purely factual manner. But, can we use terms like 'class', 'development', 'nation', or 'ethnicity' entirely without any value intrusion? Such terms may be defined in a tight way, but connotative and indexical associations will still intrude (See Chapter 3). For example, 'class' may engender positive or negative responses given the political position of different individuals, and 'development' may be seen widely as being a 'good thing', and 'underdevelopment' a 'bad thing'. Seen from this perspective, normative factors intrude into the very description of social reality with the consequence that the fact–value distinction cannot be maintained. Further, as noted previously, social science theories nearly always have some prescriptive component which, again, dooms any idea that social science can attain value freedom.

The final postulate of positivism is that there is a unity of method between natural and social science. This argument was considered in the previous chapter. To briefly recapitulate that discussion, it was suggested that there is no such thing as an agreed unity of method in *natural* science, and hence (necessarily) no obvious unity of method between the natural and the social sciences. However, the various theories that have been advanced as to what constitutes 'science' do have consequences for social science and to some extent explain some of the epistemological uncertainties extant in social science.

Behaviouralism: the development of method

Behaviouralism was the practical application of positivist ideas in social science. The most contentious area of dispute was that of values and value freedom. But there were other critiques, some of which were more justified than others. Perhaps the most obvious feature about behaviouralism was the emphasis on quantification and the development of statistical and mathematical approaches to social science. These developments were not by any means universally welcomed. The argument often became quite acrimonious. Strauss, for example, while suggesting that 'moral obtuseness is the necessary condition for scientific analysis'[36] comments on the growth of polling:[37]

Hence, the new political science lacks orientation regarding political things; it has no protection whatever, except by surreptitious recourse to common sense, against losing itself in the study of irrelevancies. It is confronted by a chaotic mass of data into which it must bring an order alien to those data, an order originating in the demands of political science as a science anxious to comply with the demands of logical positivism (p. 318) . . . Only a great fool would call the new political science diabolic; it has no attributes peculiar to fallen angels. It is not even Machiavellian, for Machiavelli's teaching was graceful, subtle, and colorful. Nor is it Neronian. Nevertheless, one may say that it fiddles while Rome burns. It is excused by two facts: it does not know it fiddles, and it does not know that Rome burns (p. 327).

One argument was that the use of quantitative methods and the adoption of science in social science presupposed a particular ontology. The world, for these methods to be effective, had to be assumed to display a degree of regularity and constancy; it had, to some extent, to mimic the uniformity of nature often assumed to underlie natural science.[38] The tendency would then be to have a social science dominated and constructed by a particular view of the world. Thus, to the extent that the world was a place where there was regularity and replicability, and where generalization was possible, the problem of uncertainty was significantly reduced. Thus, for example, Howard was willing to compare the causes of the Peloponnesian War to the outbreak of the Second World War;[39] Quincy Wright discovers that a disturbance of equilibrium is common to contemporary and primitive war;[40] Modelski and Thompson and Vayrÿnen note the appearance of cycles in great power transitions;[41] while Organski and Kugler and Gilpin stress the constancy of change as a factor in the creation of war.[42] Gochman and Maoz, indeed, explicitly stress the 'timelessness' of such relations.[43] Similarly, the notion of conflict being a reaction to intensity of interaction can sweep across time and cultures. For example, Chagnon, commenting on the war propensity of the Yanomamo indians notes (p. 113):[44]

However, there are many variations in the intensity of warfare as one moves from the tribal periphery to the tribal centre. Simply stated, warfare is more intense and frequent at the centre resulting in a different kind of cultural adaptation there . . . Briefly, villages at the centre, because of the relative proximity of neighbours, are not free to migrate into new areas at will. Instead they must confront each other politically and militarily.

While Kenneth Waltz, keen to rebut the globalist thesis, uses the same idea to express the propensity of states to 'fall into violence' (p. 81):[45] 'Interdependent states whose relations remain unregulated must experience conflict and will occasionally fall into violence. If regulation is hard to come by, as it is in the relations of states, then it would seem to follow that a lessening of interdependence is desirable.' Hence those states at the 'centre' of the international system, and with more interactions than other states, would also tend to be those that experienced more wars. Thus it is not surprising that the United Kindom and France had more wars than any other of the great powers between 1850 and 1950.

Allied to and alongside the generalizing tendency in social science, there developed the self-conscious attempt to be comparative.[46] This involved the development of a *method*. In one sense we could argue that the idea of a specific comparative method does not make much sense since all analysis is necessarily comparative; comparison is implied merely by the establishment of identity and all thought is dependent upon such establishment. However, in another sense, a distinction can be made between the self-conscious comparative endeavour and the use of unconscious comparison which is implicit in all thought.[47]

There are several claims made for the use of comparison as a scientific methodology. Perhaps the most important of these is that comparison, particularly cross-cultural comparison, is an aid to the avoidance of ethnocentricism and hence a means of 'value control'. It is easy when studying a culture, particularly if that culture is one's own culture, to take as natural a given state of affairs; through comparison the natural is often dissolved and perceived to be just one more cultural artefact. A further claim for the comparative method was that it is a substitute for experiment. In the social world where physical manipulation of the environment under scrutiny is often not possible, comparison, often aided by statistical analysis, provided a weakened version of the kind of control that can be exercised through the pure experiment.[48] The experiment thus works on the explicit articulation of a *ceteris paribus* caveat, which in the social scientific experiment is gained through matching, randomization, and control groups, in the context of an introduced experimental factor. In the comparative format the *ceteris paribus* caveat is much weakened, the degree of weakening being dependent on the degree of similarity and difference of the cases being compared. This can perhaps be illustrated by reference to an extreme case, Weber's famous 'mental experiment' concerning the role of religion in the rise of capitalism.[49] Weber 'compared' four societies in an attempt to discover why, where there was an apparent equivalent technological capacity and bureaucratic organization, capitalism arose in one and not the others. He concluded that religion was a crucial factor in the development. However, while Weber's analysis is undoubtedly profound and has rightful status as a classic work in social science, the degree of control that could be exercised was so low that the results cannot be considered to be in any sense conclusive. All other things could not be considered equal with the exception of religion.

It could also be argued that the use of a comparative methodology involved some circularity. Through the use of a general category a structure of commonality was superimposed on a recalcitrant reality which was then used to reinforce the ontological presupposition of generality. Hence, positivist and behavioural ontological perceptions of the world, which were general rather than relative, were both a presupposition and a consequence of the methods being used. It is the case that any collection of phenomena can be compared; all that is necessary is that some attribute or attributes should be present or absent. Thus whales and mice can be compared with respect to colour, weight, size, number of progeny, etc., etc. However, the attributes being compared here are in a sense 'natural' in the sense of being recognized everyday common-language features of things. The problem comes when categories are *created* for the purpose of comparison. Thus, Almond and Verba in their classic work *The Civic Culture* argue that all societies will perform communication functions, socialization functions, interest articulation functions, and interest aggregation functions.[50] Since all societies *must* perform these in order to be societies, we can therefore use these general categories to order the material of reality. In fact, of course, if the general category is so high level that while it may be true that all societies have to perform these functions, the variability in the manner in which they are performed is so great that it may be difficult to consider them as the 'same'. A spurious generality has been created. Przeworski and Teune recognize the problem and specifically guard against the difficulty by making the distinction between the *equivalence of event* and the *equivalence of meaning*.[51] By this they mean that the same event in different cultures may have a different meaning. Thus a strike in pre-1989 Gdansk would be the 'same' physical event as a strike in a liberal-democracy, but its meaning would be very different. The injunction is then to search for an event that is equivalent in meaning in a liberal-democratic polity to a strike in Poland, since events themselves cannot be used as comparative indicators. Variation in meaning, the heart of the relativist case, is thus neatly circumvented by the *assumption* that there must be comparative equivalents.[52]

A charge of the same genre can be laid at the door of the quantitative school of social science which for some represents the heartland of behaviouralism. Quantification was initially undertaken to provide 'hard data' about social science topics as an aid to theorizing about those topics. It was an attempt to remedy the 'armchair theorizing' which the behaviouralists saw as typical of a previous era. Thus data was collected and then statistically analysed to discover generalities. Two difficulties arise here. First, the problem is that in order to collect data, a theory, as a principle of selection, is needed. Data is then collected according to this theory with the consequence that the data will tend to confirm the theory.[53] The approach thus becomes self-confirmatory. Second, the use of statistics can have the effect of 'smoothing' differences and giving an entirely spurious generality. To take a trivial example, while there is enormous variation in world income, an 'average' can be derived which hides all the differences. Statisticians would themselves guard against such interpretations, but none the less an over-arching sameness can be created which owes more to the techniques used than the reality.

The general argument that the behaviouralist approach assumes a particular world has been allied to an argument that by stressing what *is*, it is not therefore laying any emphasis on what *could* be. It is thus typified as being an ideologically conservative doctrine, a doctrine of the status quo. According to this view the description of social reality acts to confirm and reinforce that reality. Thus to affirm the existence of an 'iron law of oligarchy' is to act to create that reality.[54] 'What men believe is real is real in its consequences', and to the extent that 'iron laws' are articulated as unvariable they will affect the behaviour of people. However, while there is some force in this argument, it is surely not the case that the description of the contemporary is somehow irrelevant to change and the creation of a future better world. In order to bring about change in a desired direction, surely knowledge of the world as it is, is necessary. To describe the world is not always to approve of the world, but it may lead to knowledge of the constraints to change that exist.[55] The charge of conservatism, therefore, is difficult to sustain with respect to empirical description itself but can only be justified by reference to the reasons why that study is done. Thus, if description is the *only* aim, and there are no normative or political theoretical underpinnings to the work, then the charge *may* be justified. It might also be justified if there is a belief that what the findings of research are revealing are some sort of universal social laws; to have something stated as a law is not to suggest that it is a regularity that cannot be changed. Thus when Shaw and Wong come close to saying this with respect to inclusive fitness and nepotism theory, and with the whole tenor of their argument being that war between human societies must occur because of the nature of human biology, they are indeed guilty of empirical conservatism.[56] But such conservatism is not an inherent feature of description, whether this be termed scientific or otherwise; whether it exists or not is dependent on the motives for description. Thus in some cases at least Wolin is right in his critique of some social research projects in that 'They offer no significant choice or critical analysis of the quality, fate, or direction of public life'. This is not an inherent feature of empirical social science which can, indeed, offer considerable help in the making of choice.[57] Neither can the charge of empirical conservatism be maintained through the belief or statement that there are regularities in the social world. Events in the social world are surely not random; they are constrained by structure, customs, and expectations. But it is also the case that while there may be regularities these are often specific to time and culture and thus implicitly open to change.

A further charge against the behaviouralist trend in social science was that by their emphasis on evidence and facts, such as indicators, measures, or events, they necessarily missed much of what was significant in social life.[58] In social life it is not just what happens that is significant but also what does not happen. Thus, this critique draws attention to the problem of counterfactuals (or what did *not* happen but which might have) and to factors which are not empirically observable.[59] The problem became particularly acute in the study of power, where many of the manifestations of power occurred with no physical transactions occurring that could be empirically observed or measured.[60] Knowledge of power is frequently sufficient to affect behaviour without any need for that power to be manifested in any physical or observable manner.

Conclusion

The argument here has been that positivism and behaviouralism were in part adopted as responses to uncertainty and in part from influences emanating from outside social science. The arguments against positivism, centring around the four main postulates of positivism, are sufficient to suggest that positivism as a doctrine makes assumptions about the world that cannot be justified.

The ultimate failure of positivism and behaviouralism as the philosophy and practice of social science does not, however, mean that their appearance and propagation was in any sense a waste of time and effort. There are three reasons for this. The first is that the emergence of this approach had the effect of professionalizing social science; the social scientist was no longer a dilettante but a scholar with tools and techniques with which it was necessary to be acquainted in order to be a social scientist. This did not mean that all social scientists were equally adept in the use of these techniques but that they were understood at least to some extent by all. The tools have outlasted the philosophy that encouraged their development with the consequence that a philosophical pluralism developed and strengthened in social science, a pluralism with respect to what social science was and how it should be conducted.

Further, the debate about positivism both clarified the methodological issues and provided a diversity of responses to those issues with the consequence that life after positivism became much more complex. Hence phenomenology emerged and developed into the extreme theory of ethnomethodology; critical and action-orientated theory emerged, along with poststructuralism and postmodernism; and postbehaviouralism was stated, wherein the centrality of values and the importance of 'value-control' was asserted. Rather than attempting the impossible task of ridding social science of values, values were seen as giving meaning to social science.

Finally, methodology was moved to the centre of disciplinary debate and became a major component in the socialization and induction of social scientists. Methodology was conceived of in two ways, as over-arching philosophical approaches and as specific research techniques. No course or qualification in social science henceforth would be able to ignore methodological issues, and methodology became a major factor in the evaluation of research output. In that sense, the positivistic debate made doing social science a much more rigorous, if more difficult and complex, activity.

Notes

1. For elaboration of the problems of prediction see Chapter 8.
2. Bacon, Francis (1901) 'Novum Organum', Book 1, XIX, p. 386, in Devey, J. (ed.) *The Physical and Metaphysical Works of Lord Bacon*, London: George Bell. Bacon writes:

    There are and can exist but two ways of investigating and discovering truth. The one hurries on rapidly from the senses and particulars to the most general axioms . . . The other constructs its axioms from the senses and particulars, by ascending continually and gradually, till it finally arrives at the general axioms, which is the true but unattempted way.

3. Hobbes, T. (1962) *Body, Man, and Citizen*, (ed.) Peters, R.S., New York: Macmillan, 72–90.
4. Comte, A. (1974) *The Positive Philosophy*, New York: AMS Press, 33–8.
5. Mill, J.S. (1875) *System of Logic*, Vol. II, Bk. VII, London: Longmans, Green, Reader, and Dyer, 469–545.
6. Marx believed himself to be engaging in a scientific activity, considering that the 'laws' he developed were necessary in the same sense as those in the natural sciences, while at other times Marx and Engels compared their ideas on the social evolution of society with those on natural evolution developed by Darwin. See McLellan, D. (1971) *The Thought of Karl Marx*, London: Macmillan, p. 124. Elsewhere Marx writes (Marx, K. (1961) *Economic and Philosophic Manuscripts of 1844*, London: Lawrence and Wishart, p111): 'History itself is a real part of natural history — of nature's coming to be man. Natural science will in time subsume under itself the science of man, just as the science of man will subsume under itself natural science: there will be one science.'
7. Herbert Spencer was also much influenced in his social thinking by Darwin.

    And just as biology discovers certain general facts of development, structure, and function, holding throughout all organisms, others holding throughout certain great groups, others throughout certain subgroups these contain; so sociology has to recognise truths of social development, structure and function, and that some of them are universal, some of them general, some of them special.

    See Spencer, H. (1971) (ed. S. Andreski) *Herbert Spencer: Structure, Function, and Evolution*, London: Thomas Nelson, p. 40.
8. Durkheim, E. (1971) (ed. S. Lukes) *Rules of Sociological Method*, London: Macmillan.
9. Weber writes:

    It has been and remains true that a systematically correct scientific proof in the social sciences, if it is to achieve its purpose, must be acknowledged as correct even by a Chinese — or — more precisely stated — it must constantly strive to attain this goal . . . At the same time, our Chinese can lack a 'sense' of our ethical imperative and he can and certainly often will deny the ideal itself and the concrete value-judgements derived from it. Neither of these two latter attitudes can affect the scientific value of the analysis in any way.

See Shils, E.A. and Finch, H.A. (1949) *Max Weber on the Methodology of the Social Sciences*, Glencoe, Ill: The Free Press, p. 1.

10. Positivism is one of those words the meaning of which has expanded over time with the two consequences that it is often used as a synonym for everything a writer does not like and is bandied around as a universal insult. A similar case can be seen with Marxism. How much change, accretion, modification, etc., does a term or theory need in order to be considered a different thing? For various perspectives on positivism see Kolakowski, L. (1972) in *Positivist Philosophy: from Hume to the Vienna Circle*, Harmondsworth: Penguin, p. 9 writes:

> The term 'positive philosophy' was coined by Auguste Comte, and it has lasted down to the present time in the shorter form of 'positivism'. Not all, however, who according to historians or critics profess the positivist doctrine, would agree to be classified under this heading . . . To respect these wishes one would be obliged, in discussing each thinker, to single out those aspects of positivism that are not to his taste, at the same time pointing out how much of the rest he subscribes to. Also, many thinkers are conscious of errors and oversimplifications that grow up around doctrinal labels, and for this reason hesitate to enroll themselves under any banner.

See also Hughes, J. (1980) *The Philosophy of Social Research*, Harlow: Longman, 16–64; for discussion within a tradition of empiricist sociology see Rex, J. (1970) *Key Problems of Sociological Theory*, London: Routledge & Kegan Paul; and for thoroughgoing rejection from a different perspective see Frost, M. (1986) *Towards a Normative View of International Relations: a Critical Analysis of the Philosophical and Methodological Assumptions of the Discipline with Proposals Towards a Substantive Normative Theory*, Cambridge: Cambridge University Press, 9–36.

11. Comte op. cit. p. 29.
12. Comte, A. (1875) *System of Positive Polity*, Vol. III, London: Burt Franklin, p. 23.
13. See in particular Comte, A. (1877) *System of Positive Polity: Instituting the Religion of Humanity*, Vol. IV, London: Burt Franklin, 8–75.
14. Comte op. cit. p. 27.
15. Rokkan, S. (1962) 'The Comparative Study of Political Participation: Notes Toward a Perspective on Current Research', in Ranney, A. (ed.) *Essays in the Behavioural Study of Politics*, Urbana: University of Ilinois Press, 47–90.
16. See in particular Spinoza (1985) 'Ethics', in Curley, E. (ed.) *The Collected Works of Spinoza*, Vol. I, Princeton: Princeton University Press, 408–617; Janet, Paul (1962) 'Introduction', in Leibniz, *Discourse on Metaphysics, Correspondence with Arnauld, and Monadology*, La Salle, Ill: Open Court Publishers, vii–xxiii; and Stace, W.T. (1955) *The Philosophy of Hegel: a Systematic Exposition*, New York: Dover Publications, 3–31.
17. For a discussion of this emergence and some consequences of it see Macpherson, C.B. (1962) *The Political Theory of Possessive Individualism: Hobbes to Locke*, London: Oxford University Press.
18. Assuming a Lockean *tabula rasa* conception of man, man was the outcome of the effects of his environment. His behaviour was conditioned by the positive and negative reinforcements in respect of the stimulus he received and the mode of his response. For most of human history the nature of the reinforcements were random and unplanned. This need not necessarily be the case, however. B.F. Skinner, in his utopian novel *Walden Two*, (1962) New York: Macmillan, constructs a perfect and harmonious society based upon behaviourist principles, while Watson, perhaps the most extreme of the

school, notes in *Behaviorism* (1924) Chicago: University of Chicago Press, p. 104:

> Give me a dozen healthy infants, well-formed and my own specified world to bring them up in and I'll guarantee to take any one at random and train him to become any type of specialist I might select — doctor, lawyer, artist, merchant-chief and, yes, even begger-man and thief, regardless of his talents, penchants, tendencies, abilities, vocations, and race of his ancesters.

The essence of this approach was that extreme emphasis was put on observable behaviour. The weakness of the approach was that it dealt only poorly with the interpretive, remembered, and initiatory aspects of human behaviour, and the emphasis on the effects of observed behaviour alone eventually became a statement of faith rather than an established fact.

19. See Kirkpatrick, E.M. (1962) 'The Impact of the Behavioural Approach on Traditional Political Science', in Ranney, A. (ed.) *Essays in the Behavioural Study of Politics*, Urbana: University of Ilinois Press, 1–29; Hoffman, S. (1959) 'Review of *Introduction a la Science Politique*', *American Political Science Review*, 53, p. 1120.

20. See Eulau, H. (1963) *The Behavioral Persuasion in Politics*, New York: Random House; and Dahl, R.A. (1969) 'The Behavioural Approach in Political Science: Epitaph to a Monument to a Successful Movement', in Eulau, H. (ed.) ibid., p. 77.

21. Greer, S. (1969) 'Sociology and Political Science', in Lipset, S.M. (ed.) *Politics and the Social Sciences*, New York: Oxford University Press, 49–64; and Sartori, G. (1969) 'From the Sociology of Politics to Political Sociology', in Lipset, S.M. (ed.) *Politics and the Social Sciences*, New York: Oxford University Press, 65–100.

22. See Vasquez, J. (1983) *The Power of Power Politics*, London: Frances Pinter.

23. Rummel, R. (1977) *Field Theory Evolving*, London: Sage.

24. Perhaps the best indicator of this trend is the long series of Michigan studies of voting, developing from the Erie County study by Lazersfeld, P.F., Berelson, B.R. and Gaudet, H. (1944) *The People's Choice*, New York: Duell, Sloan, and Pearce, through Lazersfeld, P.F., Berelson, B.R. and McPhee, W.N. (1954) *Voting*, Chicago: University of Chicago Press, to Campbell, A., Converse, P.E., Millar, W.E. and Stokes, D.E. (1960) *The American Voter*, New York: John Wiley, and beyond. In Britain the genre is perhaps best represented by Butler, D. and Stokes, D. (1974) *Political Change in Britain: the Evolution of Electoral Choice*, London: Macmillan and the series of voting studies emanating from the University of Essex based on the Michigan series. An influential but now somewhat dated attempt to encapsulate the emerging complexity was Mackenzie, W.J.M. (1969) *Politics and Social Science*, Harmondsworth: Pelican. Mackenzie comments (p. 19):

> The barriers between political science and political economy are wearing thin in the age of mixed economies. Public and private institutions, public and private decisions are inseparable; the theory of welfare economics is a kind of political theory, administrative theory claims applicability to all large-scale organisations, reasoning about freedom now has to be made applicable to a complex of political, economic, social and legal institutions. Similarly, it is nonsense that there should be three disciplines — political science, political sociology, social psychology — which are distinct in organization, yet inseparable in the study of political behaviour.

25. This was not due primarily to factors internal to social science itself but to the population bulge following the ending of the Second World War. This,

together with an acceptance of welfare economics and the more inter-
ventionist state, changes in norms regarding the availability of education,
and the perceived need for a more highly educated populace in industrial
societies, led to a massive expansion of the university system in almost all
developed countries. A major feature of this expansion was the growth and
popularity of social science.

26. This point is made by Nicholson, Michael (1989) *The Formal Analysis of
International Relations*, Cambridge: Cambridge University Press, p. 1. See
also Krippendorf, Ekkart (1989) 'The Dominance of American Approaches',
in Dyer, H.C. and Mangasarian, Leon (eds) (1989) *The Study of
International Relations: the State of the Art*, London: Macmillan, 28–39.

27. See, for example, Kolakowski, L. (1972) op. cit.; Hughes, J. (1980) op. cit.;
Rex, J. (1970) op. cit.

28. See Berlin, Sir Isaiah (1968) 'Verification', in Parkinson, G.H.R. (ed.) *The
Theory of Meaning*, London: Oxford University Press, 15–43.

29. What it would mean is that a questionnaire would be devised to measure
'dogmatism', and levels of dogmatism in individuals would be a consequence
of the results of the questionnaire. A set of previously unknown or
unconstructed 'facts' has been created. See for a description of this process
Rokeach, M. (1960) *The Open and Closed Mind*, New York: Basic Books
Inc. passim; and for applications see DiRenzo, G.J. (1967) *Personality,
Power and Politics: a Social-Psychological Analysis of the Italian Deputy
and his Parliamentary System*, Notre Dame: University of Notre Dame Press;
and Sartori, G. (1969) 'Politics, Ideology, and Belief Systems', *American
Political Science Review*, Vol. 63, 398–411.

30. Lukes, S. (1978) 'The Underdetermination of Theory by Data', *Aristotelian
Society*, Supplementary Vol. LII, 93–107.

31. For a summary of the debate see Brodbeck, May (1968) 'Social Facts, Social
Laws, and Reduction', 239–44, and for exemplars of the debate see the
contributions by Ernest Gellner, J.W.N. Watkins, and May Brodbeck in
Brodbeck, M. (ed.) *Readings in the Philosophy of the Social Sciences*, New
York: Macmillan, 254–303.

32. The debate goes back far beyond the inception of social science. For
example, David Hume writes:

> A very material question has been started concerning abstract or general ideas,
> whether they be general or particular in the mind's conception of them. A great
> philosopher [Bishop George Berkeley] has disputed the received opinion in this
> particular, and has asserted, that all general ideas are nothing but particular ones
> annexed to a certain term, which gives them a more extensive signification, and makes
> them recall upon occasion other individuals, which are similar to them.

See Hume, D. (1962) *A Treatise on Human Nature*, Vol. I, Book I, Part I,
Section VII, London: Fontana, p. 61.

33. The syllogism is a form of logical argument which at its most simple takes
the following form:

> All men are Greeks
> Socrates is a Man
> Therefore Socrates is a Greek

If the first (major) premise and the second (minor) premise are correct, then
the conclusion must also be correct, since it is 'embedded' in the previous
statements.

34. See Hume, D. (1972) *A Treatise of Human Nature*, Vols II & III, Book III, part 1, Section 1, London: Fontana, p. 203.

35. See A.J. Ayer's influential (though subsequently revised) (1967) *Language, Truth, and Logic*, London: Victor Gollancz Ltd.

36. Strauss, L. (1969) 'What is Political Philosophy? The Problem of Political Philosophy', in Eulau, H. (ed.) *Behavioralism in Political Science*, New York: Atherton Press, 93–108.

37. Strauss, L. (1962) 'An Epilogue', in Storing, H.J. (ed.) *Essays in the Scientific Study of Politics*, New York: Holt, Rinehart, and Winston, 305–27.

38. See North, R.C. and Willard, M.R. 'The Post-Behavioural Debate: Indeterminism, Probabalism, and the Interaction of Data and Theory', in Banks, M. (ed.) (1984) *Conflict in World Society: a New Perspective on International Relations*, Brighton: Wheatsheaf, 22–38: '. . . for the employment of method assumes, even requires, that the world be of one kind rather than another if techniques are to be effective.'

39. Howard, M. (1983) *The Causes of War and Other Essays*, London: Temple Smith, 9–10: 'The causes of the Great War are thus no more complex or profound than those of any previous European War, or indeed than those described by Thucydides as underlying the Peloponnesian War: "What made war inevitable was the growth of Athenian power and the fear this caused in Sparta".'

40. Wright, Q. (1965: rev. ed.) *A Study of War*, Chicago: University of Chicago Press, p. 41 and p. 105.

41. Modelski, G. and Thompson, W.R. (1989) 'Long Cycles and Global Wars', in Midlarski, M.I. (ed.) *Handbook of War Studies*, London: Unwin Hyman, 23–54; and Vayrÿnen, R. (1983) 'Economic Cycles, Power Transitions, Political Management and Wars Between Great Powers', *International Studies Quarterly*, 27, 3, 389–418.

42. Organski, A.F.K., and Kugler, J. (1980) *The War Ledger*, Chicago: Chicago University Press; and Organski, A.F.K., and Kugler, J. (1989) 'The Power Transition: A Retrospective and Prospective Evaluation', in Midlarski, M.I. (ed.) ibid., 171–94; Gilpin, R. (1981) *War and Change in International Politics*, New York: Cambridge University Press.

43. See Gochman, C.S. and Maoz, Z. (1984) 'Militarized Interstate Disputes, 1816–1976', *Journal of Conflict Resolution*, 18, 588–615.

The image of the British armada off the coast of Argentina and the struggle for those desolate isles that the British call the Falklands may strike one as remarkably 'nineteenth centuryish'. Yet these events bring home, as perhaps no scholarly discourse can, the constancy and timelessness of basic interstate relations. Technology has changed; the objectives, motives, and methods of states remain the same.' (p. 615).

44. Chagnon, N.A. (1968) 'Yanomamo Social Organisation and Warfare', in Fried, M., Harris, M. and Murphy, R. (eds) *War: the Anthropology of Armed Conflict and Aggression*, New York: Natural History Press, 109–59.

45. Waltz, K. (1982) 'The Myth of National Interdependence', in Maghoori, R. and Ramberg, B. (eds) *Globalism Versus Realism: International Relations' Third Great Debate*, Boulder: Westview Press, 81–96.

46. See, for example, Blondel, J. (ed.) (1969) *Comparative Government*, London: Macmillan; MacIntyre, A. (1973) 'Is a Science of Comparative Politics Possible?', in Ryan, A. (ed.) *The Philosophy of Social Explanation*, London: Oxford University Press, 15–32; Rokkan, S. (1962) 'The Comparative Study of Political Participation: Notes Toward a Perspective on Current Research', in Ranney, A. (ed.) *Essays in the Behavioural Study of Politics*, Urbana:

University of Ilinois Press, 47–90; Bendix, R. (1963) 'Concepts and Generalizations in Comparative Social Studies', *American Sociological Review*, 28, 532–9; Przeworski, A. and Teune, H. (1970) *The Logic of Comparative Social Inquiry*, New York: John Wiley; Dogan, M. and Palassey, D. (1984) *How to Compare Nations: Strategies in Comparative Politics*, Chatham, NJ: Chatham House Publishers; Lipjhardt, A. (1971) 'Comparative Politics and Comparative Method', *American Political Science Review*, 65, 682–93; Gantzel, K.J. (1981) 'Another approach to a Theory on the Causes of International War', *Journal of Peace Research*, 1, 39–55.

47. Sartori, G. (1970) 'Concept Misinformation in Comparative Politics', *American Political Science Review*, 64, 1033–53.

48. For discussion of experimental design in social science see Nachmias, C. and Nachmias, D. (second ed.) (1981) *Research Methods in the Social Sciences*, London: Edward Arnold, 75–126.

49. See Gerth, H.H. and Wright Mills, C. (eds) (1970) *From Max Weber: Essays in Sociology*, London: Routledge and Kegan Paul, 267–359; and Weber, M. (1930) *The Protestant Ethic and the Spirit of Capitalism*, London: George Allen and Unwin.

50. Almond, G. and Verba, S. (1957) op. cit.

51. Przeworski, A. and Teune, H. (1970) *The Logic of Comparative Social Inquiry*, New York: John Wiley, 113–31

52. Nicholson, M. (1989) *Formal Theories in International Relations*, Cambridge: Cambridge University Press, p. 17 rejects the idea that there is any opposition between the general proposition and the variation of particular cases. He writes:

> A patient might be diagnosed as manic-depressive. There are some underlying characteristics of his condition which he shares with other manic-depressives. If there were not there would be no reason or even basis for making the categorisation in the first place. This common structure enables some sort of approach to be made to its alleviation or cure. However, every instance of manic depression will be different from every other in important respects.

See, however, MacIntyre, Alasdair (1973) 'Is a Science of Comparative Politics Possible', in Ryan, A. (ed.) *The Philosophy of Social Action*, London: Oxford University Press, 171–88, for a severe critique of this perspective.

53. This is part of a more general critique by Feyerabend that all theory tends to self-confirmation. Feyerabend writes:

> Observational results, too, will speak in favour of the theory, as they are formulated in its terms. It will seem that the truth has at last been arrived at. At the same time, it is evident that all contact with the world has been lost and that the stability achieved, the semblance of absolute truth, is nothing but the result of an absolute conformism. For how can we possibly test, or improve upon, the truth of a theory if it is built in such a manner that any conceivable event can be described or explained in terms of its principles.

If Feyerabend is right here regarding the tendency towards self-confirmation, then the criticism of behaviouralism in particular on these grounds cannot be sustained since it is true of all theories. See Feyerabend, P. (1978) *Against Method*, London: Verso, p. 45.

54. See Michels, R. (1959) *Political Parties*, New York: Dover Publications.

55. The obverse could indeed be true. An example here would be Meadows, D. et al. (1974) *Limits to Growth*, London: Pan Books. Commissioned by the Club of Rome, the report examines a number of dimensions such as

population growth, pollution and resource depletion, and concludes that radical change is necessary since if the trends extrapolated do indeed continue, the predicament of mankind will be dire. The analysis of what is, therefore, stimulates a consideration of what could be.

56. Shaw, R. Paul and Wong, Yuwa (1989) *The Genetic Seeds of Warfare: Evolution, Nationalism, and Patriotism*, London: Unwin Hyman, p. 39.
57. Wolin, S.S. (1969) 'Political Theory as a Vocation', *American Political Science Review*, 63, 1062–89.
58. Kim, K.W. (1965) 'The Limits of Behavioural Explanation in Politics', *Canadian Journal of Economics and Political Science*, 31, 315–27.
59. For discussion of the problem of counterfactuals see Barry, B. (1980) 'Superfox', *Political Studies*, 28, 136–43; and Elster, J. (1980) 'The Treatment of Counterfactuals: Reply to Brian Barry', *Political Studies*, 28, 144–7; Morriss, P. (1987) *Power: a Philosophical Analysis*, Manchester: Manchester University Press, 216–21.
60. See Bachrach, P. and Baratz, M.S. (1962) 'Two Faces of Power', *American Political Science Review*, 56, 947–52; Bachrach, P. and Baratz, M.S. (1963) 'Decisions and Non-Decisions: An Analytic Framework', *American Political Science Review*, 57, 632–642; Bachrach, P. and Baratz, M.S. (1970) *Power and Poverty: Theory and Practice*, London: Oxford University Press; Crenson, M. (1971) *The Un-politics of Air Pollution: a Study of Non-Decisionmaking in the Cities*, Baltimore: Johns Hopkins Press; and for a further radicalization of the critique Lukes, S. (1975) *Power: a Radical View*, London: Macmillan; and for a contemporary discussion see Clegg, S.R. (1989) *Frameworks of Power*, London: Sage, especially 1–20, 86–128.

7
EXPLANATION IN SOCIAL SCIENCE

....

Introduction

The central object of this chapter is to examine the idea of explanation in science and to discover the degree to which this is generalizable to social science. It will be suggested that while the subject matter of social science and science are very different, there is none the less a similarity in the structure of explanation. This is not because the notion of explanation extant in science is in some sense a model for social science, but because both social science and science are examples of a more general model of explanation. However, while a similarity is stressed, there are also dissimilarities, and it is these differences that have important consequences for the understanding and practice of social science. Hence a 'strong' version of the explanatory model will be distinguished from a 'weak' version; the strong scientific version is merely an accentuation of the notion of explanation used in everyday life. The adoption of the weak version helps to understand the relationship between social science and explanation of the past, present, and future.

Some preliminary points about explanation

Somewhat confusingly, while we shall argue that explanation always implies a general framework, it is also the case that there can be many explanations for the same event. These may be commensurable or incommensurable; it is not necessarily the case that incommensurable explanations, in the sense of non-additivity, means that one of the explanations must be wrong. If we take the Second World War as an example, we can discover many proffered explanations for why it occurred. It could be suggested that it was essentially the terms of the Versailles Settlement, particularly the policy of reparations, the limitation on the size of the army, and the lack of indigenous control over important territories that led to a sense of injustice and outrage in the German people. Or, we could suggest that it was the rise of Fascism, with its romantic emphasis on the 'volk', German destiny, and *lebensraum* that was the central causal agent. An economic explanation could be suggested; here the battle of the left and the right, the depression, and the reflation of the economy through Keynsian arms spending could be wedded to a view of capitalism. Or, a more individualistic explanation may be sought, relating war-proneness to the personal qualities of Hitler; here the charismatic 'world historical figure' is seen taking and shaping his age to his image, in much the same way as, from this perspective, Napoleon and Lenin determined the destinies of their eras. Or, yet again, we might refer to the geo-political situation of Germany, recently unified and between East and West, and the uncertainties regarding security that this necessarily set up. Or, an explanation may be sought in terms of power transition. Germany by the end of the nineteenth century had surpassed the United Kingdom in industrial output and was seeking a political role consonant with her economic strength which was denied by the status quo powers; from this point of view the Second World War was merely playing the second-half of a power game. Or, from a psychological point of view, both the First and Second World Wars were a reflection of the authoritarian nature of the German people derived from the nature of the German family, particularly with respect to the *Junker* heritage.

All or some of these explanations may be right or some more right than others. They may or may not be complementary in an additative sense and may even be contradictory. For example, emphasis upon an individualistic explanation may not coexist easily with an explanation couched in geo-political terms. What this example brings out is that what counts as an explanation will depend upon the universe of discourse within which it is proffered which means, by extension, that all explanation is *explanation from a point of view*. Hence an explanation in terms of psychology will be substantially different from an explanation in sociology, economics, or in international relations. Logically, there is no necessary limit to the potential number of explanations; if all phenomena have an infinity of attributes, as was argued previously, the number of explanations of aspects of any phenomenon is likewise potentially infinite. This means that there is not *an* explanation but only *explanations*.

A further problem arises here, however, as to whether an explanation is an explanation if it is wrong. There may be many different plausible and appropriate explanations of an event, but there may also be incorrect explanations. Hence, we may ask whether phlogiston was an adequate explanation of combustion at the time when it was commonly believed, when it was later shown to be incorrect. The hard line here, which might be termed the logical version, would be that an explanation is only an explanation when it is correct, but here, in line with the arguments about tentativeness developed in Chapter 5, it would then have to be admitted that we can never be sure about an explanation. An explanation would always have to be held tentatively, particularly if we are attempting to explain complex social phenomena. A different view, which might be termed the psychological view, would suggest that an explanation is an explanation to the extent that it performs an explanatory function for the recipient, that is, it satisfies the receiver by reducing the unfamiliar to the familiar and increases comprehension of the novel event by relating it to what is known or believed, even though it may be wrong. Thus an astrological explanation of an individual's life chances may be an explanation for someone with those beliefs even though, from my point of view, it would not suffice. From my point of view, I may believe that life-chances are more likely to be affected by class position at birth, ability, health and contingent social events. The implication of this is that the correctness or incorrectness of an explanation cannot be established through the structure of explanation *per se* but only in relation to factors external to the explanation such as the criteria of validity noted in Chapter 5.

Since explanation is always from a point of view, and is related to and adequate only within a universe of discourse, it means that an explanation for one person may not be an explanation for another person. Someone unfamiliar with the working of the internal combustion engine would remain mystified by the explanation of engine failure that suggested 'the engine won't work because the rotor arm in missing'; similarly, a psychologist might remain mystified by reference to 'power transition', which for the scholar of international relations would instantly summon up an entire explanatory framework. Hence, just as we noted previously that observation is selective, so also is explanation.

Shortly we shall be arguing that something is explained in so far as it can be seen to be an example of a general class of events. This is sometimes thought to lead to a contradiction between the generality of a phenomenon (that which it shares with other similar cases) and its individuality (that which is unique to it). It is, in fact, no contradiction to argue that all things are both unique and general; if in nothing else, everything is unique in a spatio-temporal location, while also being general in the aspects or attributes it shares with other phenomena. Two simple examples will demonstrate this. Every man and woman is unique in the peculiar aggregation of attributes that each possesses, while at the same time having characteristics (legs, desires, age, etc.) that are shared by other men and women. Similarly, every war is unique; the Vietnam War in some ways *was* a unique and never to occur again event, and yet it shared many characteristics with other wars that have occurred throughout history. Uniqueness is composed of a constellation of particular characteristics each of which may be general, but which have never before occurred in that combination. There is, therefore, no contradition between the unique and the general.

We can also argue that to explain means to make reference to a theory, even though in many real cases the theory in question is unarticulated or implicit. In this unarticulated sense, as noted previously, some conception of the way the world is is needed for observation. A theory in a more formal sense is, to use Popper's term, a 'crystallisation of a point of view' but is always dependent for its explanatory usefulness through its function in relating the unknown to the known. A generalization is an abstraction of characteristics or attributes of things from some point of view, and the point of view is always related to some theory of the world. Hence the generalization, 'Revolutions never succeed where the military remain wholly loyal to the regime' is embedded in a larger theory about the nature of revolutions and the way people behave. A theory is or contains generalizations relating to some aspect of the world. Hence the theory of cognitive dissonance in psychology or relativity in physics are generalizations about the nature of the world and hence the basis for explanation.

Further, a distinction needs to be made between an explanation *per se* and the function of an explanation. There are numerous purposes of communication such as instrumental, control, information, expressive, social contact, alleviation of anxiety, stimulation and role-related functions. Within each of these functions explanations may be used or sought. For example, an explanation may be given with the aim of changing the definition of the situation and hence the response of the audience; this would be a case of explanation being used in a control function or perhaps an instrumental function if the idea is to persuade to some end. Similarly, an explanation of an unusual noise in the night may alleviate anxiety. The reason *why* the explanation was given may be related to a communication function, but whether it *is* a satisfactory explanation is from a logical perspective largely unrelated to function. Finally, while an explanation elicits information of various kinds, it may or may not stimulate surprise. Whether it has this effect will depend at least in part on the novelty and significance of the explanation. The vast majority of explanations in everyday life and elsewhere are mere confirmations of what is known and lead to no psychological feelings of novelty.

Generalizing versus descriptive idioms[1]

It follows from the previous section that there can be no such thing as a description of a thing that makes no reference to anything outside it. This in part is because words in themselves contain generalized meanings. Thus to describe someone as a 'tall person with red hair' is to use words that take their meanings from classes of phenomena. All explanation must, implicitly or explicitly, make reference to factors external to it. Ordinary language is redolent with general meanings. An event or phenomenon which had *no* similarity or attribute commonality with any other event or phenomenon would simply be unrecognizable and undiscussable; both the psychological response and the logical response would seek to relate it in some manner to what is known, i.e., to reduce it to the familiar. However, we can none the less make a distinction between the nomothetic (or generalizing) and the ideographic (or descriptive) *idioms*, while recognizing that each case is in reality scalar. In a sense, two ideal-types are being created.

Both science and social science are by the nature of their activities generalizing, that is, they aim at a general explanation of phenomena. Typical social science statements might be:

'The level of suicide increases with the level of social anomie.'[2]
'The greater the number of cross-national intersections a state is involved in the greater the probability of war.'[3]
'The higher the proportion of GDP a state spends on either internal or external means of coercion, the lower the rate of growth of GDP.'[4]

Such statements are essentially nomothetic in that an attempt is made to generalize beyond particular cases and to subsume many cases under the generalization. Historical analysis, on the other hand, will tend to operate within an ideographic or descriptive discipline; here the attempt consciously to generalize is minimized, and the full complexity and uniqueness of the particular case is emphasized.[5] Hence, within an ideographic idiom one could discuss the rise of Nasser in terms of his education, his relationship with his father, his role within the officer corps, his relationship with both Egyptian and Arab populaces, the quality of his oratory, or the compelling nature of his eyes. The resultant 'picture' would be individualized and specific to a single individual and a particular context and very rich in detail. If, on the other hand, one were to take Nasser as a case in a study of charismatic leadership, the range of variables selected for analysis would be much fewer. The idea of 'charismatic leadership' is well established, through theory and many other examples, and much of the detail contained in the individualized case may be irrelevant.

A further distinction can be made consonant with the nomothetic and ideographic idioms in terms of 'variable-sparseness' and 'variable-richness'. Social science, in so far as it seeks to generalize, must of necessity tend towards variable-sparseness since the activity is to generalize across cases. When generalizing, it is usually the case that only one or a few variables are utilized. When describing a phenomenon and emphasizing its uniqueness, attention is being drawn to the particular and unrepeatable combination of attributes possessed by that phenomenon. However, when looking at, for example, 'revolution', generalizations might be about 'power deflation', or the sequences of revolutionary processes, or the role of the military in the onset of revolution. But in each case the richness of idiosyncratic factors associated with particular revolutions will be lost. It is important to note, though, that all variable-sparse approaches originate in in the variable-rich domain, and variable-rich approaches can legitimately be informed by variable-sparse perspectives.

An example may illustrate this. The internal colonial model of social development arose out of the historical study of South American experience.[6] Here the idea of colonial exploitation was transferred from the international domain to explain relations within one state. The essential characteristics of that model can be transferred to the analysis of other societies to greater or lesser benefit.[7] Hence it may be argued that the condition of the Scots or the Flemish can be explained by internal colonialism. However, in such a theoretical transfer, the peculiar conditions in which the theory had its genesis will be lost in the abstraction of the theory. The theory will 'explain' to the extent that it is seen to be applicable or congruent to the new case. But it will only be congruent with respect to a limited number of features and will have little to say about a host of other situation-specific features. Variable-sparseness is thus both derived from variable-richness and can also inform and bring generality to other variable-rich applications. In the trade-off between these two models a compromise is always sought. Abstraction and high levels of variable-sparseness are always associated with the distortion of data, in the sense that merely through the activity of abstracting a theory will fail to explain all the variation in phenomena. However, to understand is necessarily to simplify and abstract from the infinity of possible attributes, and different theories are merely alternative 'searchlights' highlighting combinations of attributes which may be complementary or incommensurable. What cannot be done with any profit is to add or combine theories to any great extent to create theoretical frameworks of great complexity. If the aim of a theory is to aid comprehension through directed observation and simplification, complexity beyond a certain point will tend to defeat this end.

A model of explanation

Explanation may in general be defined as 'the reduction of the unfamiliar to the familiar'. In this sense, an explanation is proffered and understood when the phenomenom is seen to be part of a more general class of events. This is called the 'covering law' model of explanation or, more technically, the 'deductive-nomological' model. In its strict scientific usage, which we shall refer to as the 'strong' model, an event is explained if it is capable of subsumption under, or is an example of, a general law. Hempel gives the following example:[8] 'Consider, for example, the explanation of mirror images, of rainbows, or of the appearance that a spoon handle is bent at the point where it emerges from a glass of water; in all these cases the explanandum is deductively subsumed under the laws of reflection and refraction.' The logical form of this model can be expressed thus:

C1, C2, C3 . . . Cn   [Particular facts, events, etc.]
L   [General statement]
If C1, C2, C3 . . . Cn are examples of L, then they are held to be explained.

While this model can adequately cope with much scientific explanation — though it is more adequate in its strong form with respect to sciences such as physics and chemistry than meteorology or biology — it is clearly inadequate in this form when applied to social science. The major problem is that in social science there are no 'laws' in the way that there are in natural science, although there are generalizations. A scientific law may be defined as 'an empirical generalization that is accepted as true'.[9] The generalization, in order to qualify as a scientific law, would need to be framed in universal terms. There can be no laws in this sense in social science merely because of the subject matter of social science. In principle it is *always* possible for human beings to act consciously so as to falsify any particular generalization; this would be an example of the Oedipus Effect (see Chapter 8). In fact, the range of human societies and experience is such that few generalizations have any pretensions to universality. However, to suggest that there is little recourse to universality is not to suggest that the covering-law model is an inadequate model of explanation. Rather, explanation is by means of a generalization that is not universal. This can be termed the 'weak' version of the covering-law model.

Immediately a problem suggests itself. Human affairs are marked by variety and disparity, a state of affairs that can only be expected due to the human capacity to learn and behave flexibly. Hence, the same antecedent conditions can give rise to different effects, while different antecedent conditions can give rise to the same outcomes. The consequence of this is that the generalities appealed to in explanation may vary greatly in their degree of generality. If it is the case that most crime is committed by adolescent males, this statement together with additional statements about adolescent males would begin to enter into an explanation of the behaviour. But how large must 'most' be? What, then, is the degree of generality needed before a class can be considered adequate for the purposes of explanation? There can be no general rule on this, other than some conventional agreement which is always open to contestation. The normal research model, which would apply conceptually as well as in actual empirical analysis, would be to accept that which is held to be explained by some accepted generality and then seek to explain the residual, or that which is not explained.

An example may help to illustrate this in the conceptual sense. Nationalism is a central concept of both domestic and international politics. As an explanation of certain kinds of events, it has wide applicability and generality. Yet, in trying to account for the growth, mobilization, and spread of nationalism, differences are noted among different nationalisms.[10] While there are similarities among all nationalisms — hence the inclusion of cases in that category — there are also differences. It thus makes sense to sub-divide the categories so that commonalities relevant to those sub-divisions, but not to the whole class, have applicability. Hence, for some explanatory purposes it would make sense to divide the generic category 'nationalism' into 'first-world nationalism', 'anti-imperialist Afro–Asian nationalism', and 'peripheral nationalism'. Thus the 'conceptual residual' associated with 'nationalism', i.e., that which cannot be accounted for, is then accounted for by processes that are applicable and have generality within the other classifications created. The process may be repeated until in the end the generality dissolves into ideographic explanation.[11] At each stage of the process, however, generality is involved, but of constantly decreasing scope, with each conceptual or empirical residual itself being the target of explanation by generalization.

There is one further feature of the covering-law model which is significant. In the natural sciences a natural law is framed in universal terms and held, within the limits of the problem of induction (see Chapter 5), to be as true in the future as in the past. Hence the law of gravity explains events in the past but also is a prediction about the behaviour of falling objects in the future. However, in social science in particular, because of the nature of the activity, the symmetry between past and future is much less evident; we may be able to explain events without being able to predict them. The reasons for this will be examined in the next chapter.

Reasonable explanation

Jon Elster writes:[12] 'The proper paradigm for the social sciences is a mixed causal-intentional explanation — *intentional understanding* of individual *actions*, and *causal explanation* of their *interaction*.' Elster is here trying to stand astride a divide that has aroused much argument in social science.[13] The covering-law model, as it was stated in a natural science context, dealt with causes. For example, changes in the distribution of flora are *caused* by changes in climatic conditions and genetic mutation. 'Cause' as a concept, following David Hume, must be marked by 'temporal priority' (the cause precedes the effect) and 'constant conjunction' (A is always accompanied by B).[14] As such, cause, though it cannot be logically demonstrated, deals with what are usually considered to be invariant relations between phenomena. Not only are these relations invariant, but also there is no choice involved. An atom cannot decide whether to split or not; it is made to do so by another fast-moving particle. People, however, are not like this. They act on the basis of interpretations of the world, motives and desires, and constraints in the environment. Thus, if we suggest that 'migration in Ethiopia and Mozambique was caused by drought', we are in fact speaking inaccurately. What led to migration was the desire of people to stay alive and their reasonable belief that food and water were obtainable elsewhere. They *could* have behaved fatalistically — as indeed many did — but chose to try their luck elsewhere. The point is that people act from reasons rather than causes.

The issue is far from being a mere academic debate as the following context makes clear, for the language of cause-and-effect implies determination and lack of choice, while the language of reason-and-action implies autonomy and choice. Singer and Cusack, for example, in discussing the onset of war, introduce two ideas of war, 'inexorability' and 'steersmanship'.[15] In the first perspective war is seen as a natural part of the human condition, an inherent condition that can 'only be obstructed';[16] hence nations 'are continuously preparing for, actively involved in, or recovering from organized violence in the form of war'.[17] Similarly, Modelski and Thompson and Kennedy,[18] among others, have identified a cyclical process of great power transition, with the implication of cyclical continuance with its associated global wars.

In the second perspective, war is not the consequence of structural factors over which men have little control but is a question of choice and therefore of moral responsibility. Bruce Bueno de Mesquita, while emphasizing generality and identifying a common theme in the study of international relations — 'that theme is the self-interested pursuit of gain by national leaders on their own behalf and on behalf of their nations'[19] — yet within the 'framework of circumstances' he still regards leaders as morally responsible.[20] They do not *have* to go to war; it is a choice.

That people *do* act from reasons is indisputable and that there are differences between reasons and natural causes is beyond question.

Indeed, Ryan persuasively argues that there are three essential differences between reasons and causes.[21] The argument, from our point of view, however, is whether the covering-law model of explanation can adequately cope with explanations couched in terms of *reasons*. The argument is a broad one taking in many aspects of social science with tributaries going off in several directions and going back at least to Max Weber.[22] These tributaries will not be followed here; rather, the question we shall stay with is the central question of whether reasonable explanation can be accommodated within the weaker version of the covering-law perspective.

Bearing this in mind, from the point of view of explanation, we understand (i.e., reduce the unfamiliar to the familiar) by referring intentions (motives, purposes, etc.) to generally observed phenomena which need not be universal to have an explanatory function. The access to generality may be either through personal experience, or through the observation of others, or a combination of both. No reference to empathy, the generality of human needs or emotions, or universal human nature is necessary; the psychiatrist does not have to be a psychopath to recognise a psychopathic condition. It is without surprise that we observe and understand the relationship between Anthony and Cleopatra because we have observed similar cases on numerous occasions. Similarly, the actions of Saddam Hussein are comprehensible in their motives and consequences, not because we are ourselves absolutist dictators but because in history we have observed many such cases. Or, to reverse the normative direction, the sacrifices of Mother Teresa become familiar as motive and action through a knowledge of Schweitzer, Wilberforce, Fry, and a myriad of other cases.

To see the problem in this way leads to a solution to the moral dilemma, where the attribution of covering-law is linked to causality and the abrogation of moral responsibilty. We understand intentions through their generality, yet the individual still has the capacity for choice. In *fact*, people tend to behave in certain ways in particular situations, and hence we can and do generalize about their intentions and reasons. But they do not *have* to behave in those ways. The generalization is merely a description of the way in which people do behave, not a prescription or a deterministic statement. Indeed, were it not through the generality of reasons, human action would be incomprehensible and inexplicable. The fact that this generality is based on the normative acceptance of rules or upon socialized perception is neither here nor there. Neither is it relevant that at any point of time the generality can be changed by a collective act of human will. We can still argue that reasons may be morally good or bad, rational or irrational. What is important is that the understanding of reasons, and hence the explanation of human actions, is achieved through their generality.

Conclusion

It makes sense, therefore, to accept Elster's idea of a mixture of causal and reasonable explanation. The language of causality may appear more appropriate at the level of structure (i.e., higher levels of social anomie lead to [cause] higher rates of suicide) at the same time recognizing that structural 'causality' is ultimately dependent on the actions of individuals who are acting from reasons. There is little need to abandon the use of causal language in social science (i.e., large increases in unemployment cause a decrease in the level of aggregate demand) as long as it is realized that invariance is not implied and moral responsibility for actions is not avoided.

Similarly, if invariance and universality are abandoned as necessary conditions for explanation via the covering-law model, and we are happy to use generalizations that are not universal, then there is no reason why the covering-law model in its weaker form should not be seen as a general model of social science explanation.

Notes

1. Sometimes referred to as nomothetic and ideographic. 'Ideographic' is equivalent to 'descriptive', while 'nomothetic' is equivalent to 'generalizing'.
2. See Durkheim, E. (ed. G. Simpson) (1952) *Suicide: a Study in Sociology*, London: Routledge & Kegan Paul.
3. Waltz, K. (1982) 'The Myth of National Interdependence', in Maghoori, R. and Ramberg, B. (eds) *Globalism Versus Realism: International Relations' Third Great Debate*, Boulder: Westview Press, 81–96.
4. See Smith, R. (1980) 'Military Expenditures and Investments in O.E.C.D. Countries, 1954/1973', *Journal of Comparative Economics*, 4, 1, 19–32.
5. It should be noted that we are here talking about tendencies. Some social scientists will prefer to work in a purely descriptive mode, and some historians are happy to generalize.
6. Casanova, P.G. (1965) 'Internal Colonialism and National Development', *Studies in Comparative International Development*, 1, 4.
7. See, for example, Hechter, M. (1975) *Internal Colonialism: the Celtic Fringe in British National Development 1536–1966*, London: Routledge & Kegan Paul; and Webb, K. (1978) *The Growth of Nationalism in Scotland*, Harmondsworth: Pelican.
8. Hempel, C.G. (1966) 'Explanation in Science and History', in Dray, W.H. (ed.) *Philosophical Analysis and History*, New York: Harper & Row, 95–126.
9. Caws, P. (1965) *The Philosophy of Science: a Systematic Account*, Princeton: Van Nostrand, p. 82.
10. For an application of this argument in the case of nationalism and uneven development see Orridge, A.W. (1981) 'Uneven Development and Nationalism: 1', *Political Studies*, XXIX, 1, 1–15; and (1981) 'Uneven Development and Nationalism: 2', *Political Studies*, XXIX, 2, 181–90.

11. The process of analysis described here is not too different from that noted by Przeworski, A. and Teune, H. (1970) *The Logic of Comparative Social Inquiry*, New York: Wiley Interscience.
12. See Elster, J. (1982) 'Marxism, Functionalism, and Game Theory: The Case for Methodological Individualism.' *Theory and Society*, 11, 4, p. 463.
13. For an annotated bibliography of the debate see Doyal, L. and Harris, R. (1986) *Empiricism, Explanation, and Rationality: an Introduction to the Philosophy of the Social Sciences*, London: Routledge and Kegan Paul, 70–2.
14. See Hume, D. (1955) *An Inquiry Concerning Human Understanding*, New York: Bobbs-Merrill, 46–68.
15. Singer, J.D. and Cusack, T. (1981) 'Periodicity, Inexorability, and Steersmanship in International War', in Merritt, R. and Russett, B. (eds) *From National Development to Global Community*, London: Allen and Unwin, 404–22.
16. See Eckstein, H. (1980) 'Theoretical Approaches to Explaining Political Violence', in Gurr, T.R. (ed.) *Handbook of Political Conflict*, New York: The Free Press, p. 139; and Webb, K. (1986) 'Inherent and Contingent Theories of Conflict', *World Encyclopedia of Peace*, Vol. 1, Oxford: Pergamon Press, 431–4.
17. Morgenthau, H. (1954) *Politics Among Nations: the Struggle for Power and Peace*, New York: Knopf, p. 25.
18. Modelski, G. and Thompson, W.R. (1989) 'Long Cycles and Global Wars', in Midlarski, M.I. (ed.) *Handbook of War Studies*, London: Unwin Hyman, 23–54; Kennedy, P. (1987) *The Rise and Fall of the Great Powers, Economic Change and Military Conflict from 1500 to 2000*, New York: Random House.
19. Bueno de Mesquita, B. (1989) 'The Contribution of Expected-Utility Theory to the Study of International Conflict', in Midlarski, M.I. (ed.) *Handbook of War Studies*, London: Unwin Hyman, p. 143.
20. Bueno de Mesquita, B. (1981) *The War Trap*, New Haven and London: Yale University Press, p. 5.
21. Ryan, A. (1970) *The Philosophy of the Social Sciences*, London: Macmillan, 117–20.
22. See Weber, M. (1947) (ed. T. Parsons) *Theory of Social and Economic Organization*, New York: Oxford University Press, 87–123.

8

THE PROBLEM OF PREDICTION

....

Introduction

It has often been said that man differs from animals in his ability to plan. To 'plan' means to have a more or less articulated vision of the future and some idea of the means to achieve that vision. Man differs in that he is often conscious in his planning, for in the animal kingdom the blueprint for action is mostly laid down in the genes in the form of instinct, something lacking in the human creature. This genetic blueprint is something that has evolved through natural selection, with the organism progressively adapting to a given ecological niche and environment. In a sense, an inductive knowledge of the past is contained in the inheritance of animals. In the world of animals, however, the limitations of a knowledge of the future as laid down in the genetic and instinctive blueprint are a lack of flexibility. The consequence of this is that a change in a given environment can have disastrous effects upon a particular species which is dependent upon the constancy and maintenance of that environment. Animals, except in a very limited way and to the best of our knowledge, do not plan in any conscious or coherent manner. Mankind, on the other hand, is a planning creature in every aspect of his existence. There is almost no aspect of his life which is not affected by some vision of the future. Human action — defined here as 'meaningful behaviour' — is normally marked by at least three characteristics: an awareness of the past, a vision of the future, and a sense of the rightness and wrongness of actions. But the point is that the future is never something that is vacuous or empty; rather it is a mental space that is filled with expectations, hopes and fears, and with strategies and policies designed respectively to maximize or minimize them. This is true in all spheres of life.

It is thus not a question as to whether man plans and predicts or does not plan or predict; the only point at issue is the best means of planning and predicting and the consciousness or unconsciousness of such a process. Most of the time in our daily lives we do not think about 'prediction' as such, but in reality prediction is built into the pattern of expectations we have about the future. Further, such expectations are predicated on theories or beliefs about the world, even though they may not be articulated as such. Even such a simple act as going to the refectory for lunch is based on a theory of human motivation — the cooks etc. have to earn a living and will thus usually turn up to do their work — and upon our experience of the regularity of past performance. We have no choice but to predict the future and to act on the prediction, but, paradoxically, we do so in the sure knowledge that often the future will not be as we foresaw. It is thus foolish to suggest, as some do, that it is not the business of social science to predict or to study the practice of prediction, since this is a significant dimension of human experience.

The philosophical problem of prediction

The problem of prediction follows as a consequence of the problem of induction and the search for certainty. Early theories of science, for example those of Francis Bacon or John Stuart Mill, attempted to suggest that we could readily accept that the future would be like the past. The ideas of David Hume with respect to induction were, if not disregarded, somewhat downgraded in importance. Science appeared to have discovered laws of nature that were invariable in time and space. Hence there were arguments that sought to establish the likelihood of the future being like the past. Sir Roy Harrod's argument, for example, attempts to get around the problem of induction by reference to probability theory.[1] Other arguments sought to establish the uniformity of nature; if nature were the same everywhere and for all time, then there is no problem of induction for the future will be like the past.[2]

Within science as a set of practising disciplines the problem of induction has often been little more than an interesting philosophical quibble.[3] Given the behavioural invariability of inanimate matter, the future can be assumed for practical purposes to be like the past. Indeed, the idea of prediction assumes this as part of the hypothetico-deductive model of science; an experiment is held to be validated to the extent that the predicted outcome occurs, and the more often it occurs then the greater the degree of certainty. Within this context the covering-law model of explanation (see Chapter 7) is held to be competent with respect to both explanation and prediction; the variable feature — the temporal position of the observer — is not significant if the future is like the past.

Prediction in the social sciences, while there may be some shared features, is not like prediction in the natural sciences for three reasons. First, behaviour is not invariable, as is frequently the case with matter in natural science. Second, consciousness is a factor in human behaviour whereas it is not a factor in the behaviour of matter; what you say about an atom will not affect its behaviour, and its behaviour will not be changed by the way in which it defines situations. Third, while prediction is often used in natural science as a way of validating an experiment — a theory or an hypothesis is often seen as confirmed if the expected result occurs — the nature of prediction in the social sciences frequently precludes its use as a means of validation.

Finally, it should be noted that while prediction is a poor means of validating theories of social science, social science theory frequently contains expectations about the future. Often theory is an abstraction of key and interacting features of a phenomenon that is believed to explain that phenomenon. For example, the theory of relative deprivation suggests that given certain social and psychological conditions, there will be a tendency to engage in some form of dissent.[4] But this does not mean that dissent will *always* occur. The theory of relative deprivation, being a political–psychological abstraction, does not deal very much with economic or religious effects on behaviour. Many other factors will also influence behaviour as well as a sense of relative deprivation, with the consequence that the expectation embedded in the theory may well not come to pass. As we shall see below, it is frequently possible to explain past behaviour without being able successfully to predict future behaviour.

Prediction as a problem in social science

People have to predict, and governments have to predict. And yet the philosophical basis of such an activity is fraught with problems. Some of these problems have been dealt with by Karl Popper.[5] First, we may draw attention to the well-known Oedipus Effect, or the self-fulfilling or self-defeating prophecy. The argument here is that, unlike natural science, the prediction will itself become a factor in the decisions taken by people, and they will act to falsify or fulfil the prediction. Here we may perhaps make a distinction between two types of prediction, an *intentional* prediction and an *outcome* prediction. An intentional prediction is a statement about the future that indicates the disposition of an actor to behave in a certain way in the future. For example, 'I will be in London on the 18th December 1996'; whether this is a true prediction or not will depend upon the veracity of the statement, the maintenance of the intention, and my capacity to ensure the prediction. An outcome prediction, on the other hand, is far more independent of personal or actor intentions. 'Due to changes in the technology of communication there will be an increase in inter-nation interdependency' would be an example. Both kinds of prediction may lead to an Oedipus Effect. Making personal plans, for example, is a case of indulging in intentional prediction, and the plans may stimulate opposition which may defeat the plan. A plan, on the other hand, may be a response to a possible future that is seen as more or less likely. For example, I may look at some economic indicators and decide that there is a recession on the way, and that in all probability my job will be at risk, with the consequence that I will be unemployed. A prediction has been made which leads, for example, to emigration and a job somewhere else. Thus I am not unemployed. The prediction that I will be unemployed has been falsified because the prediction itself led to action to falsify it. A policy is typically an intentional prediction — a statement of future intent — that is predicated on an outcome prediction; a state of affairs in the future environment is perceived that is not desirable and action is taken to amend the future. And, as part of our equipment as human beings, there is also the capacity to, at least some of the time, anticipate the responses of others and even our responses to their responses. This point will be picked up later.

An argument against prediction in social science also emanating from Popper — and also indirectly from the problem of induction — relates to the discovery of new knowledge. His argument here is that the progress of the human race is dependent upon new discoveries. Since we cannot anticipate new discoveries (or we would already know them), we cannot predict the future of human society. Whether this is useful or not as an argument will clearly depend on the scale or scope of the prediction. With respect to the scale of prediction, a British prime minister, pondering on his alliance attachments, may well anticipate that the United States will still be the dominant military and economic world power in a month's time, but he would be foolish given human history to argue with great conviction that this will still be the case in 2050 AD. If we are attempting to predict the human future on a grand scale, then many things, including new discoveries, may interfere with such an ambitious project. But most of the time we are not engaged in such projects; hence the force of the argument is somewhat lessened.

At the same time we may on occasion anticipate certain discoveries or developments. Here we may make an analogy with weather forecasting. In forecasting the weather tomorrow the layman can do nearly as well as the most sophisticated meteorologist merely by anticipating that the weather tomorrow will be the same as the weather today; if the number of days when the weather changes are significantly fewer than the number of days when it stays the same, then there is a good probability of being right in one's predictions. What the layman cannot do, though, is to anticipate the changes when they do occur. What can be argued, however, is that there are trends that can be expected to extend into the future which will have other effects. This is partly based on induction and hence subject to the problem of induction, but also partly based on a realization of the inter-connectedness of social, economic, and political forces that raises the likelihood of the continuance of a trend to a very high probability. The development of new technologies through discovery will not necessarily alter the direction of the trend but will be far more likely to either reinforce or moderate a trend. Thus Comte's prediction in the early nineteenth century with respect to the universalization of Western means of production, or Cipolla's prediction regarding the movement to ever more efficient means of energy utilization, or predictions regarding the growth of world population are unlikely to be invalidated because of the number of supporting processes that reinforce the trend. There will be more people alive next year than this year. It is 'inevitable'![6]

With respect to the scope of prediction, it is sometimes the case that the general can be predicted in a way that the specific event cannot be predicted. This is well established in particle physics; the emission of any particular particle cannot be predicted but over a given period there is a regularity in the number of particles emitted. Thus, given the end of a war and major demobilization, it can be predicted that there will be a rise in the birth rate while the sexual fate of any particular soldier cannot be predicted with any certainty. Or, again, the massive oil and price rise in 1974 immediately made new prospecting an economic proposition, brought economically marginal oilfields into production, and stimulated research and development into other technologies of energy production. This was predicted at the time by *The Economist*. However, the particular and precise developments could not be predicted.

At the same time, whether something can be predicted or not will often depend on the resources which are devoted to a particular research programme. *Some* discoveries are not the random creation of a great mind but rather are eagerly sought through research programmes. While specific discoveries may not be predictable, the direction of such discoveries may well be predictable. Hence, given the enormous scientific resources being devoted to AIDS, it is predictable that eventually a means will be found to treat or even cure the disease, just as the enormous resources devoted to the conquest of cancer have led to a vast decrease in the mortality rate from the disease. Similarly, the vast resources being devoted to the mapping of the human gene, while they will undoubtedly throw up many surprises, will also have some effects which are highly predictable such as the identification of genetic causes or predispositions for many human conditions. Thus some discovery, though not all, may itself be somewhat predictable. Indeed, part of the thrust of the critique launched at the neo-Malthusian Club of Rome report on the future was that the dolorous prediction disregarded human inventiveness and adaptability.[7] One aspect of the critique effectively argues (inductively) that where resource scarcity occurs material substitution occurs, and while we cannot anticipate such substitutions none the less they will happen in response to shortage and cost.[8] For example, if China — one-third of the human race — continues to industrialize and develop at her current rate, many more demands will be placed on all kinds of resources, including oil. If the price of oil becomes high enough due to shortage, substitution will occur. This may be the development of the hydrogen engine, increasing sophistication of electric engines, the adoption of alcohol as a substitute for oil, the refining of petrol from vegetable sources, or greater dependency on nuclear power. While agreeing with Popper, therefore, that new discoveries will have an effect on the human future, it is not obvious that this is always relevant to our predictions — in part this will depend on the time-scale of the prediction — nor is it obvious that these discoveries are unsought or liable to interfere with trends in human life.

A further argument advanced by Popper relates to the possibility of prediction through comparison. The argument rests on the notion that in order to predict there must be equivalent cases from which induction is possible. For example, if there were only one acorn, then the growth of an oak tree could not be predicted; or if there were only one chrysalis, then the emergence of a butterfly could not be foreseen. As there is only one human history, the future of the human race cannot be foretold. This argument rests, of course, on the idea that there is only 'one history' and is an attack on the use of induction as a basis of prediction in human affairs. It makes sense, however, and historians and social scientists have always done this, to break up human history into smaller units for comparative purposes. Thus we can speak of the fate of firms on the basis of many examples of commercial enterprises, or the development of nationalism on the basis of many such developments, or the causes of wars on the basis of many examples. This will not enable us to comment too much on 'the future of the human race', but most of the time our ambition is rather more limited. While there will always be problems with respect to the limits of comparison, the investigation of those limits is an empirical rather than a logical problem. For example, if we were comparing nationalist movements, there is little doubt that there is a connection between the emergence of nationalism in Europe and the emergence of nationalism in the Third World as an anti-colonial rhetoric. The latter is not independent of the former. In general, then, we may reject the 'one history' argument, though accepting the cautionary implications regarding contagion embedded in it. Thus, while we may be happy to speak of different nationalisms, we should recognize that in all probability these are not wholly unrelated to each other.

A further and very serious difficulty with prediction in social science has been called the 'zebra principle'.[9] Even if we were to accept the covering-law model of explanation in either its stronger or weaker forms (see Chapter 7), and it is difficult not to, it does not follow that if we can explain we can therefore predict. The evolution of that strange creature the zebra could not be predicted because it was due to a myriad of random genetic changes, but once having occurred it could quite reasonably be explained by reference to genetic and Darwinian evolutionary theory. Or, to use the example given by Nicholson, if a sea wall breaks and floods the surrounding land, the event could not be predicted because the decayed condition of the concrete was not known, though in retrospect it can be explained by a combination of the laws of gravity and hydraulics, the presence of spring tides, and the condition of the sea wall. Hence, to predict the initial conditions need to be known. The problem is that in many cases in the social sciences, the initial conditions are not known. Often the initial conditions are not tangibles, such as economic resources or number of tanks, but rather are states of mind or the definitions of the situation. In the study of politics these are often not known to the social scientist or, more importantly to the decisionmaker, in advance. And, even if they were known at one time, it is possible for a state of mind or a perception of a situation to change. One of the more amusing aspects of the Gulf War was the large number of pundits — often old warhorses — who were recruited by the television companies to comment on the run-up to the outbreak of military action. A great deal of their contribution was an attempt to predict what was going to happen, this often based on what they assumed to be Saddam Hussein's state of mind, and his behaviour in the past. Needless to say, many of them got it wrong.

A further problem of prediction in social science that should concern us is the problem of contingency. At its most extreme the notion of contingency in history is a critique of any rational explanation of history based on generalization. As H.A.L. Fisher once wrote: 'Men have discovered in history plots, rhythms, etc. I see only one emergency following another.' Another version of the same theme is the Cleopatra's nose idea of history: if Cleopatra's nose had been a centimetre longer would Mark Anthony have fallen in love with her and would the history of the Roman Empire have been the same? Thus the destiny of the Roman Empire was dependent upon the the length of Cleopatra's nose. Yet another version of the same theme is the 'great man' theory of history; the great man emerges — a Napoleon, Lenin, or Hitler — and through his understanding and insight shapes the future. In all these perceptions of history the central theme is that the past is shaped by contingent or accidental events which cannot be accommodated within any generalized models with the consequence that the future must be seen as being unpredictable.

From one point of view, whether the contingency thesis is right or wrong is irrelevant; even if it were correct, man would still plan. We could not live and remain sane in a world that was totally composed of contingent factors — this is one of the points made by Kafka — and while we adapt and modify our behaviour when contingency does occur, on a day-to-day basis we work on the (correct) assumption that all is not contingent. The future will be like the past in at least some respects, though in some cases it will not be. Indeed, the possibility of contingency is built into our everyday language to the extent that in many cases the contingent, while necessarily unexpected, is unsurprising. Just as any statement of regularity with respect to past experience is in the final analysis only acceptable as a probabalistic statement (this is implied by the problem of induction), so our expectations of the future are at best probabalistic. And, with any statement of probability, however implicit and unarticulated the actual degree of probability may be, there is also an implied likelihood of the event not being true.

Even though the contingent event cannot be predicted (i.e., the Lockerbie air disaster; the Salman Rushdie affair), the social world is made up not only of events but of responses to events. If responses and events were equally contingent the world would indeed be unpredictable, but given that there is a degree of consistency in responses the seriousness of the contingency of events is lessened. The manner in which responses can be considered as consistent will be discussed in the next section.

A further factor that inhibits prediction is that in social science the same kind of event does not always have the same set of causal antecedents, and similar causal sets may not always have the same effects. For example, the transformation to an industrial society in Britain had very different causal antecedents than the industrial transformation in Taiwan or South Korea. The former occurred in a somewhat *ad hoc* manner, while in the latter two cases industrial transformation was a planned process. There is not, therefore, always sufficient invariability to extrapolate from causes to effects. This is not really a problem so long as we do not mis-identify cases. For example, while 'nationalism' is a widespread phenomenon, the processes leading to it will vary in different periods and contexts. Thus we may speak of European nationalism, anti-colonial postimperialist nationalism, and peripheral nationalism, each of which emerged in different circumstances and with different causal antecedents. So long as we are aware of the differences, the fact of variation in causes and effects should not alarm or surprise us.

Another factor affecting our ability to predict is the very complexity of social explanation. It is necessarily the case that the theories we use to explain social events are simplifications. No theory is ever able to explain *all* the facets of the phenomenon to which it refers. Without simplification analysis would not be possible, but with simplification comes the exclusion of factors which on occasion can be significant for the event to be explained. A theory sets a boundary around a set of variables and dictates what is or is not to be considered relevant. If it did not do this it would be of little use. A theory thus idealizes by abstraction. This is not a situation that is unique to social science. Karl Popper gives the example of an oak leaf that falls off a tree; while the theory of gravity makes certain predictions in an ideal case (i.e., in a vacuum), in real life the path of a specific falling oak leaf is unpredictable due to wind, humidity, density, etc. What we can say with reasonable assurance is that at some time and some place the leaf will fall towards the earth. Similarly, while there may be many variations on a pattern that are the result of contingent factors, the pattern exists in spite of the contingent effects. Thus the historical processes of statebuilding and industrialization may have happened in very different ways, but the consequence is still the existence of cleavages, such as class and religion, in European society. In the explanation of past events we can more easily cope with divergence from theoretical expectations due to the fact that we have knowledge of external interfering factors. With prediction, however, we do not have the advantage of hindsight with respect to the antecedent conditions. We are in the midst of the antecedent conditions, and the event is at some point in the future. For example, while we have theories of capitalist development, and may reasonably expect the development of a market economy in Russia, we can be reasonably sure that it will not go 'according to plan'. The economic model of development will not include political, social, religious, or psychological variables, all of which have the capacity to impinge on the expected course of capitalist development. The event — or some class of events — can only be predicted on the basis of some theory which is itself an abstraction and will in all cases deviate from perfect explanation of particular cases. Whether prediction is possible will depend on two things, the scale on which the prediction is made and the strength of the social process involved. With respect to the former, while the precise event cannot be foretold the direction of events may be discernable in the same way that the exact path of a river may not be predictable but its descent to the sea is. With respect to the latter, if there is a well-established social process validated comparatively, then irrespective of divergence and variation in events in particular cases, some degree of predictability is attainable.

There are two further notions that throw some light on the problem of social prediction, catastrophe theory and chaos theory. Catastrophe theory — somewhat misnamed because the events are not always catastrophic in the common sense — deals with the mathematics of sudden change. Many social changes are incremental, in the sense that change is steady and reasonably predictable. But some social changes are very unlike this: the change is sudden and often unexpected, catching even knowledgeable observers by surprise. There is a sudden 'flip' in the system, rapid change occurs and a new form of stability occurs. For example, when cooking an omelette increments of energy are added to the pan with little noticeable effect; at a certain point, however, a sudden change of state occurs and you have an omelette. Similarly, with 'the straw that broke the camel's back': straws are added incrementally and eventually one particular addition leads to a radical change in the state of the camel. The problem is that, in social life, we frequently do not know *which* straw will lead to the radical change. Two examples may help to demonstrate this. The first is drawn from Smelser's value-added theory of conflict. Smelser argues that for a particular type of conflict to occur certain kinds of conditions are necessary such as structural conduciveness, the spread of generalized beliefs, and a diminution in authoritative response. But as well as these factors, a specific instigating event which coalesces and focuses the other factors is necessary. We may know that a particular situation is 'ripe' for a riot, but not know when, where, or how — or even if — an instigation will occur. As a second example, we can look at political authority in China. China is going through a rapid process of economic transformation that is based on private ownership and production. The growth rate of the economy is one of the highest in the world. Soon Hong Kong — an advanced capitalist economy — is to be incorporated. At the same time the old forms of political authority and the ideology that accompanies it remain in place. A deep disjuncture is developing between economic liberalism and political authoritarianism. The situation is ripe for political and social disturbances of a high order, of which Tiananmen Square may have been a foretaste. We cannot, however, know when this will occur. Thus we may reasonably predict — and base policies on these predictions — without the ability to be precise. Sometimes, we can on good theoretical grounds surmise that there will be change but not be able to specify exactly when that change is going to occur.

Chaos theory, like catastrophe theory, is also mis-named, in the sense that in the ordinary use of the word chaos is not always the result. What chaos theory does argue, however, is that *in principle*, some things are inherently unpredictable. Thus it is not due to the fact that our measurements or theories are inadequate — it would not matter how good they are — we would still not be able to predict some things. One consequence of this way of thinking is that very small changes in the past may in the long run have very large effects: the beating of a butterfly's wings in an Amazonian rain forest may lead to a hurricane in New York. We can think of any process of change or development as a series of movements down a path, a sequence. At any moment in that sequence there is the possibility of 'bifurcation', or division. The direction of the path may change. In theory there are an infinite number of potential bifurcation points. If we accept that social change or development is 'path dependent' — that later states are dependent on former states —

and that random bifurcation is always possible, then the prediction of some social developments may in principle be impossible. However, whether the fact of chaos is or is not important will in part depend of the time-scale of the prediction. If we were attempting to predict the balance of international power in 2050, and there are chaotic elements in social change, then we would almost certainly have problems. On the other hand, if our prediction was limited to the next five years, the probability of our being right would be much greater, merely because the deviations and divergences caused by small bifurcations are likely to be much smaller.

In this section some of the philosophical difficulties with prediction have been discussed from the point of view of the social scientist. The conclusion is that from both logical and empirical points of view particular predicted outcomes can never be guaranteed. None the less, we have to predict and we do predict and often with success. When we predict unsuccessfully we are often able reasonably to explain the failure of our predictions.

Prediction and the search for certainty

The social scientist is in a privileged position in that he or she is often able to observe and analyse without the necessity to act. The policy-maker is in a different position in that action is unavoidable. In such a position, not to act is often to act, in the sense that not taking a decision will be interpreted meaningfully and will have behavioural consequences. The policy-maker, therefore, does not have a choice as to whether to act or not to act. The only choice open is over what action to take. Further, it is reasonable to suggest that with contemporary communications and increased interdependency in the world, together with the interventionary nature of modern government in the economy and society, the number and range of issues requiring decision are greater than ever before. As Harold Wilson was reported to have said, 'a fortnight in politics is a long time'. Issues can rise and disappear with alarming rapidity; given the efficiency of communications and the relationship between attention and overload, to keep an issue on a national or international agenda requires as much effort and resources as getting it there in the first place. And, a frequent ocurrence, the past prediction is redefined in terms of the later outcome thus disguising failure.

What is certainly true is that the political leader does not have the time to ponder long on the ultimate consequences of actions. National leaders do have longstanding policies based on particular analyses, and they also have priorities and preferences — such as a belief in market forces — but much international (and domestic) behaviour conforms more to an action–reaction model than anything else. But to argue that much of the day-to-day operation of politics is reaction politics is not to suggest that the political world as seen by the policy-maker is wholly contingent, that is, that the development of history is completely unpredictable. Two factors are important here. A great social scientist wrote many years ago, 'What men define as real is real in its consequences'; in so far as there is some mutuality and stability in the definition of reality, then the behaviour of others, at least in the short term, can often be predicted. Second, as noted previously and following from this point, while events may not be predictable, the responses of social actors are frequently very predictable. If we know how an actor has behaved in the past, what interests he or she has, and what pressures and constraints are operative, then we have a good chance of forecasting that actor's behaviour. Contingency and predictability therefore coexist. Policy-makers are often 'trapped' by past decisions and their responses are often (but not always) constrained by both past decisions and by the social and political environment within which such decisions are made. It was inconceivable, for example, because of the question of national sovereignty and the creation of a precedent, that the British foreign secretary would concede to Ayatollah Khomeini's demands with respect to Salman Rushdie in spite of the considerable economic and political costs of rejection.

The philosophical problems of prediction in a world of whirl and action are of little moment. Philosophically we may be aware of the dangers and limitations of predicting the consequences of actions, but the policy-maker has to act irrespective of these problems, and these actions will be based on a particular assessment of the future. To do so he or she will seek *certainty*, not in a philosophical sense, but in the organization of the world. To the extent that the world is unchanging and to the extent that the responses of others are constant, prediction is possible and the task of policy-making that much easier. But how is such certainty in any complex political environment to be guaranteed? Basically, it cannot be guaranteed in politics any more than it can be guaranteed philosophically, but there are three ways in which policy-makers have sought to increase certainty and predictability. Each of these is dependent on ways of *controlling* the behaviour of others so that they become predictable.

The first is through coercion and the use of power. The second is through the manipulation of self-interest. And the third is through the development of trust. These should be seen in terms of ideal relationships which will in particular cases often be intermixed. Entering into an alliance, for example, involves trust, a perception of the interests of the alliance partner, and an extension of power with respect to a perceived potential adversary.

It is within the context of power, interest, and trust that uncertainty is reduced. However, as the prior discussion should have indicated, these three factors are interconnected in an intimate manner. Power or coercion are rarely used gratuitiously — to do so would be uneconomic — but are used in the pursuance of interest. Further, the use of naked power is justified in moral terms, either with respect to a relevant constituency (the right of the people to *lebensraum*) or with respect to some principle deemed valid (sovereignty, democracy, etc.). Similarly, constancy based upon self-interest that can only be attained through the maintenance of the interests of others, implies the capacity to deliver and the capacity to do otherwise, while trust in a practical world can only persist where there are sanctions available in case of a breach of trust. Trust is definitely not in my interest if others are wholly free to betray that trust. Thus in any situation there will be all features present but in different amounts.

The attempt to use power and coercion to guarantee the responses of others has always been a major factor in social life. Coercion, or the threat of coercion (which is always more useful if possible), entails certain costs. As with all politics, the maximization of one goal has costs with respect to other goals. The aggregation of the means of coercion may lead to a loss of development in other ways; the more that is spent on the means of coercion in order to apply sanctions to others, the less there is to spend on other valued goals. Further, to the extent that coercion or the threat of coercion is used to maintain a constancy of response, there will be a tendency to diminish the possibility of the development of a mutuality of interest; the use or threat of the use of coercion thus inhibits the ability to rely on the constancy of the environment in other ways. In addition, the maintenance of the response will only be successful in so far as the power ratio remains unchanged. Since most actors do not like being in a subordinate position, there will be a tendency for them to change the ratio in their favour with a subsequent increase in uncertainty. Finally, in some cases the very attempt to ensure the responses of others through the use of power or coercion may be self-defeating in that it creates uncertainty — especially if they also have resources — in the minds of others and hence a loss of certainty regarding their responses. Hence, while power in one of its many forms is present in most social relationships, to use it as a tool to control the future is fraught with difficulties.

The second approach to ensuring a degree of certainty in the social environment is through the maximization of mutual self-interest. This approach has a long history. Bishop Butler, in a critique of Hobbes's belief in egoism and self-interest, argued that true self-love implied reciprocity with respect to the interests and needs of others, since in a community one's own needs could only be supplied through others.[10]

Hence, according to this view, the responses of others can be guaranteed in so far as it is in their *interest* to behave in particular ways. Thus, in the functional analysis of international relations, peaceful responses by international actors are believed to be enhanced by increased social, political, and economic ties. Indeed, one of the major impetuses behind the creation of the European Union was the desire to build common interests between France and Germany so that war would not be a practical response to conflict. Similarly, the instability in many Third World countries can be partly attributed to a lack of social and economic reciprocity, and hence a sense of common interest, due to the absence of material and other resources to satisfy the interests of others.

Interest can create (and destroy) the relative certainty it seeks to bring about. If mutual self-interest is to be the basis of a constancy of response, certain conditions have to be met. There has to be a relative equality in the importance of the interests. If something is a major interest of mine, but only a very minor issue for you, then I may be foolish to expect any great constancy in your behaviour, just because it does not matter to you. If, on the other hand, the reciprocity is important to both parties, then breaching the norms of behaviour is liable to be damaging to both parties. Further, there is liable to be greater constancy of behaviour if there are multiple interests involved. This is due to the fact that misbehaviour in one area is likely to spill over into other areas and hence interfere with reciprocity in other areas. In addition, a mutuality of interests may be dependent on the correct appreciation of both parties of the interests of the other side. If this is misperceived then the relationship is liable to be short-lived. Allied to this is a time dimension; the longer the reciprocity has existed, the more likely it is that it will not be breached. Finally, if reciprocity is going to persist, there has to be some relationship between short term and long term goals. Hence, it may be in my interest to cooperate with you in the short-term, but in the long-term my interests may lie elsewhere. It may, indeed, be the case that it is worth while trading off short-term deficits in a relationship in order to satisfy long-term goals.

If these various conditions are satisfactorily met, a consequence might be the development of a 'pseudo-morality'; provided that there is no change in the prevailing structure of interests, long-term considerations will ensure that the behaviour engaged in appears to be moral behaviour. This may also entail the use of moral language in the sense that people 'should' or 'should not' behave in particular ways. The difference between moral and non-moral behaviour resides in the motivation for the piece of behaviour, although the behaviour itself may be identical. Moral behaviour stems from a belief in the intrinsic rightness of certain kinds of behaviour, while behaviour from interest stems from a perception of benefiting from the action.

Thus to ensure the satisfaction of your own interest, reciprocity must be engaged in, and a constant endeavour made to recognize and satisfy the interests of others. In this way a system of obligations is built up. In addition, the constancy of transactions may well lead to the development of a culture of interaction, where the question of whether this is or is not in my interest recedes as practice becomes custom. Once practice is sufficiently hallowed by custom and acceptance it becomes legitimized; the move has been made from interest to trust. It becomes unthinkable (or nearly unthinkable) that an actor could renege.

The essential characteristic of a trust relationship is the moral element that is embedded in it. It is impossible to think of morality except in the context of a relationship. The idea of the moral noble savage existing in isolation is an absurdity. It is a mode of regulating relationships. Whereas, in the pure case, relationships are regulated by power through the implicit or explicit threat of sanctions and in the case of interest through the mutual advantage of parties, morality is a mode of regulating relationships between parties on the basis of mutually agreed more or less explicit principles that give meaning to the concepts of 'right' and 'wrong'. This does not imply that there is necessarily any thorough systemization of principles for there to be morality — in any particular case principles may conflict — but that there should be grounds of appeal to decide whether an act is right or wrong. What is of interest about morality, however, is that it pervades every aspect of human existence; the idea of a wholly amoral man or non-moral existence is synonymous with either madness or non-humanity. Notions of justice, fairness, or right invade all aspects of life. The most horrific acts of destruction are 'justified' by appeal to moral principles, and from time immemorial wars have been fought over whose moral perceptions are to prevail.

While morality is an unavoidable part of every human relationship, there is frequently a gap between discussions of morality in the literature on ethics and morality as practised in the real world. For morality, while it may be justified on long-term utilitarian grounds (though of this we cannot be certain), it is in many cases opposed to self-interest. To behave morally is often not to maximize your self-interest, even though, when self-interest is paramount, it will often be justified morally. The literature on moral philosophy will often seem to discuss morality as autonomous from other social effects. In reality, of course, any particular set of moral beliefs would not survive very long unless sanctions were also incorporated as a support for disinterest and as a barrier against self-interest. In the personal case these sanctions might range from socialized feelings of discomfiture, to excommunication, or to acts by others of a more stringent nature. In the case of a polity, minimal morality is encapsulated in law, with sanctions spelled out in detail. However, while it is the case that sanctions do accompany morality in the real world, the primary thrust of trust is not based on sanctions; sanctions are merely a back-up or fail-safe system should trust fail. This implies that even where there is a trust relationship, the maintenance of some means of coercion is not entirely without point.

Conclusion

This chapter has examined some of the many problems surrounding prediction. There are many of them. But while prediction in social life is difficult, we have no alternative but to predict every moment of our conscious lives. And, in spite of all the difficulties, we are often right in our predictions. Partly this is because quite often the future is like the past, and partly because we know where people are 'coming from'. Sometimes, on the basis of this, uncertainty can be reduced by anticipating the responses of others. The problem with the future is not just that it does not conform to our expectations — sometimes this can be delightful and exciting — but that often it leads to uncertainty and anxiety and thus to unpredictable behaviour. Where there is uncertainty and anxiety, actors may engage in a 'worst case analysis' and thus set in train events that were neither desired nor predicted, in that other actors may act similarly. In the face of this uncertainty, human beings will both attempt to predict the behaviour of other actors, and often, if possible, to control that behaviour in an attempt to attain some certainty. There are various ways of controlling the behaviour of others (and of others controlling our behaviour), but all of them are imperfect. The one thing that is certain is that any simple scientific model of prediction is inadequate in a social scientific context where complexity and uncertainty are constant companions.

Notes

1. See, for example, Bacon, Francis (1901) *Novum Organum*, in Devey, J. (ed.) *The Physical and Metaphysical Works of Lord Bacon*, London: George Bell; and Mill, J.S. (1875) *System of Logic*, London: Longmans, Green, Reader, and Dyer. For details of Sir Roy Harrod's argument see Caws, P. (1965) *The Philosophy of Science: a Systematic Account*, Princeton: Van Nostrand, 256–8.
2. See Wild, J. (ed.) (1930) *Spinoza Selections*, Letter XXXII, Letter XXXV, New York: Charles Scribner's Sons, 440–6; and Berkeley, G. (1967) *The Principles of Human Knowledge and Three Dialogues Between Hylas and Pholonous*, London and Glasgow: William Collins, p. 197.
3. See Campbell, N. (1952) *What is Science?*, New York: Dover Publications, p. 76.

4. Gurr, T.R. (1970) *Why Men Rebel*, Princeton: Princeton University Press.
5. Popper, K.R. (1974) *The Poverty of Historicism*, London: Routledge and Kegan Paul.
6. By 'inevitable' we normally mean that we cannot conceive of any force or power preventing an occurrence. A philosopher once gave the example of a train approaching a car stranded on a level-crossing; a mile away there were many imaginable interferences, a quarter of a mile away an accident was highly probable, while an inch away the event is 'inevitable'.
7. Meadows, D. *et al.* (1972) *Limits to Growth*, London: Pan Books.
8. Cole, H.S.D. *et al.* (1973) *Thinking About the Future: a Critique of the Limits to Growth*, London: Chatto and Windus.
9. Nicholson, M. (1983) *The Scientific Analysis of Social Behaviour: a Defence of Empiricism in Social Science*, London: Frances Pinter, 157–61.
10. See Sermon 11 in Butler, J. (1855) *The Analogy of Religion to the Constitution and Course of Nature: Also Fifteen Sermons*, London: Religious Tract Society.

9
THE COMMITMENT OF THE
ACADEMIC IN SOCIAL SCIENCE

Introduction

In many subjects the question 'what use is it?' seems inappropriate. For example, subjects such as the history of art or archaeology are held to be justified merely through their contribution to human knowledge, as part of the development of civilization. In the natural sciences a distinction is sometimes made between 'pure' and 'applied' science. Pure science is seen as being both justified in its own right and as having *potential* application. In some areas, such as astronomy, it is difficult to see how theories about the nature of the Big Bang or the nature of gravity in a black hole can ever be applied in any useful way. In none of these cases would we consider the subject illegitimate merely because it cannot be applied. Social science, however, seems to have a more direct applicability than many humanities or science disciplines and is often justified by its relevance to human problems. The main reason for this is that the theories of social science nearly always have easily identifiable prescriptions built into them. It is difficult to have a theory of economics, or a theory of juvenile delinquency, without these having some kind of implications for human action. Because we are dealing with people, and researching and writing about people, it is more difficult for social scientists to be dispassionate and distanced from their subject matter as is the case, for example, with natural science. Social science research, therefore, nearly always has implications for social policy.

It is also the case that many students go to university or college to study social science at least partly motivated by humanitarian concerns, with a desire to do something about the world. It is interesting in its own right, but it is also often seen as holding the key to the solution of some of humankind's most pressing problems. These problems may be on a macro scale such as the cycle of debt and poverty in the Third World or may be on a micro scale such as the problems of child abuse, dyslexia, or delinquency. When they begin studying these subjects, however, a degree of disillusion often sets in. For what they are confronted with is not the 'truth' about Third World debt or delinquency but a range of interpretations and theories about these subjects. Not only will there be dispute about the theories themselves, but there will be disputes about the validity of data or the way in which social things are measured. Any belief in 'truth' is soon lost among the myriad of conflicting interpretations and theories. At this stage the intelligent student will often ask: 'what is the use of social science if social scientists cannot agree amongst themselves?' The more cynical may come to the conclusion that the social scientist is merely selling his or her subjective values under the guise of a rigorous discipline, or that the various competing theories of social science are little more than ideologies wrapped in academic jargon. In the face of criticisms such as these, it is pertinent to ask what the role of the social scientist is, and what contribution he or she has to make to the policy-making process. The belief expressed here is that the social scientist *does* have a role in the process, but it is a role that is constrained by the nature of the academic profession and is best performed at some distance from the political process of policy-making. This does not mean that the academic is necessarily dispassionate, or neutral, or value-free but merely that he or she will perform and be of more use in the long run by avoiding close involvement in policy-making. The world of practice and the world of scholarship are two very different worlds, and each will benefit from the other if they remain relatively disengaged and loyal to their own roles.

The role of the policy-maker

The policy-maker in contemporary society is usually a bureaucrat. High policy may be decided by politicians, but the implementation of policy is usually the business of bureaucratic professionals. It is often the case that academics have a very negative image of bureaucratic decision-makers, often believing that they would do the job better. It is, however, doubtful that this would be the case, for once engaged in policy-making they would come under the same kind of pressures that bureaucrats suffer. It is also the case that in many countries policy-makers have a negative image of academics, believing them to be unrealistic and stuck in their 'ivory tower'.[1] Neither image is fully justified; it is just that they live in different worlds and follow the imperatives of their different occupations. What is unrealistic is either the Platonic notion of the philosopher-king, where the men and women of knowledge become the wielders of power because of that knowledge, or the idea that the academic can become an *éminence grise*, whispering into the ear of power. Apart from anything else, anyone who has seen some academics operating on university committees would have severe doubts about any automatic right to power.

In many ways it is possible to argue that in the contemporary world the role of the policy-maker has become more problematic, and it is because of this increased difficulty that there is a role for the academic. There are three reasons for the increased difficulty of policy-making: the increased complexity of modern life, the transparency of the policy-making process, and the abundance of information for analysis.

In one sense we can think of 'development' or 'modernization' as an increased density of interaction and interdependence between different sectors of society. Modern society functions through the dovetailing and complementarity of many varying and contrasting sectors of life. Functional interdependency has always been a part of social life, but in the past three hundred years it has moved from primarily parochial interaction to intense functional interdependency within states and is now rapidly moving towards global interdependency. While normally this has the effect of making modern and developed states more stable, in that any perturbation in a state has to affect multiple interacting sectors of society to be significant, it also has the effect as far as policy-making is concerned of linking policy areas intimately. This means that making policy in any one area of social life affects many other areas, increasing the complexity of the process considerably and bringing many more affected interests into the process. If one then adds the international dimension, and this is increasingly important, yet another layer of complexity is added. Whether we are talking about water, privacy, fish, or money, the complexity of domestic decision-making is overlaid with international obligations and constraints.

A second factor making the life of the policy-maker more difficult is the transparency of the policy-making process. By this is meant the public *observability* of the activity. This has perhaps gone further in the United States than in other places, due to greater freedom of information, but in all developed countries policy-making takes place in an increasingly public manner. One reason for this is the role of the media. For our purposes we may consider this to be the newspapers, radio, and, perhaps most importantly, television. Scandal, incompetence, inefficiency, and corruption are all meat and drink to the media, and if discovered are exploited to the full with the aim of increasing the audience. Even if policy-making is conducted in a proper and efficient manner, it is still a matter of public contestation among different political proponents, a kind of theatre communicated through the media with the 'public' assumed to be a judgemental audience. A consequence of this is that the agenda of policy-making is often set elsewhere, in the media or in the international environment, with the consequence that the policy-maker is often just responding to external pressures. Perhaps the one thing that saves the policy-maker from permanent pilloring is that the media, like a hyperactive child, has a short and inconstant attention span; today's burning issue is tomorrow's cold news. The degree of transparency may increase still further as a consequence of modern technology. In America at both the state and federal levels, a great deal of legislation and planning is on public-access electronic bulletin boards. Congressmen, senators, bureaucrats, and even the president, can all be contacted by electronic mail. Pressure groups have both high levels of information and direct access to decision-makers. What is true of the United States now will probably become true for other developed countries. In such circumstances, while the policy-making process is open, observable, and transparent, the life of the policy-maker has become much more difficult.

A third factor that makes policy-making more difficult is the sheer abundance of information in modern society. Modern society exists in a sea of information, and we are constantly deluged by it through radio, television, newpapers, and the host of other communication facilities that are available. The photocopier, the telephone, the fax and the telex, together with the networked computer and the capacity to create and access vast databases both nationally and internationally, give the contemporary decision-maker amounts of information undreamt of by his predecessor. Long gone are the days when, for example, Lord Palmerston, as foreign secretary, could read and reply to all the mail coming into his office. During the Gulf War there were around 2,000 communications coming into the Foreign and Commonwealth Office each day. It might be thought that making decisions would be easier the more information there is available. To some extent this is true, but if the amount of information becomes so overwhelming that it becomes impossible to absorb it — or even read it — in the time available, its usefulness declines. Information is only useful in so far as it can be 'managed', and where this is not possible short-cuts and simplification processes occur. Just as assumptions have to be made where there is a shortage of information, so they are also made when there is an unmanageable amount of information.

The problem is heightened by the pressures of time. Most decisions are made by people who are working very hard all the time. The idea that bureaucrats, civil servants, and policy-makers do not work hard is far from the truth, a stereotype propagated largely for political purposes. Indeed, it might be argued that in general they work so hard that there is little time left for reflection, for stepping back from the grind of busy office life to take an over-view of what they are doing. Indeed, Tom Millar, an academic who was seconded to a department in the Australian civil service writes:[2] 'most civil servants, I discovered . . . had little time to read outside their work. Just wading through the day's telegrams and dispatches, preparing briefs or submissions to the Minister, and engaging in the necessary civilities, took up every moment in a long day.'

Further, decisions are made not only on bureaucratic grounds under pressure of time but in a political context. By a 'political context' we mean that decisions are taking place in an arena of contestation where some will benefit from a decision and others will lose. In this sense the bureaucrat decision-maker is *responsible* in a way that the academic seldom is. Bureaucratic decisions have consequences for peoples' lives, and yet they are made in a manner that often departs radically from any ideal model of rational decision-making. As Weiss notes:[3]

Policy-makers know that public policies are not the product of rational problem-solving. They recognize the overwhelming pressure to take account of the political interests of important segments in society and to adapt to prevailing ideologies. Whilst they also realize the importance of good information for their actions, they usually believe that they are deluged with more information than they have time to absorb.

The life of the policy-maker is complex, busy, and in most cases extremely difficult. Given the nature of the problems, it is difficult to see that the social scientist would perform any better than the professional decision-maker; pondering deeply on epistemological or ontological problems, or worrying about the statistical procedures used to establish a particular theory would not in general aid the professional decision-maker in attempts to deal with a balance-of-payments' problem where an answer is required today or tomorrow. It is highly probable that the social scientist would perform far worse. By the time a professional becomes a significant decision-maker he or she has usually become accustomed to the problems of decisional complexity and is familiar with the use of power, bargaining, negotiation and summation in a way that social scientists are not. It is not self-evident that the social scientist would have the political or bureaucratic skills of the professional. The social scientist, however, has other skills and capacities usually not possessed by the professional.

The skills of the social scientist

Many academic social scientists in many disciplines do have a belief that they can contribute to the betterment of society. Many students choose to study psychology, sociology or politics not just for their future careers but through a real interest in the subject and often with a humanitarian concern about the human condition. The problem, however, is what best the academic social scientist can contribute and how best he or she can contribute. The argument here is that the social scientist has much to contribute to the professional — and to policy-making — but not by becoming a kind of second-order decision-maker. Lusting 'after the possibilities of pulling the levers of power' diminishes the role of the academic and the contribution that can be made.[4] The best contribution that the academic can make is *as an academic* and not as a surrogate or pseudo decision-maker.

One of the factors that separates the academic study of social science from the perception of the decision-maker is the emphasis of the former on paradigms, theories, or approaches. Many practitioners would find the paradigmatic view of the world incomprehensible. The professional has his or her imperatives, goals which are perceived to be in 'the national or public interest', and acts in 'the real world' to achieve those goals. What is not of prime concern is what sort of world it is. Questions like this, however, are the life blood of the academic social science in all disciplines. Further, the time-scale of academic scholarship and practice are often very different; the academic can wander over the decades and the centuries, while the professional must act today.

Paradigms (theories, approaches, models, research programmes etc.) arise from the academic activity of theorizing. A theory, to use Karl Popper's phrase, is a 'crystallisation of a point of view'. Given a basic point of view — that international politics is fundamentally about military power, or that it is driven by economic relations between actors — the academic will go as far with the theory as it will go. The consequence is multiple theories about the world. A theory, to be useful, has to be a simplification of reality, a construct that points out and selects what is significant in the world. It will have self-confirming tendencies in that it states what is significant about the world and is partially confirmed by the discovery of those factors. In this way it becomes a research programme, with a body of supporting literature, with advocates who are to some degree 'tied' to that approach by past literary and scholarly allegiance. In addition, unlike the natural sciences, where experimentation, prediction, or application tend to validate or invalidate theories, social science theories are always in contestation with no clear-cut or unambiguous means of deciding among them. This is not to suggest that there are no criteria of validity in social science — the problem is that there are too many criteria and they point in different directions — but that these criteria are never ultimately decisive. If a theory does come under heavy intellectual fire, typically it transmutes into another and more fireproof version of itself. Hence, early Marxist theories of international relations were plugged by the theory of imperialism, functionalism was reinforced and reinterpreted to become neo-functionalism, while the grand old man of international relations theory — realism — succumbed to the welter of criticism to become structural or neo-realism. Theories in social science rarely entirely disappear but change and emerge dressed up in a different way.

The sensible thing to do when faced with this plethora of approaches and theories is to admit that 'there is something in all of them'. What cannot be done is to add or combine all these approaches into one large 'meta-theory'. The consequence of this would be to create a theoretical structure which would begin to approach the real world in complexity with a resulting loss in the utility of the theory as a tool of analysis. If a theory is useful only in so far as it simplifies and selects particular features of a phenomenon as significant — what Karl Popper would call the 'searchlight' theory of theories — then any great increase in complexity is going to reduce the usefulness of the theory. I suppose, if a theory or a model became too complex, then you would need theories about it to simplify it and make it useful.

A further consequence of the social scientist's proclivity for multiple theorizing is the generation of multiple prescriptions for action. It is not the case that the theories of social science are in any sense value-free with respect to policy. All of them are redolent with prescription. In this sense social science theories share much with ideology; they are interpretations of the world that lead to prescriptions for action. To be a monetarist or a Marxist economic theorist is to see the world in a particular way, to identify the root causes of the world's problems, and to see the way to rectify those problems. However, while particular theories may resemble ideology, a social science discipline with multiple theories within it is not merely a collection of ideologies but something rather different. Functionally they are different; while it is a central goal of ideology to mobilize a clientele, it is difficult to see the works of Talcott Parsons, Harold Garfinkel, or Bruce Bueno de Mesquita mobilizing anything. Similarly, it is the aim of an ideology to produce unity in its clientele, while for a social science discipline schism, disparity, argument, and debate are typical. Social science also differs markedly from ideology in the degree of openness and the acceptance of the legitimacy of other points of view.

This view of social science has other implications. First, it means that social science is forever in a situation of 'Cartesian anxiety', forever concerned with its epistemological and ontological roots.[5] We can never aspire to the Kuhnian ideal of science because we can never achieve agreement over fundamentals. Second, to be an academic social science expert is to know a range of interpretations about the world and to have beliefs about the strengths and weaknesses of those perspectives. To be a 'functionalist' theorist does not mean an exclusion or a miscomprehension of other perspectives but merely a preference for one approach to others. Indeed, if any empirical work is to be done, some approach that delineates the significant has to be adopted at some stage. Third, to be a social science expert is to see in the world a richness that is largely denied to the ideologist or the practitioner. Each theoretical interpretation of the world draws attention to different aspects of reality, counterposing them one against the other. Fourth, this view of social science implies that there is not a disciplinary view of any particular discipline; there are only views. Thus, when it comes to policy prescription social scientists will be found on all sides of every question, each perspective tending to advocate a different policy. For the professional, seeking advice or guidance from the academic, the question is therefore 'which academic?' or 'which perspective?' The utilitarian answer often adopted by the practitioner is to select the academic who tends to agree with the professional's own views.

But there is one further implication of this view of social science which is important to the subject matter of this chapter and which bears heavily on the relationship between the academic and the professional. The academic has perforce to exercise a degree of epistemological dispassion. This is not the same as 'value-freedom', nor even 'disinterest', for, as has been noted, the many theories of social science come complete with values and policy prescriptions. It is not possible for the academic, or any group of academics, to persuade definitively the discipline of any one view, and hence it is necessary to live permanently with controversy. In so far as the academic is incapable of wholly persuading others, 'knowledge' within the discipline must always be held as tentative. The individual academic may be committed to a particular view, but the discipline never is; the nature of society, as it is now and as it was and will be, is ever in dispute.

Perhaps an example will illustrate this. The work of Modelski and others argues that there is a 'long cycle' that describes the transfer of hegemonic power.[6] This cycle, approximately one hundred years of hegemonic peace followed by a transfer period of thirty years of war, has occurred five times since 1495. The statistical regularity claimed by the model is reinforced by mechanisms that explain the decline of the hegemonic power, particularly the diffusion of technology and the lack of domestic investment as a consequence of maintaining global reach. If this model is extrapolated into the future, and if 1946 is taken as the 'moment' of the US accession to hegemonic status, then we can expect a further global war around the middle of the next century. However, the simple situation outlined by Modelski and others is subject to ontological uncertainty; is the world of 1995 the 'same' world as previously? If it is the same world in all important respects, then an argument can be made for the repetition of the cycle; after all, the world of 1815 was very different from the world of 1914 in many ways. Many pluralists, from complex interdependence to world society theorists, would argue that the world has undergone a radical transformation in the last fifty years and that any simple inductive extrapolation is doomed to failure. Further, it may be the case that the availability of nuclear weapons will make any hegemonic struggle in the future very different from the past. It should be noted here that this kind of debate about the nature of the world cannot easily be decided by resort to evidence — for in many instances in the social sciences theory is underdetermined by evidence — but is a very typical debate within the academic study of international relations and social science more generally.[7] Knowledge, from the perspective of the discipline, must be held as being tentative since no academic or group of academics can demonstrate their beliefs in an incontestable manner.

If it is the case that academic knowledge is distinguished from ideology by openness and tentativeness, a further implication follows regarding the world of practice. If an academic engages in policy-making as an actor, that is, becomes a practitioner or a professional, he or she necessarily loses the dispassion which is the hallmark of scholarship. 'Action' cannot be tentative, in the sense that tentative action or inaction is still positive action in the world of practice. Further, the academic will become tied to policies; rather than being a free-floating disputacious wild spirit, the academic will of necessity be forced to adopt a party line. The past, in terms of policy commitments and institutional loyalty, will become a prison, and entrapment will occur. The academic will cease to be an academic and certainly cannot claim academic authority for his or her actions. As Flack notes:[8]

The experience of the twentieth century has made it obvious that an alliance between intellectuals and power-orientated organisations is problematic. The logic of states and parties requires the subordination of truth to that of organisational maintenance and growth. The organisationally mobilised intellectual is, by definition, not free to set his or her agenda of inquiry, to publish freely his or her knowledge and understanding, or to say fully what is in his or her mind. The organisationally linked intellectual is to at least some extent required to sacrifice the very freedom he or she most needs to fulfill the vocation of the intellectual.

To summarize, briefly, the position of the academic. First, there will be concern with theory (paradigms, research programmes, perspectives, approaches, etc.) and the structured explanation of events and relations. Second, there is an acceptance of the legitimacy of multiple views of the world. Third, social science is defined in terms of unresolvable debates among perspectives. Fourth, the academic is forever concerned with fundamentals. Fifth, academics will be found on all sides of every question; hence there can be no academic view as such, only academic views. Sixth, the time frame of scholarship will often differ from that of the professional. And, finally, academic beliefs about the world are necessarily held in a tentative manner.

The role of the academic in the policy-making process

The argument here has been that the world of the professional and the academic with respect to social science is very different. Congruent with this are the different roles which they have. It has been suggested here that the nature of academic work makes the academic unsuitable to be a policy-maker in any direct sense; to engage in policy-making is to diminish openness and independence. Yet, the academic has got a valuable role to play in policy-making, but it is a role that derives from the strengths of scholarship. It derives from the acceptance that roles can be both different and complementary. In particular, it is suggested here that the academic can perform four functions in the policy-making process that are congruent with his or her role and expertise and which would be performed less well by the professional. These four functions are the provision of alternatives, information, sensitization, and criticism.

The provision of alternatives

In is in the nature of an academic discipline — particularly a social science discipline — that there are different ways of viewing it. Indeed, this has been described earlier as typical of the academic activity. What the various approaches to social science within different disciplines are doing is drawing attention to different empirical aspects of the world based on theoretical and coherent understandings of the world. It will follow that, both within and between schools, prescriptions for action will vary. And, in the dialogue between perspectives, the limitations and potential consequences of a perspective and its prescriptions will be exposed. In this sense, what the academic community can do is explore the social environment unencumbered by the imperatives of action or power and provide alternative menus. It matters little that some of these menus will be considered 'unrealistic' (that in any case will depend upon a point of view) but that they can successfully counterpose a view against any particular normality or orthodoxy.

Information

It was noted previously that the decision-maker is frequently over-whelmed by information, and it was suggested that in the contemporary world with the communications revolution and the centralization of decison-making this is even more the case than in the past. The problem is not information as 'bits' of knowledge about the world, but the structuring of information in a meaningful way. The academic, whose primary strength is the theoretical ordering of reality in different ways, can bring this to the management of information. Further, while the academic will rarely be able to compete with the professional in terms of information about what happened yesterday, his or her ability to put what happened yesterday into an historical socio-political context is without parallel. A considerable reservoir of structured knowledge about empirical aspects of the world exists, and yet this empirical understanding is not utilized by the professionals. In this context the question of time is important. The academic is rarely under the same pressures of time as the practitioner. There is the space to assimilate, codify, and to interpret, in a way that is rarely possible for the policy-making professional.

Criticism

The value of criticism, argument, and debate to understanding has long been recognized; Edmund Burke noted that, 'he that wrestles with us strengthens our nerves and sharpens our skill. Our antagonist is our helper.' Within the arena of social science, academics are observers trained in criticism and as such, are a resource to be utilized. While this may often be uncomfortable at times (as most academics will acknowledge from their experience), the outcome of such criticism in terms of re-orientation is often of great value. Criticism can come in a number of forms. It can be directed towards the ends of policy and thus be questioning of the goals adopted by the professional. It can be questioning of the means for the attainment of goals, or it can be speculation on the consequences of particular policies. The information on which the policy is based may be queried. Perhaps more important than any of these, however, is the ability of the academic to question the nature of the world, to examine the often implicit and unexamined assumptions about the social environment.

Sensitization

The world is a complex place, ever changing and always in motion; as Heraclitus is reported to have said: 'You never step into the same river twice . . . all is flux, nothing stays still.' Academics from their vantage point of relative intellectual freedom are able to study the structural changes in the world in a way that is not always easy or possible for the professional to do. What, for example, are the consequences of economic liberalization in China? A quarter of the world's population is engaged in a massive revision of long-established economic practice. Is it possible to have economic liberalization without some degree of political liberalization? What lessons can we draw from change in Eastern Europe or developments in South Korea or Taiwan? What are the consequences of even a modest rise in the standard of living in China in relation to demands on world resources? Or, to take another example, is the democratic movement going to sweep through Africa? Cases abound from Kenya to Namibia of a move towards democracy, partly consequent upon the delegitimization of the alternative political model following the collapse of the Soviet Union. But, with democracy such a fragile plant in the Third World, should it not be given more fertile soil to flourish in through the abolition of debts? There are a myriad of questions such as these in any analysis of social science, questions which draw the analyst into speculation, comparison, and theorizing. They are the sort of questions about which the academic is able to sensitize the professional. It is not that the professional is unable to think about these and many other problems — they certainly do and often in an intelligent and structured manner — but in general they have neither the time nor the training to develop such ideas to their fullest extent.

Conclusion

The attempt in this chapter has been to suggest a practical and positive role for the academic. However, what they can contribute usefully they contribute as academics and not as would-be decision-makers, for they have little claim to competence in that arena. If the professionals are going to benefit from the academic, and the academic from the professional, there do have to be institutional opportunities for this to occur. Some institutional arrangements are in place in most countries, but in general these need to be deepened and given more positive purpose. If the academic *is* going to communicate with the policy-maker, some attempt needs to be made to do so in terms that are readily understandable by the professional. The professional may well not have had a social science training, and the terminology and theoretical constructions may not have much meaning outside narrow disciplinary boundaries. However, while the academic can make valuable contributions to the policy-making process, he or she should also exercise a modicum of modesty regarding expectations about his or her role. Policy-making is a complex process involving many actors with different interests. The academic input is only one among many others and should be seen as such.

Notes

1. For an extended eight-nation cross-national discussion see, for example, Girard, M., Eberwein, W.-D., and Webb, K. (eds) (1994) *Theory and Practice in Foreign Policy Making: National Perspectives on Academics and Professionals in International Relations*, London: Pinter Publishers.
2. Millar, T.B. (1991) 'Academics and Practitioners in Foreign Affairs', *The Round Table*, 319, 275–83.
3. Weiss, C.H. (1986) 'Research and Policy-Making: A Limited Partnership', in Heller, F. (ed.) *The Use and Abuse of Social Science*, London: Sage, 214–35.
4. Groom, A.J.R. (1984) 'Academics and Practitioners: Towards a Happier Relationship', in Banks, M. (ed.) *Conflict in World Society*, Brighton: Wheatsheaf Books, 192–208.
5. Bernstein, R.J. (1983) *Beyond Objectivism and Relativism: Science, Hermeneutics, and Praxis*, Philadephia: University of Philadelphia Press, p. 18.
6. Modelski, G. and Thompson, W.R. (1989) 'Long Cycles and Global War', in Midlarski, M.I. (ed.) *Handbook of War Studies*, London: Unwin Hyman, 23–54.
7. 'Underdetermination' here means that the same evidence can be interpreted differently when seen from different theoretical perspectives. This means, necesarily, that the evidence cannot be used to decide among competing theories. See Ryan, A. (1981) 'Is the Study of Society a Science?', in Potter, D. *et al. Society and the Social Sciences*, London: Routledge and Kegan Paul, 8–33.
8. Flack, D. (1991) 'Making History and Making Theory: Notes on How Intellectuals Seek Relevance', in Lemart, C.C. (ed.) *Intellectuals and Politics: Social Theory in a Changing World*, London: Sage Publications, 3–18.

10
JUSTIFIED BELIEF VERSUS UTOPIAN REJECTIONISM

....

Introduction

A central aim of this book has been to examine some areas of uncertainty in social science and the 'social scientific' response to these problems. In the course of this discussion a point of view has emerged regarding the possibility of a study of society that can broadly be termed an empiricist, though non-positivist, perspective. An important distinction is made between 'positivism' and 'empiricism'. Bertrand Russell, for example, recognizes this distinction between varieties of empiricism by defining it broadly as the belief that knowledge 'rests wholly or partly upon experience'.[1]

The view of positivism taken here is a strong view as encapsulated in the four basic principles of positivism, as noted previously in Chapter 6. What is not being done here — but which is so often done — is to conflate positivism with empiricism with the consequence that all facticity is then termed positivist. As Gellner, in his witty attack on postmodernism suggests in a discussion of the Frankfurt School: 'Those were the days when a "positivist" was a man involving fact against Marxism; nowadays he is anyone who makes use of facts at all . . .'[2] What, essentially, is the difference between positivism, which is a variety of empiricism, and the view of empiricism espoused here? The distinction rests basically on the rejection of the four postulates but the maintenance of a belief in facticity as important to the study of society and that while multiple interpretations and constructions of social facts are possible, the range of plausible interpretations is not infinite. There are thus limitations on the degree of conceptual anarchy in social science.

The fact that positivism is a failed doctrine should not, therefore, lead us to a rejection of all forms of empiricism. In numerous ways throughout this book attention has been drawn to the interpretive activity of the observer but without at the same time denying the essential facticity of the social world. The fact that all observation is interpretation does not deny the proposition that there is something to be observed even though there may be different ways of observing it. This leads, of course, to a request for information on the 'it' that is being observed; if 'it' can be meaningfully interpreted in a number of different ways, how can we ever know what it is? To say that there is a reality 'out there', but without constraint on interpretation, is, in fact, not to say too much at all about the empirical world but merely to rephrase idealism in empirical terms. This was one of the problems faced by Kant and solved by him through the introduction of the *synthetic a priori* categories (quantity, quality, relation, and modality); in other words, things are, for him, as they are because we are as we are.[3] A more recent argument in the same vein, but regarding language and the structure of mind, would be that made by Noam Chomsky.[4]

The answer given in this work with respect to social science is twofold: first, that there are criteria of validity that enable us to make judgements about the world that are reasonable if not certain, and second, that the nature of the activity of social science limits the scope of variation of interpretation. The latter view comes reasonably close to what Habermas refers to as an 'ideal language situation' in that it emerges from the clash of views.[5] An example of this convergence can be seen in the treatment in Chapter 3 of 'essentially contested concepts', where knowledge is seen in the disciplinary acceptance of a range of usages, and the reasons for variation in usage, with the consequence that a term can both be recognized to be essentially contestable and yet also used incorrectly.

The other aspect of the argument was the acceptance of criteria of validity, as previously specified. These are seen as the terms within which contestation occurs. A.J. Ayer, in a justly famous work, argues that to know that something is the case three conditions must pertain — that what we claim to know is true, that we are sure of it, and that we have the right to be sure.[6] In both social science and science these conditions cannot be met in any conceivable way apart from dogmatic statement. In the end all we can argue for persuasively is 'justified belief', the acceptance of fallibalism and the tentativity of knowledge. This does not mean, however, as, for example, the sceptical postmodernists would have it (see below) that there are no grounds for the acceptance or rejection of knowledge propositions but merely that what we mean by 'knowledge' (the term 'justified belief' is to be preferred since it does not imply absolutism with respect to knowledge) is not to be associated with certainty. Certainty can only be accepted with respect to analytic statements within an accepted system of conventions (i.e. '2+2=4') and never with respect to empirical domains. To ask for more, and then retreat into a 'hysteria of subjectivity'[7] when this is not available, is not to understand the nature of knowledge. This has through the ages always been the case; claims to knowledge have been made and resisted through sceptical argument, and yet belief as such persists when plausibly justified. Bishop Berkeley, indeed, pushed that argument to the degree that I could not be philosophically justified in believing the existence of something I could not observe, such as the wall behind me, but the fact that there is such philosophic doubt does not lead me to accept non-existence but rather to argue that there are good grounds for a justified belief in the possibility of a constant reality in spite of philosophic doubt.

If it is accepted, then, that philosophic doubt is just *philosophic* doubt, and that certainty cannot be a condition of empirical knowledge, then the grounds of the argument change to the conditions necessary for justified belief. The argument changes from the illusory, quixotic, and utopian quest for the absolute foundations of knowledge to the criteria for the establishment of justified belief. It was argued earlier, in the context of social science, that there are such criteria, and that these, with others, are embedded in various philosophies of science, each of which attempts to establish the pre-eminence of particular criteria over others. The argument here has been that the historical social science concentration on 'science' and philosophies of science has overlooked the important feature that we use many criteria of validity all the time as terms of debate in the contestation that occurs in the establishment of a point of view. The methodology of social science should therefore overtly concentrate on criteria of validity as they pertain to social science claims and ostensibly junk, ditch, and forget the legitimizing myth of 'science'.

The postmodern critique of social science

Postmodernism denies most of what is asserted here on what seem to this author rather dubious grounds. Postmodernism as a 'radical' critique of contemporary forms of social science has in recent years made considerable inroads into the literature of social science. It is advanced as a critique of positivism and a rejection of 'traditional' methods of doing social science, although, as some postmodernists point out, post-modernism is not necessarily antithetical to the use of empirical data. However, while postmodernist analyses do make reference to facts, given the denial of any relevant criteria of validity and the extreme anti-realist and idealist stance, it is difficult to maintain that empirical analysis can have the same significance in postmodernist writings as in other approaches. The movement has its origins in several traditions — linguistics, literary criticism, a particular analysis of modern society, a rejection of Marxism, and an analysis of the nature of power. Given the diversity of the roots, it is unsurprising that its contemporary expression is somewhat incoherent with Gellner, for example, in choleric fashion exclaiming that 'it is not altogether clear what the devil it is', while Umberto Eco suggests that it is a term that 'is applied today to anything that the user of the term happens to like'. In a sense, the lack of clarity about the activity and the diversity of the protagonists of the approach is both a defence strategy and also congruent with the arguments of at least some of the adherents. It is a defence strategy in that the diversity and lack of definition make it an intangible moving target in a mist, but this may be said to be congruent with some postmodernist statements that postmodernism is not a position or theory but precisely the reverse.

It is also suggested that postmodernism as an approach (theory, performance, project) is not amenable to traditional forms of analysis. There are two obvious responses to this state of affairs. The first is not to bother at all, which might be perfectly sensible since, on the admission of at least some postmodernists, they have nothing to add to the cumulation of knowledge and, indeed, deny it. The second, in good Millsian liberal fashion, is to believe that there is something there if so many people who are believed to be not stupid are persuaded of it, however unclear, ill-defined, or diverse it may be.[8] A further reason is that were consideration of the novel not to be undertaken as a general procedure, then the result would be stasis in the same way that the acceptance of everything is (see below).

Rosenau, in her wide-ranging survey of the postmodernist literature in social science, attempts to bring some order to the field by making a distinction between 'skeptical' and 'affirmative' postmodernism, the distinction largely residing, according to Rosenau in the degree of distrust, pessimism, and belief in action. 'Affirmatives' 'seek a philosophical and ontological intellectual practice that is nondogmatic, tentative, and nonideological', all of which is admirable from the point of view generated in this work.[9] However, if it is the case that the affirmative tendency is 'doing another Marx' to the Bourgeoisie — using an analytic approach to undermine opponents but being unwilling to accept the consequences of that analysis for their own approach (and hence denying reflexivity) — then it is clearly unacceptable and self-contradictory. Given that postmodernism is anti-foundational, relativist, and in some views nihilistic, it is difficult to see how the affirmative postmodernist can indeed be socially, politically, ethically, or philosophically affirmative without at the same time denying the logic of postmodernism. Indeed, as seen in Chapter 2, the relativist position is uncomfortable, and the affirmatives are following a well-trodden path in attempting self-escape once the opposition has been deconstructed or destroyed through anti-foundational analysis. For this reason this chapter will largely concentrate on the sceptical expression of this movement.

Much of this book has been about the investigation of uncertainty in social science, this seen from the standpoint of empiricist social science.

The idea of science was seen to be incoherent, in that social scientists very frequently adopted science in a naïve manner. However, at all stages it was argued that an ameliorated social scientific view that changed the level of concern, from science writ large to criteria of validity, made empirical activity in social science much more acceptable. However, throughout it was also noted that uncertainty was never entirely removed, particularly as relevant criteria of validity, which of themselves make sense in particular situations, may collectively have alternative implications. Such uncertainty is both a cause of continuing epistemological debate and a source of substantive creativity. From this point of view, the postmodernist, rather than being free and liberated as he or she would claim, is seen to have a very low tolerance of ambiguity and a kind of inverted authoritarianism. Because there is uncertainty and philosophic doubt, this does not have to lead to disengagement, the rejection of justified belief, and automatic oppositional stances as a matter of principle. Because an adolescent discovers that sex is not perfect union, a transcendental and blissful blending of souls, this does not usually lead to the abandonment of all sex but to the realization that there is better and worse sex.

The adoption of an oppositional logic effectively simplifies the world.[10] But is it *really* the case that either philosophers or social scientists have simplified the world into a series of dichotomies. Just five of the oppositions cited by Gregory — who is a fairly mainstream sceptic — demonstrate this point but also demonstrate a certain contempt for previous scholarship. The 'general/particular' opposition has been modified, discussed, and debated not only in the context of induction but also through the introduction of probability; the 'rational/irrational' opposition has been extensively examined by generations of scholars and broken down into a number of complex categories: the '*a priori/* empirical' opposition ignores the whole history of discussion from Kant onwards regarding the *synthetic a priori*; the 'peace/war' opposition ignores an entire structuralist literature going back at least thirty years that has argued (persuasively) against such simplicity. Neither is the idea of the 'truth/falsity' opposition nearly as simple as suggested; philosophers throughout the ages have investigated the problems interminably. Scholarship would indeed be a simple matter if everything were in terms of simple oppositions and dichotomies, but unfortunately neither scholarship nor the world is like that. This, again, is a demonstration of the low tolerance of ambiguity shown by the desire to avoid complexity and reduce things to unacceptable simplicity. To then attack such simplicity as if a sophisticated critique, revision, and subversion is being undertaken is merely a linguistic sleight of hand that loses all interest once the shallowness of the procedure is recognized.

The error is compounded by the further argument that one term of the opposition is 'privileged' or 'dominant', leading to a 'hierarchical struggle'. This, of course, is nonsense given that it is premised on a prior argument that is in most cases palpably false. The same kind of oppositional case can frequently be made with respect to the targets of postmodernist attack, on the excessive need for an 'authority' to be 'undermined' and 'subverted'. As a recent example we might take Richard Ashley's article.[11] The title of the article is a play on the word 'border', this being used in both a positional sense with respect to the author's relationship to and self-perceived place with respect to the profession and with reference to the substantive conclusions of the piece. While being a general defence and advocacy of a particular approach, the case is substantively argued that international relations as a discipline should be located at the border of domestic and international society. There is nothing wrong with this argument, but it is presented as a *novel* critique of (a particular expression of) realism and in apparent ignorance of much of the literature that has concentrated on this nexus from functionalism to world society to regime theory. It can only be 'disturbing' or 'unsettling' to someone who hasn't read anything. A reason for this approach, the need for an authority to subvert, as suggested by Ellis, lies in one of the roots of the emergence of post-structuralism and postmodernism in French philology: there *was* in that case the dead hand of tradition and authority to be subverted.[12] But to transpose that experience to all areas, disciplines, or traditions, making the assumption that there *must* be an authority, is surely not acceptable. Further, to extend Krippendorff's argument, the excessive emphasis on naïve realism and the discovery of 'margins', 'silences', etc. could be construed as a somewhat ethnocentric emphasis upon particular (but by no means all) American views to the exclusion of other traditions of thought.[13] Oppositional logic, to make sense, must have something to oppose, but it makes little sense to set up an imaginary target and attack it with righteous indignation; one is reminded of Don Quixote.

It can also be argued that the radical nature of postmodernism is more illusory than real. The term 'radical' can be used in a number of different ways which are often not distinguished. The two main senses for our purposes are the ideas of political and, more importantly, methodological radicalism, and in the modes of change and novelty. Politically, if the incoherence of the affirmative postmodernist position is accepted, the postmodernist can have no sustainable basis for action. This was, indeed, recognized by their antecedant anti-foundationalists, the Greek Sceptics and Sophists; recognizing that they had no philosophical or ethical basis for change-based political action, they in the main for the sake of convenience opted for acceptance of the prevailing political system even while recognizing that the system itself had no ethical foundation. A further point, which has both political and methodological consequences, is that the abandonment of criteria of validity is also the abandonment of change; if there are no good criteria for the acceptance of theories, then there are no criteria for the rejection of theories. Progress, therefore, in the sense of moving to better theories, explanations, or understandings of the world is necessarily impossible. All that one can have is a myriad of kaleidoscopic images juxtaposed for eternity. This is, indeed, sometimes acknowledged in the rejection of 'the enlightenment project' — which is a gross simplification of the multitudinous strands that made up that historical development — with its belief in progress and human betterment, and also in the deconstruction of traditional theories *and* the retention of those theories.

The anti-foundationalist argument, as noted above, has a long history and is hardly radical in either its political or methodological implications, considering the term 'radical' as innovation or novelty; Gellner, for example, considers postmodernism as merely 'a living and contemporary specimen of relativism'.[14] In other important ways the postmodernist approach is far from novel. For example, while there is considerable variation in the way that the term 'logocentricism' is used — it is sometimes used to refer to any and all recourse to foundational beliefs[15] and sometimes to refer to the direct relationship between words and things[16] — in the latter sense it is merely a restatement of the rejection of essentialism which is and has been commonplace at least since Wittgenstein. No one believes in simple representation, which as a target of attack went out with the ark.

This rejection and the corollaries for the transfer of meaning were discussed at some length previously. A further example would be the rejection of any dichotomizing logic based on the Law of the Excluded Middle, typifying this as the traditional mode of Western logic.[17] This radical rejection seems to have occurred with little cognizance of other work of far more profundity in the same direction, such as fuzzy set theory or Boolean logic, although reference is sometimes made to Hegel as a precursor in this respect. The point is that the rejection of dichotomized categorization is by no means novel or radical and is, in fact, routinely applied in certain arenas.

Similarly, through the extension of the idea that because of intertextuality and the deferment of meaning, authorship and construal are transferred to the reader — there being no privileged reading of a text — with the consequence that the author's real meaning is both uninteresting and inaccessible, is really just a convoluted restatement of the 'intentional fallacy', discussion of which is a mainstay of first-year undergraduate seminars in literature.[18] If indeed, this were wholly the case, I could argue with complete *consistency* (but with little sense) that the *Federalist Papers* and *Mein Kampf* actually meant the same thing. This, again, is an example of the low tolerance of ambiguity displayed by the postmodernist; authors do mean something specific when they write, and it is of interest to the reader to attempt to understand this, and yet different readers may have different interpretations of a text. We are not led to an anarchy of subjective interpretation but rather to numbers of plausible interpretations that are open to contestation and through which comes deeper understanding of the text and its possible implications.

Perhaps the final aspect of 'novelty' noted here is the postmodernist tendency to linguistic and neologistic fecundity with the consequence of making texts obscure to the main body of a particular discipline, in spite of Ashley's blithe belief in their current familiarity.[19] This existence of disciplinary strangeness[20] is not entirely new; at the inception of behaviouralism terms such as 'smallest space analysis', 'beta weights', or 'Kendall's tau' had the similar effect of mystifying and dividing the cognoscenti from the disciplinary laggards and creating 'two cultures'.[21] Strangeness, however, in this case is not a by-product but lauded in its own right in that its use is supposed to make others look afresh at well-known phenomena and see them in a new light. If it does indeed do this, then it is to be appreciated. However, whether something is insightful and creative does not depend on neologism or strangeness but on the intrinsic worth of what is being said. An example might be taken from a recent work, Shapiro's linkage of the language of politics with the language of sport.[22] This is a fairly 'conventional' piece of discourse analysis pointing out a linguistic interpenetration of two discourses. While the article is suggestive, what it does not do is attempt to discriminate between the political use of the language of sport as a means of political communication — to express political ideas to a mass audience — and an identification of international conflict as a kind of sport, that is, as a way that international decision-makers perceive the world. This, indeed, would be far more difficult to do but also far more interesting and significant. An approach *per se* cannot guarantee or justify an outcome — this is ultimately dependent on the wit and perspicacity of the author — with the consequence that it is the nature of the outcome and what it contributes that is significant. Hence, in the final analysis, in spite of an almost Messianic propagation of the creed, it will not be that something is postmodernist or that someone is a postmodern author that will be important but whether what is produced is interesting or significant. In this context there is perhaps some parallel with behaviouralism; as noted previously it was not that something was a behavioural piece that guaranteed it but whether it added something to justified belief or debate. Popper, indeed, noted this years ago; there is no method by which to have good ideas. Postmodernist analyses may sometimes be interesting, but it is not because they are postmodernist but because the ideas are themselves interesting.

In the discussion in Chapter 3 on stipulation and classification, the point was made that both can be very creative activities. Thus in the view presented in this book there is no proscription on neologism. Where such activity is engaged in procedural rules were given that made the activity acceptable. Hence the introduction of terms such as 'regime', 'structural violence', or 'hypergame' (regardless of their general acceptance) would have been acceptable as linguistic introductions to be debated. What is not acceptable, and what has been demonstrated to have happened above, is the introduction of new terms to describe what is already well known either in the search for strangeness or in the belief that something novel is being indicated. This at best can only lead to obscurantism and at worst to an admission of ignorance.

Meaning, for the postmodernist, is something forever intangible, 'a dynamic process, much more like an interaction between particles — a spark, a field of conductivity, the play of signifiers'.[23] The argument begins with Derrida's analysis of the relationship between signifiers and signs, with the rejection of any form of representational epistemology: that is, that the meaning of a word, and by implication any theoretical presentation, is not to be found in the structure of reality itself but in the construal of reality. Reality, or things, therefore, are not presented to us in any direct form but are the consequences of the mental act of interpretation. This denial of realism is, of course, far from new; few philosophers these days would argue for any simple theory of realism or representation, and in this sense the postmodernists who follow Derrida are reiterating a commonplace.[24] For example, the notion that reality is a mental construal — that its observation and interpretation is theoretical — has been accepted in the philosophy of science at least since Popper and, indeed, was previously noted by Goethe. Having accepted, though, that the construal of the world is an interpretative act does not lead us on to an acceptance that either words or theoretical constructions are arbitrary. We can accept that the sign, whether it is phonetic or graphic, is arbitary in the sense that any other sign would perform the same function equally well — to wit 'inverno' or 'winter' — but their use is in practice non-arbitrary and constrained by the practices of a community and the rules of language itself. This, indeed, accords with one of the main thrusts of Habermas's attempts to develop a foundational theory. This is, in fact, recognized by many postmodernists in the use of terms such as 'stock of signs', 'representational practices', 'knowledge regimes', or 'interpretive communities' but without acceptance of the consequences that Habermas perceives.

The rejection of the notion of linguistic arbitrariness, with respect to reality, may, however, be given another interpretation. While we have accepted as commonplace the idea that there is no direct relationship between reality and language, that is, the rejection of realism and simple representationalism, it is equally difficult to deny that there is *some* relationship. It is as foolish to say that language is wholly independent of reality as it is to say that it represents reality. Let me be traditional here and use the concept of 'warmth' to demonstrate this since it is used by both Berkeley and Ellis.[25] It is obvious that the world can be categorized in a myriad of ways; this was noted in Chapter 3 with the additional point that re-categorization can be a highly creative activity. Further, not only can there be numerous categorizations but within categories scalar properties can vary. It is a *fact* (a situation or circumstance about which there does not seem to be valid room for disagreement) that there are hot, warm, and cold days, but this facticity is a consequence of the significance of the experience to us, with both the dimension and its scalar properties a matter of cultural or other agreement. If, for example, we could conceive of an isolated island where through inbreeding the entire population was born with little sense of temperature, then the concepts of hot and cold and their scalar properties would probably have little significance, with a consequential change in facticity. Seen from this perspective, there is a 'world', but it is represented to us through categories of significance (to which Habermas would refer as 'constitutive-interests') which are themselves reflections of ideas about the world and subject to change. This, indeed, accords with some contemporary theories of science, such as those of Popper and Lakatos, where knowledge is both fallibalistic and based on assumptions which cannot be demonstrated to be true. This would also accord equally well with a pragmatist conception of knowledge as a hypothesis subject to modification. The error lies, as Ellis points out, in going from the statement that 'something is not a fact of nature' to the assumption that it must then be a 'fact of language' and nothing else. Again, there is the assertion of an unacceptable simplicity, with consequences that lead to 'external absurdity'.[26]

A further aspect of the postmodernist theory of meaning derives from the idea and implications of 'intertextuality'. A 'text' in this sense is a term inherited from French postmodernist and poststructuralist literary criticism and is a blanket term used to refer to aspects of the world. Rosenau in her glossary draws attention to its vagueness by terming it 'all phenomenon, all events';[27] or, in less pretentious terms, a text is a 'thing', presumably with at least some definable though permeable boundary as a basis for identification. Intertextuality at its simplest means the necessary inter-penetration of 'discourses' or 'texts' such that any text implies or infers a multitude of other texts so that its complete meaning as an individual text can never be established. 'Meaning' is thus permanently postponed or 'deferred'. The inter-penetration of meaning is held to apply both to words within a language and to texts themselves. At the level of words, the commonplace idea that words take their meaning from contrast or difference was taken by Derrida to mean that part of the meaning of the word was always elsewhere and not immediately present, with the consequence that there is an infinite 'play of differences'.[28] It is as if when contemplating one English word, the observer had to have in mind at the same time the complete *Oxford Dictionary* in order properly to appreciate the meaning of that word. This is, of course, nonsense but a nonsense based on a seductive half-truth. The half-truth is that the meaning of a word is derived in part from what it contrasts with and is merely another way of saying what was conventional in Oxford linguistic philosophy — that 'the meaning of a word is dependent on the context of its use'; Wittgenstein clearly recognized this in his discussion of 'language games'. Derrida's error here lies in neglecting the point that to choose a word is to *not* choose other words, and the not-choice amplifies rather than detracts from the specification of meaning. In other words, Derrida got it the wrong way round. Ellis puts this rather well:[29]

The meaning of one word does indeed depend on the meaning of many others; but to choose one word from a system is to employ *all* the systemic contrasts with other words at that moment — the process of contrasting does not stretch into the future.

Hence, the more precise the use of words — as for example in the best forms of poetry — the greater the number of relevant contrasts and the greater the specificity of meaning. This, of course, does not deny that there are connotations or indexical meanings — as described in Chapter 3 — that make implicit or explicit reference elsewhere, but these too are present at the moment of choice and not deferred. It is often the case that an author will choose allusion elsewhere — much of T.S.Eliot's work is redolent with allusion — but this is done to aggregate meaning not to defer, lose, or send meaning elsewhere. Hence, in the terms of this text, as explicated through the discussion and examples of stipulation in social science in Chapter 3, the specification of a term with greater subtlety and distinction has the function of increasing the contrasts and hence the transfer of meaning. To believe otherwise is fundamentally to misunderstand the nature of language.

A similar, though perhaps more complex argument, can be made with respect to the intertextuality of texts, as opposed to the interpenetration of words. This will be discussed in the context of theory in so far as this is the primary locus of discussion in social science. Theory, as described earlier, is the elicitation and elucidation of what is believed significant about a particular phenomenon, class, events, or relations between them. This is largely in line with Popper's view of theory as 'a crystallisation of a point of view'. It is the point of theory to be selective with respect to the environment (the term 'selective' is preferred to 'privilege' or 'make dominant' even if the consequence is to 'tame' or 'domesticate' post-modernist linguistic radicalism). Hence, to make a theoretical choice, to choose to look at things in a particular way, is to choose not to look at things in a different way. In the social sciences there is fecundity in theoretical expressions and a plethora of points of view, and to choose a point of view is to contrast that point of view with other possible expressions. The meaning of the choice is a function of and is partially dependent on what is not chosen but, as with the deferral of meaning in language, does not imply the interpenetration of texts but the specification of theoretical perspectives. This argument can, indeed, be pushed further. Earlier it was argued that the more theoretical perspectives there were in a discipline, the better it is for that discipline in terms of contestation of programmes and relevant substantive empirical content of the discipline; meaning, from this point of view, becomes *more* specifiable the more contrasts there are.

Perhaps an example will demonstrate this. If I choose to adopt the world society approach to the explanation of international relations — a plausible but certainly unfinished programme — I am at the same time not adopting realism, neo-realism, sociobiology, structuralism, functionalism, critical theory, or other versions of pluralism. I am making claims about the world that have both an autonomous status in the terms of the discourse of the chosen theory but also a disciplinary positional specification with respect to other points of view.

A necessary consequence of this is that there will always be areas which are not covered by a theory. It has long been recognized that because theory is an abstraction it cannot explain all events within its domain; this was noted in a practical context in the discussion of prediction in a previous chapter. Popper makes the same point in a natural science context: in spite of what we know about gravity, in reality the path of an oak leaf falling from a tree cannot be predicted. The idea of the 'silence' and the 'margins' of theory — as an accusation of the usefulness, privileging, or dominance of theory — is meaningless once the meaning of 'theory' is properly understood. All theory by its nature has to be 'silent' (though most of us would prefer the term 'not covered' rather than the neologistic use of 'silence') with respect to aspects of reality, and if it were not then it would be useless for the purposes intended. Whether drawing attention to the 'silences' of theory or drawing attention to the 'margins' of theory is interesting or useful does not depend on the fact of silences or margins (the world society approach has little to say about degenerative diseases) but whether that to which attention is being drawn is in itself interesting. And it is only interesting if in some way it illuminates in some significant manner, which must, in the final analysis, make recourse to the original theory itself. An example will demonstrate this. It was previously noted in

Chapter 3 that in the view of a number of scholars there was a deficiency in theories of war and peace. Galtung, Schmidt, and Curle were mentioned in this respect. In the new terminology they were 'silent' on what Curle termed 'unpeaceful' relationships, and what Galtung, Schmidt, Hoivik, Alcock, etc. referred to as 'structural violence'. The introduction of this (contentious) view into the discipline was significant in so far as it was interesting, significant, and fecund with respect to extant theory rather than merely because it pointed out silence or the margin of theory.

Similar kinds of points can be directed at the idea of 'forgetting' (or ~~forgetting~~). This is advanced as a critique of contemporary theory in so far as that theory has superceded or rejected previous approaches. Since, in the view of at least some postmodernists, there can be no progress, to 'forget' is to reduce the richness of the points of view open to us. In one sense, this is obviously true; to accept one view is, again, not to accept another. Further, it may be the case, as Lakatos points out, that 'degenerative' theory (though the postmodernist would not accept the term) is always open to rehabilitation through new discovery. What the postmodernist is doing here is pointing out theoretical opportunity costs. This is acceptable in so far as many now unregarded theories may have an intrinsic interest for either historical or other reasons. Further, it will probably be the case that the approaches that we adopt today will be superceded by other theories more appropriate to future time and place. But the question is whether we really wish to maintain past theories or perspectives in the sense of giving them equal status with those extant. The ancient Greek theory of the sun as a God riding a chariot across the sky is interesting in so far as understanding it makes reading Greek literature more comprehensible and leads to at least some understanding of a mind-set where explanation was by myth, but do we really want to 'remember' it to the extent of considering it to have equal validity with contemporary cosmology? Whether 'forgetting' is important or not is dependent on what is forgotten and its contemporary significance, and not merely on the fact that it has been downgraded in the scale of believable things. There may be good reasons for such downgrading. It is not forgetting *per se*, but rather what is forgotten.

Finally, a brief discussion on the postmodernist view of meta-narratives or the logocentric idea. This is the belief that there can be no reference made to external sources of validation since such sources do not exist; there can be and are no immutable foundations for the postmodernist and any attempt to posit knowledge on the basis of such foundations is doomed to failure. This writer would largely agree with the point of view expressed in that there are no absolutely incontestable foundations for knowledge, but whereas the postmodernist would then suggest that there are no reasons for belief, I would sharply disagree: while there are areas of uncertainty, there are also the limitations on that uncertainty.

Frequently, in postmodernist thought, the idea of a meta-narrative is allied to the failure of the 'enlightenment project' and the belief in progress. 'Progress', of course, is a complex idea, an example of an essentially contested concept. What is seen as 'progress' is from a point of view; to a conservative disposition the improved position of women in Western society would seem retrogressive, even an attack on the sanctity of the family; while from a different perspective it would seem progressive and emancipatory. The twentieth century, from the overt violence of the concentration camps of the Boer War, to the Holocaust, to the horrors and atrocities of Kampuchea and Bosnia, and to the structural causes of poverty in the Third World, could indicate a continuity in the barbarism of mankind, a lack of progress of the most terrible kind. But there is another side. Throughout the twentieth century there has been a spread of humanitarian belief that, while far from even or perfect in spread, still marks a change in the condition of mankind even if, from a gloomy disposition, this is not seen as progress. The idea of international responsibility is with us today as never before, whether this is marked by United Nations peacekeeping, international aid, the spread of the idea of human rights as a global concept, increased medical facilities, awareness of ecological issues, or merely a growth of consciousness regarding the plight of others. Both interpretations of the human condition are possible, but one interpretation accepts potential while the other is self-fulfilling defeatism. In so far as the interpretation of the human condition is contestable, for the sake of the human condition it makes far more sense to adopt a Pascalian 'wager' position. This argument, advanced to demonstrate that there are good cost-benefit reasons to believe in God, can equally well (but with much more plausibility) be used to sustain a belief in the betterment of the human condition.[30]

Progress, in terms of social science rather than general comment on the condition of mankind, is similarly complex. What do we mean by progress in social science? Certainly what we don't mean is advancement in terms of some positivist dream of perfect explanation and verification by prediction. As noted earlier in this book, neither position is tenable. Yet, many would reject the idea that social science is akin to, say, the study of literature (and hence would not accept approaches that might make some sense in literary studies as being relevant to social science) with respect to the greater degree of subjectivity that is involved in interpretation in that area. In terms of this book, it has been suggested that empirical criteria are relevant to the assessment of social science output but that these are not always decisive.

Progress, however, can be seen in another way. One of the aims of social science has been, rightly or wrongly, to gain an understanding of the social world of human beings. This world, since the Renaissance, the rise of science and technology, the spread of capitalism, and the Enlightenment, is in constant motion. Whereas in times past change was much slower, often brought about by natural factors such as disease, famine, and migration, in contemporary society change is an inherent necessity of the economic system. 'All is flux', suggests Heraclitus, 'you never step into the same river twice', or, in the words of Carl Becker, 'whirl is king'.[31] What 'progress' would mean in this sense would be keeping up with the changing human environment through constant interpretation and reinterpretation. What may have been useful insights and theories a few years ago no longer have the same persuasive power today. Theoretical understanding may change due either to changes in the external environment or to changes in theory itself, or, more usually, to some interaction between these. The concern, for example, with the Cold War has passed, leaving new problems and issues to understand in the post-Cold War era. The changes in human organization and environment will require continual revision of interpretation, affecting constantly what the social scientist has to offer to the policy-maker and society.[32] To argue that the 'Enlightenment Project' was misplaced or that the fragmentation of culture is such as to render coherent understanding impossible are both defensible positions intellectually, but it is questionable whether they are defensible positions morally given the nature of sceptical withdrawal.

Progress may be seen in another way. It is one of the arguments of this book, deriving from the idea of triangulation, that the understanding of phenomena is enhanced by the possession of multiple means of viewing. As social science proceeds it becomes increasingly rich in the traditions that it can draw on; far from 'forgetting', the variety of interpretation, and hence potential ways of understanding, increases. This does not mean that *all* past views are accepted, or that *everything* stays but that the analytic plethora and richness of the discipline develops. Hence, in the field of conflict analysis, it is as legitimate to call on the ideas of SunTzu, Herodotus, or Thucydides as it is to invoke Deutsch, Bueno de Mesquita, or Burton.

In general then, this author finds little in the recent upsurge of postmodernism that is of interest, but in line with the intellectual liberalism that underlies this work would not (even if able) attempt to proscribe the practice of the approach. This for two reasons. As J.S. Mill noted many years ago, beliefs become unexamined rhetoric unless challenged, and hence challenge itself can be seen as healthy. Second, also as noted earlier, approaches sometimes take many years to develop and will often change in development. It is not inconceivable that some postmodern works will in time add substantially to the the insights available to social science. Finally, however, to engage in radical anti-foundationalism appears morally indefensible, in that the affirmation of humanitarian values becomes meaningless, and further, ignores the fact that while we can never attain certainty there are still grounds for justified belief.

Notes

1. Russell, B. (1964) *Problems of Philosophy*, London: Oxford University Press, p. 75.
2. Gellner, E (1992) *Postmodernism, Reason and Religion*, London: Routledge, p. 33.
3. See, for discussion, Korner, S. (1967) *Kant*, Harmondsworth: Penguin, 70–104.
4. Chomsky, N. (1968) *Language and Mind*, New York: Harcourt, Brace and World.
5. See, for example, McCarthy, T. (1982) 'Rationality and Relativism: Habermas's 'overcoming' of Hermeneutics'; and Habermas, J. (1982) 'A reply to my critics', in Thompson, J.B. and Held, D. (eds) *Habermas: Critical Debates*, London: Macmillan, 57–78 and 219–83.
6. Ayer, A.J. (1966) *The Problem of Knowledge*, Harmondsworth: Penguin, p. 35.
7. Gellner, op. cit., p. 29.
8. An illiberal response would be to dismiss the entire approach as a fad. Gellner, op. cit., p. 46, comes close to this by arguing that universities are staffed by people who are rewarded for creativity, and where cumulation is not obvious or easily measurable, the creation of 'artificial obsolescence' enhances career patterns.
9. Rosenau, P. (1992) *Post-Modernism and the Social Sciences: Insights, Inroads and Intrusions*, Princeton: Princeton University Press, p. 16.
10. See, for example, Gregory, D.U. (1989) 'Foreword' in der Derian, J. and Shapiro, M.J. (eds) *International/intertextual Relations: Postmodern Readings of World Politics*, Lexington, Mass: Lexington Books, p. xv; and Kellner, D. (1988) 'Postmodernism as Social Theory: Some Challenges and Problems' in *Theory, Culture and Society: Explorations in Critical Social Science*, 5, 2–3, Special issue on postmodernism, p. 240.
11. Ashley, R.K. (1989) 'Living on Border Lines: Man, Poststructuralism and War' in der Derian, J. and Shapiro, M.J., op. cit., 259–321.
12. Ellis, J.M. (1989) *Against Deconstruction*, Princeton: Princeton University Press, 82–6.
13. Krippendorff, E. (1989) 'The Dominance of American Approaches in International Relations' in Dyer, H.C. and Mangasarian, L. (eds) *The Study of International Relations: the State of Art*, London: Macmillan, 28–39.
14. Gellner, op. cit., p. 24.
15. Rosenau, op. cit., p. xii.
16. Ellis, op. cit., p. 35.
17. See, for example, Lewis I.R. and Langford, C.H. (1959, second edition) *Symbolic Logic*, New York: Dover Publications, p. 34; and Cohen M. and Nagel, E. (1963) *An Introduction to Logic*, London: Routledge, 181–5.
18. See, for example, Wimsatt, W.K. (1964) *The Verbal Icon: Studies in the Meaning of Poetry and Two Preliminary Essays with Munroe C. Beardsley*, New York: Noonday Press.

19. Ashley, op. cit., p. 259.
20. See Gregory, op. cit., p. xiv, where the activity of making something 'strange' (difficult, odd) is noted with approbation.
21. See for discussion Nicholson, M. (1989) *Formal Theories in International Relations*, Cambridge: Cambridge University Press, 10–13.
22. Shapiro, M.J. (1989) 'Representing World Politics: The Sport/War Intertext', in der Derian and Shapiro, op. cit., 69–96.
23. Gregory, op. cit., p. xvi.
24. The rejection of realism is part and parcel of most idealist philosophic perspectives, in which category postmodernists must be placed. However, while most but not all idealists would adhere to some form of a coherence theory of knowledge, it is a part of some postmodernist belief that contemporary culture has become fragmented. See, for example, Baudrillard, J. (1992) 'Simulcra and Simulations' and Jameson, F. (1992) 'Postmodernism and Consumer Society' in Brooker, P. (ed.) op. cit., 151–79. In one sense, few philosophers of science these days would adhere to simple realism; if Russell's definition of 'idealism' is accepted as 'the doctrine that whatever exists . . . must in some sense be mental' then many of us are idealists. See Russell, B. (1964) *The Problems of Philosophy*, London: Oxford University Press, p. 37. Perhaps this point is well made by a consideration of Roy Bhaskar's (1989) *Reclaiming Reality*, London: Verso, where the version of realism advocated is termed 'transcendental' or 'critical' realism. A good example of the rejection of simple realism, again to emphasize the non-novelty of the argument, would be George Berkeley's 1709 *Essay Towards a New Theory of Vision* (1963) London: Dent; while perhaps the most persuasive recent attempt to establish a form of realism would be through the idea of 'sense-data' with perhaps G.E. Moore being a prime example. For comment see Bouwsma, O.K. (1967) 'Moore's Theory of Sense-Data' in Warnock, G.J. (ed.) *The Philosophy of Perception*, Oxford: Oxford University Press, 8–24; and for extended discussion Ayer, A.J. (1956) *The Problem of Knowledge*, Harmondsworth: Penguin, 84–133.
25. Ellis, op. cit., 46–9; and 'First Dialogue' in 'Three Dialogues Between Hylas and Philonous in Opposition to Sceptics and Athiests' in Berkeley, op. cit., 199–240.
26. This term is used by Pauline Rosenau (1990) in 'Internal Logic, External Absurdity: Postmodernism in Political Science', *Paradigms*, 4, 1, 39–57.
27. Rosenau, (1992) op. cit., p. xiv.
28. Derrida writes: 'the significant concept is never present in and of itself, in a sufficient presence that refers only to itself. Essentially and lawfully, every concept is inscribed in a chain or in a system within which it refers to the other, to other concepts, by means of a systematic play of differences.' See Derrida, J. (ed. P. Kamuf) *A Derrida Reader: Between the Blinds*, New York: Harvester Wheatsheaf, p. 63.
29. Ellis, op. cit., p. 55.
30. Pascal, B. (Trans. J.M. Cohen) (1961) *The Pensees*, Harmondsworth: Penguin, 155–9. Pascal, in this famous argument is suggesting that in situations of uncertainty, sensible decision is aided by reflecting on the costs of various actions in response to that uncertainty. A similar argument has been used by ecologists with respect to scientific uncertainty regarding global warming.
31. Becker, C.L. (1932) *Heavenly City of the Eighteenth Century Philosophers*, New Haven: Yale University Press, p. 1.
32. See for extended discussion, Girard, M., Eberwien, W.-D. and Webb, K. (eds) (1994) *Theory and Practice in Foreign Policy Making*, London: Francis Pinter.

INDEX